# INTELLECTUAL IMBALANCE, LOVE DEPRIVATION AND VIOLENT DELINQUENCY

# INTELLECTUAL IMBALANCE, LOVE DEPRIVATION AND VIOLENT DELINQUENCY

## A Biosocial Perspective

*By*

### ANTHONY WALSH, Ph.D.

*Department of Criminal Justice*
*Boise State University*
*Boise, Idaho*

*With a Foreword by*
**Lee Ellis, Ph.D.**

CHARLES C THOMAS • PUBLISHER
*Springfield • Illinois • U.S.A.*

*Published and Distributed Throughout the World by*

CHARLES C THOMAS • PUBLISHER
2600 South First Street
Springfield, Illinois 62794-9265

© *1991 by* CHARLES C THOMAS • PUBLISHER

ISBN 0-398-05757-5

Library of Congress Catalog Card Number: 91-23444

*Printed in the United States of America*
SC-R-3

**Library of Congress Cataloging-in-Publication Data**

Walsh, Anthony, 1941–
   Intellectual imbalance, love deprivation, and violent delinquency
: a biosocial perspective / by Anthony Walsh.
      p.   cm.
   Includes bibliographical references and index.
   ISBN 0-398-05757-5
   1. Juvenile delinquents — Psychology.   2. Violent crimes —
Psychological aspects.   3. Juvenile delinquency — Idaho — Case
studies.   4. Juvenile delinquency — Ohio — Case studies.   I. Title.
HV9069.W3   1991
364.3′6′019 — dc20                                                      91-23444
                                                                          CIP

# FOREWORD

Anthony Walsh has written a book from a perspective with which most criminologists quite frankly do not agree. I can state with certainty that the biosocial perspective is fairly unpopular among criminologists based upon a survey an associate and I conducted a few years ago among about 180 persons who attended the 1986 convention of the American Society of Criminology in Atlanta (Ellis & Hoffman, 1990). While our survey will need to be repeated in order to identify trends, it clearly showed that supporters of the biosocial perspective are in a minority. But, to those working from this perspective, that is the bad news; the good news is that the support is probably not as shallow as they fear.

Among other things, respondents to our survey were asked which theory they thought currently enjoyed the greatest empirical support. Opinions were fragmented to say the least, and the theories which were seen as having the greatest support were somewhat unexpected. Leading the list, *control theory* was picked by 27 percent of the respondents and *general social learning theory* was picked by 18 percent. Third place went to *behaviorist social learning theory*, with 8 percent identifying it as having more empirical support than any other theory. *Biosocial theory* tied with *differential association theory* in fourth place, each with 6 percent of the respondents believing that these theories currently have the greatest empirical support.

Since what is called *biosocial theory* is probably more appropriately considered a fairly broad perspective rather than a specific theory, it may not have been entirely appropriate to compare it to fairly specific criminological theories (such as differential association theory). Nevertheless, our survey suggested that while the biosocial approach is certainly a minority perspective in criminology, it is by no means insignificant.

A couple of ironies are noteworthy in regard to the results of our survey. First, what is now the apparent leading theory in criminology—

control theory—is no longer specifically advocated by Travis Hirschi, the theory's foremost proponent (see Gottfredson & Hirschi, 1990; Tittle, 1991:1610). Second, even though the biosocial approach appears to be as popular as differential association theory, the former still is rarely mentioned in most criminology or delinquency texts, while references to the latter is obligatory in every text that is published.

With a clear recognition of its minority status within the criminology community, let us ask what the biosocial perspective really is, and how it specifically relates to the study of criminal behavior. Contrary to what some critics contend, those working from a biosocial perspective do not consider learning and social environmental variables irrelevant to crime causation. Rather, as the present book aptly illustrates, biosocial theorists contend that social learning is important, although its full significance can only be understood within a biological context.

To follow through on the above point, most biosocial theorists are what I call *neurologically specific* in their theorizing. This means that they explicitly recognize something that environmentalists ignore, i.e., that it is the unique functioning of each person's brain which is the most immediate controller of all human behavior. Thus, instead of assuming that social environmental variables are simply being filtered through some "rational thought" processes to impact behavior, biosocial theorists conceive of both genetic and environmental variables as impinging upon numerous brain functioning variables to impact behavior. Of course, biosocial theorists are not of one mind in what they consider the most important neurological, genetic, or environmental variables, or how these variables interrelate.

I am pleased to see that Walsh's book is replete with references to various possible brain functioning variables which may mediate the impact of both genetics and environment on criminal behavior. The book begins by describing the basic nature of the biosocial approach to criminology (and to the study of social behavior in general). In my opinion, Walsh fairly depicts the sterility of pure environmentalism, and forcefully shows why it is important for criminologists to remove the blinders that continue to prevent them from looking carefully at biological contributors to criminal behavior. Stripped of these blinders, Walsh's book provides readers with a panoramic view of criminology through a clear biosocial lens.

I totally concur with his separating the *biosocial perspective* from what is called *sociobiology*. Whether intended by most of its proponents or not, sociobiology has come to be primarily confined to the application of neo-Darwinian evolutionary theory to the study of social phenomenon (Hapgood, 1984:96; Archer, 1986:48; Boorman & Levitt, 1980:214). Although the biosocial perspective in no way excludes the application of modern evolutionary theory to the study of criminal behavior (see, for example, Ellis, 1990a), this is not its primary focus. Rather, the biosocial perspective concentrates upon how physiological factors may interact with the environment to alter behavior. The most frequently considered physiological variables are those pertaining to the functioning of the brain (although numerous hormonal factors that continually alter brain functioning in response to environmental experiences are also important to consider) (Ellis & Coontz, 1990).

Another admirable feature of this book is that it deals forthrightly with some of the most sensitive issues in the field of criminology, such as how intelligence, social stratification, and race relate to criminal behavior. Unlike writers who skirted these issues, downplay their importance, or actually distort the nature of the evidence, Walsh confronts the facts with unusual clarity and honesty. In particular, his treatment of the well-documented tendency for persons who are prone toward crime to be deficient mainly in verbal intelligence (VIQ) rather than in spatial reasoning intelligence (or so-called performance intelligence, PIQ) is insightful. His inquiries in this interesting relationship may eventually link up with proposals that the left and right hemispheres of the neocortex play somewhat different roles in crime causation (Ellis, 1990b).

Overall, I would say that even those who are still skeptical of the merit of a biosocial approach to criminology will gain from reading this book. In the long run, I hypothesize that it will help to increase the popularity of the biosocial perspective in criminology, and possibly in social science generally.

LEE ELLIS, PH.D.

## References

Archer, J. (1986). Animal sociobiology and comparative psychology: A review. *Current Psychological Research and Reviews, 5,* 48–61.

Boorman, S. A. and Levitt, P. R. (1980). The comparative evolutionary biology of social behavior. *Annual Review in Sociology, 6,* 213–234.

Ellis, L. (1990a). The evolution of violent criminal behavior and its nonlegal equivalent. In L. Ellis and H. Hoffman (Eds.), *Crime in Biological, Social, and Moral Contexts* (pp. 61–80). New York: Praeger.

Ellis, L. (1990b). Left- and mixed-handedness and criminality: Explanations for a probable relationship. In S. Coren (Ed.), *Left-Handedness: Behavioral Implications and Anomalies* (pp. 485–507). North-Holland: Elsevier.

Ellis, L. (1990). Androgens, brain functioning, and criminality: The neurohormonal foundations of antisociality. In L. Ellis and H. Hoffman (Eds.), *Crime in Biological, Social, and Moral Contexts* (pp. 162–193). New York: Praeger.

Ellis, L. and Hoffman, H. (1990). Views of contemporary criminologists on causes and theories of crime. In L. Ellis and H. Hoffman (Eds.), *Crime in Biological, Social, and Moral Contexts* (pp. 50–58). New York: Praeger.

Gottfredson, M. R. and Hirschi, T. (1990). *A General Theory of Crime.* Stanford, CA: Stanford University Press.

Hapgood, F. (1984). Notes of a naturalist. *Science, 84,* 5 (October), 96–97.

Tittle, C. R. (1991). Book review. *American Journal of Sociology, 96,* 1609–1611.

# PREFACE

The primary purpose of this book is to bring evidence from the biological sciences and neurosciences to bear on the problem of violent delinquency. I do this not in the belief that current sociological criminology is "wrong" but in the belief that it can be improved and extended by integrating insights from the more basic sciences into it. The pollination of ideas across disciplines enriches them by bringing fresh perspectives to old problems. The biological sciences can perhaps help to resolve some of the conflicts and issues existing within and among contending criminological theories.

This work examines the effects of intellectual imbalance and love deprivation on violent delinquency. As far as I am aware, this is the first book to examine how these variables are related, and how they are both related to violent delinquency. My primary aim is to present a comprehensive review of the theoretical and empirical literature relevant to these topics and to place them in a biosocial framework. While the work can stand alone as described, original data are used to support, clarify, or illustrate certain points. These data consist of a sample of 585 juvenile delinquents processed through juvenile probation departments in Idaho and Ohio in the early 1980's. Only delinquents who had completed their delinquent careers, i.e., had reached the age of majority, were included in the study. All findings reported from the original data must be considered exploratory, suggestive, illustrative, and heuristic rather than explanatory in any strict sense because I lack a control group of non-delinquents. A control group is often—and rightly—considered essential if one is nominating a cause of delinquency. Lacking a control group of non-delinquents, one is left uninformed about whether or not such a group would show results comparable to those obtained from delinquents.

However, absent a control group, one is not prevented from exploring *within*-group differences along dimensions of interest. Neither is one prevented from comparing sample means of certain variables, such as IQ, with established population norms. In other words, in some instances population norms serve as controls, and in other instances the delinquent group serves as its own control (e.g., "Does an increase in X lead to an increase in Y within this sample?). Nevertheless, this work should not be viewed or judged as a piece of empirical research testing a series of hypotheses. Rather, it should be viewed as a theoretical work that is hypothesis-*generating* and that is buttressed at certain points by additional empirical evidence.

Chapter One defines the biosocial perspective and makes a case for its usefulness in criminology. The biosocial perspective recognizes the inseparability of the social milieu and the biological baggage the individual brings to it. It has absolutely nothing to do with "born criminal" or "bad seed" explanations of criminality, nor does it claim that there are "crime genes" (but it does not deny that there may be genes that influence physiological processes that may in turn influence the risk of criminality in certain environments). The biosocial perspective merely recognizes the interactive and mutual influencing nature of the biological and the social.

Biological studies of criminal behavior have been criticized on the grounds that no quality can be found in acts defined as criminal that distinguishes them from non-criminal injuries; criminal behavior is a legalistic label, not one that is descriptive of actual behavior (Fishbein, 1990). Critics assert that criminal behavior is such a highly variable phenomenon and is so infused with culture-specific and moral overtones that it is nonsensical to search for biosocial "causes."

It is true that to ask "What causes crime?" is as useless a question as to ask "What causes disease?" In both cases the specific crime and the specific disease would first have to be defined before an answer could be attempted. This study takes the advice of Mednick, Gabrielli, and Hutchings (1984) in searching for specific traits that put certain individuals at risk for criminal labeling. Violent criminal behavior is one such phenomenon for which identifiable individual traits can be sought (Fishbein, 1990).

Criminology is concerned with breaches of the criminal law, including criminal violence. It is not concerned with "legitimate" violence as practiced by nations and their agents, which is usually more cruel and destructive than illegitimate violence. The problem of legitimate violence is more properly the domain of political science and sociology, not criminology. Legitimate violence can be seen as behavior that conforms to the expectations of society; criminal violence is behavior that violates those expectations. Although at some levels of analysis the causes of legitimate and illegitimate violence may be identical, the criminological explanation of illegitimate violence revolves around exploring the relative inability of those who engage in it to learn to control its expression and to learn the norms and values of society relating to prosocial behavior. Buikhuisen (1989) considers this to be axiomatic for any theory of delinquency. The relative inability to learn suppression of violent impulses and the norms and values of prosocial behavior may be reflected in IQ scores.

Chapter Two explores the nature of intelligence as measured by IQ tests, the issue of bias in IQ testing, and the concept of heritability. Although many criminologists believe IQ tests to be biased, the prestigious National Academy of Sciences insists that they are not (Linn, 1982). Likewise, the idea that IQ is to some extent heritable does not sit well among many social scientists, although those best acquainted with the data (geneticists and developmental psychologists) do not doubt it (Snyderman and Rothman, 1988). Test bias and heritability are concepts that must be adequately addressed in a work that proposes that IQ has a lot to do with delinquency.

The environmental effects on IQ, which may be considerable, are addressed in Chapter Three. These effects are explored mostly in terms of the effects of experience on the developing human infant brain. IQ scores do vary across different kinds of environments, and neuroscientists have described the mechanisms thought to be responsible for much of this variation. There is ample evidence that various kinds of socioemotional deprivation experienced at important periods of central nervous system development adversely affects the structure and functioning of the brain.

More important in understanding delinquency than full-scale IQ are discrepancy scores between the verbal and performance subscales of the Wechsler IQ test. A significant discrepancy between performance IQ (P) and verbal IQ (V), in the direction of performance greater than verbal (P > V), has long been considered a marker of psychopathy among clinical psychologists. A significant deficit—either V > P or P > V—is indicative of intellectual imbalance. An imbalance in the direction of V > P, that is, a person who has excellent verbal skills vis-à-vis his or her performance skills, is considered a marker of good behavior. These claims are examined with data presented in Chapter Four. Differential autonomic nervous system functioning is examined as one of a number of possible psychophysiological determinants of intellectual imbalance.

In Chapter Five the connection between IQ and delinquency is explored, paying special attention to race, SES, IQ and opportunity, the spuriousness argument, differential association and IQ, and the differential detection hypothesis. Does the introduction of race and/or SES render the IQ/delinquency relationship spurious, or does IQ have similar effects across races and levels of SES? Is differential association largely a function of "like seeks like," and is the similarity perhaps a function of similarity of IQ? Do brighter delinquents avoid detections, thus artificially inflating the correlation between official delinquency and IQ? The data presented will show IQ to be an important variable explaining violent delinquency, but in terms of intellectual imbalance rather than full-scale IQ.

Chapter Six looks at the effect of love deprivation on violent delinquency. Love deprivation is a "blanket" variable that encompasses many affective disadvantages suffered by a child such as physical and psychological abuse, parental rejection, parental substance abuse, and so forth (Walsh and Petee, 1987). It has been asserted by too many researchers to cite here that nothing is more powerful in explaining violence of all kinds than love deprivation.

It will also be shown that love deprivation has an important effect on cognitive development, especially in terms of producing the $P > V$ profile. Love deprivation will be contrasted with $P > V$ discrepancy in terms of their respective power to explain variance in violent delinquency within different environments. Genes are units of potential that are free to most fully express themselves in environments that are both homogeneous and advantaged. To the extent that IQ is a genetic trait, it should be most fully expressed in terms of its link to violence in an homogeneous advantaged environment, such as the upper 10 percent of the SES distribution. Conversely, IQ should have less impact within disadvantaged environments, where environmental variables should be more powerful.

Chapter Seven explores violent delinquency among females. Females are examined separately because violent behavior among females is comparatively rare, and because the psychological literature advises that males and females should not be "mixed" when IQ is a component of any statistical model (Saccuzzo and Lewandowski, 1976). It also appears that the various social disabilities impacting on delinquency have different and interesting effects across the sexes, and that the threshold of these disabilities is usually higher before females cross from conforming to delinquent behavior. Differences in the extent of violent delinquency between the sexes are explored primarily in terms of biological sexual dimorphism (gonadal hormonal and neurophysiological differences).

Other variables impacting on IQ and delinquency, such as birth order, family size, broken homes, illegitimacy, and substance abuse, are examined in Chapter Eight. Broken homes and, to a lesser extent, family size are usually considered sociological variables and are therefore quite extensively treated in the criminological literature. Birth order is considered more a "psychological" variable and is one that rarely appears in the criminological literature. I have yet to see a criminological study in which the focus was on illegitimate birth. This is quite strange because many social disabilities—lack of social support networks, father absence, lower class, abuse and neglect, and so forth—are correlated with illegitimacy (Walsh, 1990).

The final chapter summarizes the research and offers some thoughts on the amelioration of the problem of violent delinquency via the biosocial perspective.

A.W.

# CONTENTS

# INTELLECTUAL IMBALANCE, LOVE DEPRIVATION AND VIOLENT DELINQUENCY

# Chapter One

# THE BIOSOCIAL PERSPECTIVE: ISSUES AND CONCERNS

## The Biosocial Perspective Defined

A biosocial perspective of human behavior is one that seeks to understand that behavior from a point of view that includes insights from the biological sciences. It is *not* simply a biological perspective, for it is fully aware of the role of social, psychological, political, historical, and economic factors in human behavior. In no sense can it be considered a hierarchical theory in which macro phenomena are deduced from a small number of principles rising in a deductive pyramid to arrive at an encompassing general principle. The biosocial perspective is just that—a perspective or view of the subject matter that recognizes the social, psychological, and biological aspects of human behavior. As Lancaster et al. (1987:2) put it: "Recognition of the continuous, mutual, and inseparable interaction between biology and the social environment is one of the critical foundations of the biosocial perspective." The biosocial perspective offers no grand schemes or ultimate causes of human behavior; rather it seeks to understand how biological factors interact with other factors to produce observed behavior. It does not seek to "reduce" complex behavior to the level of biological processes in isolation from environmental influences.

The biosocial perspective is not coterminous with sociobiology. Sociobiology has a more ambitious agenda; it has a grand theory, and it seeks ultimate causes (Green, Morgan, and Barash, 1979). Sociobiology's grand theory, from which sociobiologists believe that most of the more important human behaviors can be deduced, is evolutionary theory. Sociobiologists believe that we humans carry within us a number of patterned behavioral predispositions bequeathed to us by our evolutionary history. These predispositions are encoded in our genes, but are overlayed by culture. Culture can channel them in diverse ways, but it can rarely defy them altogether. Another way of putting this is that culture envelopes the human organism, penetrates it, but never entirely fuses with it.

3

Confronted with a proximate cause of a piece of behavior, whether it be aggression, sexual behavior, altruism, or whatever, the sociobiologists ask themselves ultimate questions like: "How has this behavior contributed to the inclusive fitness of the species?" Asking such questions, however, does not stamp sociobiologists as genetic determinists, nor does it render them blind to cultural input. As the father of sociobiology, E. O. Wilson, himself has put it.

> Human behavior is dominated by culture in the sense that the greater part, perhaps all, of the variation between societies is based on cultural experience. But this is not to say that human beings are infinitely plastic. . . . Assisted by sociobiological analyses, a stronger social science might develop. An exciting collaboration between biologists and social scientists appears to have begun (Wilson, 1978:xiv).

There is little doubt that general human traits arose from the evolutionary history of the species. Behavioral traits that somehow contribute to species survival exert pressure for selection into the repertoire of traits characterizing the species. Nonetheless, to say that Jimmy rapes and kills because lust and aggression are male mammalian traits that have been selected by evolutionary pressures begs an awful lot of questions. Jimmy's behavior is the result of phylogenetic characteristics he shares with his species, his unique genetic endowment, the functioning of his nervous system and its present state of arousal (hormonal and neurotransmitter activation), his prior experiences, the immediate activating stimuli, and how all these factors permutate and interact. Because species characteristics, by definition, do not vary qualitatively (even if they do so quantitatively) but the other mechanisms enumerated do, the criminologist is least interested in species characteristics and most interested in identifying the other mechanisms.

For instance, the sociobiologist and the biosocial criminologist would attempt to explain the phenomenon of human rape quite differently. Sociobiologists would look at how evolution has shaped the basic reproductive strategies of human males and females. Females, they reason, shed a one or more of a finite number of ova on a periodic basis. If she is to reproduce and push her genes into the future, she must mate at a time when a number of integrated biological events — sexual receptivity, optimal uterine environment, and the presence of a fertile ovum — occur in synchrony (Naftolin, 1981). Since the human infant maintains a long period of dependency, its mother invests tremendous personal resources in bearing and rearing it. Because she has few opportunities to reproduce relative to the male and because she must assure herself that she has male support in child rearing, she has to discriminate among males with whom she will copulate. She has to refuse copulation to males who do not appear to have the resources necessary to provide for her and her offspring. (This is not true today, but phylogenetic behavior has to be evaluated in terms of the conditions that existed at the time that the behavior was being selected into the behavioral repertoire of the species.)

If the males reproductive pattern were also periodic, it would require that sperm shedding, sexual arousal, and the aggression necessary to ward off competing males would have to be synchronized with the female cycle. Such a double synchronicity would be unlikely and would afford little opportunity for individual males to push their genes into the future. The optimal reproductive pattern for the male, then, would be one in which the male is constantly producing fertile gametes and in which he is constantly sexually ready (Naftolin, 1981). We are thus confronted with two conflicting reproductive strategies: the female strategy, which is discriminating and periodic, and the male strategy, which is indiscriminate and non-periodic. When male demand is confronted with female denial, rape is sometimes the result. As Thornhill and Thornhill (1987:286) put it: "... human rape is a maladaptive consequence of an adaptive general mating strategy of men."

Such an implied view of rape as "natural" (albeit "maladaptive") is guaranteed to rattle many cages. Scientists working from a biosocial perspective may accept that certain behaviors are, at bottom, the result of eons of evolutionary selection. But I think that they would also agree that any attempt to explain a complex phenomenon like rape by appealing to such remote ultimate causes is analogous to blaming the length of Cleopatra's nose for the Second World War.[1] The biosocial scientist would want to know the contexts in which rape typically occurs, the family background of the rapist, his capacity to learn social prescriptions and proscriptions, his moral orientation, the status of his neurohormonal system, and many other biological and social factors before attempting a causal analysis.

## Of Theory and Censorship

Violent juvenile delinquency has long been a source of concern. Like the weather, everyone talks about it, specialists study it and make predictions about it, but they have difficulty explaining it. Not that they don't try; we suffer from an embarrassment of theoretical riches in this area, so much so that a comprehensive listing of the them would fill a couple of pages. Theories come and go and are resurrected and buried according to the ideological tenor of the times. There is nothing like the unanimity found among scholars in the hard sciences as to what matters constitute established fact, or about which phenomena have satisfactory explanations. Students in introductory criminology or juvenile delinquency classes are immediately introduced to the thickets of ideological controversy surrounding these areas. The multitude of conflicting theories within criminology is a strong indicator of the softness of our science. There are areas of disagreement in the hard sciences also, but the amount of knowledge about which there are no disagreements that students must assimilate is so vast that controversies are rarely introduced until students reach graduate school.

Much of the "noise" coming from criminology and juvenile delinquency studies surely has a lot to do with the infancy of our science. After all, physics and chemistry have been around for a long time, but scientific attempts to study human behavior are only about one century old. But it also has a lot to do with the stubborn refusal on the part (perhaps the majority) of criminologists to consider anything but the "environment" to be responsible for crime and delinquency. The antipathy to non-environmental explanations for any kind of human behavior is exemplified by the well-known responses, many of them physically violent ones, that greeted the works of Jensen, Eysenck, E. O. Wilson, Herrnstein, and others of similar persuasion. The only "crime" these men are guilty of is trying arrive at some plausible explanation for how the environment "gets into" the individual to produce the behavior both they and their detractors are interested in.

A self-imposed quasi censorship does exist when a topic proposed for publication is seen as distasteful: "Standards of evidence are elevated when one is defying the zeitgeist," writes Sandra Scarr (1981:523). Scarr asks why it is that environmentalists are not required to consider alternative genetic explanations for their findings just as researchers who offer genetic explanations are required to posit environmental alternatives. "Our work," she writes, "is subjected to the scrutiny of an electron microscope when the rest of psychology is examined through the wrong end of a telescope" (1981:524). Sarnoff Mednick (Buikhuisen and Mednick, 1988:6) reports that he was told to burn data implicating genetic factors among the causes of crime. Gordon (1980) has written a revealing piece about the politics of publishing works that "defy the zeitgeist," and

Durden-Smith and deSimone (1983:20) relate how their proposal for a book on sex and the brain was dismissed by one reviewer with the words: "this book ought not to be done." Not that their proposal was poorly done or that the authors were ignorant of the literature, but because to explore the biological bases of sex differences was ideologically unacceptable to the reviewer as "sexist" and "anti-humanist."

Ideological soulmates of Durden-Smith and deSimone's reviewer may likewise pepper their thoughts of the present work with epithets like "reductionist," "biological determinist," "racist," "sexist," or even "fascist," for I touch on the subjects of sex and race as well as IQ. While I categorically reject such labels, I do recognize that the violation of taboos has the tendency to evoke them. Let us not fool ourselves: there are taboos in criminology. It is also true that the defenders of the environmentalist faith use their positions as reviewers and editors to make such statements as "this book (article, research project, etc.) ought not be done."

There must be some limits to scientific research; the horribly cruel experiments of Hitler's SS physicians, crossbreeding of humans and animals, and the use of human beings to experiment with dangerous drugs come immediately to mind. But the statistical analysis of data on behavioral differences among people that may be explicable in biosocial terms should not be taboo just because it may cause psychic pain for some. After all, the works of Copernicus, Darwin, Freud, and of many other scientists who bucked the ideological tide caused great psychic pain in the religious community, a community which also went to great lengths to convince others that such works ought not be done. We should not reduce ourselves to the level of book burners, for in the maelstrom of conflicting ideologies the one unifying force is science.

## Violence: Social and Individual Explanations

FBI figures for 1989 indicate that violent crime increased five percent between 1987 and 1988. The increase in violence among juveniles is particularly troubling (Romig, Cleland, and Romig, 1989:130). Although the incidence, that is, the rate, of violence has shown steady and troubling increases for a number of years, the evidence seems to indicate that the prevalence (the proportion of consistently violent offenders) remains relatively stable over time. Increasing incidence and relatively stable prevalence leads to the conclusion that a small minority of offenders are committing more and more acts of violence.

Consider the 1945 birth cohort study of Wolfgang, Figlio, and Sellin (1972). They found that 6.3% of the 9,945 subjects committed 71% of the murders, 73% of the rapes, and 82% of the robberies attributed to the birth cohort. In a follow-up study of a larger (28,338 subjects) birth cohort born in 1958 (Tracy, Wolfgang, and Figlio, 1985), the incidence of violent delinquency was three to five times greater than found in the 1945 cohort. However, approximately the same percentage of individuals (7.5%) again committed the vast majority of violent crimes. In the 1945 cohort, 34.9% of the subjects were arrested at least once, and 33% in the 1958 cohort. Similar findings are reported among a 30,000 strong Copenhagen cohort by Wilkin et al. (1977). Thus, although the percentage of the respective cohorts who became delinquent, as well as the percentage who became chronic recidivists, remained essentially the same, the chronic recidivists are committing more violent crimes than ever before.

Despite excellent data like those provided by the cohort studies, sociological criminology still turns for explanations to forces outside the individual to explain his violence. The causes of violence are seen as poverty, social class, white racism, capitalism, variations of the subculture of violence thesis, poor schooling, or any combination or permutation thereof. Staunch advocates of cultural explanations disavow any kind of causal explanations that speak to individual differences, often dismissing such attempts as dated relics of a positivistic past (Taylor, Walton, and Young, 1973). "Whenever we find a high rate of delinquency," writes MacIver (1960:123), "we can be sure that the root trouble lies not in the youths themselves, but in the social and environmental conditions to which their families have been exposed." It appears that Hirschi and Hindelang (1977:571) were quite correct when they wrote: "Few groups in American society have been defended more diligently by sociologists against allegations of difference than ordinary delinquents."

This is not to say that explanations favored by sociologists lack cogency. There is no doubt that certain environments are more conducive to violence than others, and that given certain situations anyone is capable of reacting violently. We only have to peruse the data across cultures and time periods to realize that the cultural milieu has a tremendous influence on the rate of violence and on crime in general. But this observation should not prevent us from asking why individuals experiencing identical environments behave quite differently. Why do some individuals raised in the stench of the ghetto become productive members of the community while others raised in relatively benign environments become criminals? Why do most individuals arrested once or twice not get arrested again (as we see from the cohort studies) while others go on to become serious recidivists? Why do some steal without resorting to violence while for others violence is part and parcel of their criminal activities?

The data from the cohort studies appear unequivocally to indicate that the problem of serious and protracted delinquency, especially violent delinquency, lies with relatively small groups of *individuals* within our society. All behavior is the result of individuals operating in environments, and different people react differently to their environment. Criminologists have enjoyed very little success in explaining the prevalence as opposed to the incidence of violence with reference only to the sociocultural environment. If we are to adequately confront the problem of violence *within* any given cultural milieu in addition to attempting to identify aspects of the milieu that are conducive to violence, we must study those individuals most responsible for it. This means that we must address the psychology and biology of such individuals, as well as their environment. As Jeffery (1990:377) has pointed out: "The brain, hormones, and the neurotransmitter system are critical to an understanding of violent behavior." This means that criminology must become an interdisciplinary science, for I agree with Jeffery (1990:273) that "Sociological criminology, separate from other disciplines, is not a viable enterprise."

### Reductionism and Emergence in Science

The great physicist Percy Bridgman always maintained that the first step in understanding any system—atomic particles, chemical compounds, cells, individual organisms, societies—is to understand the elementary units comprising the system. He considered this just as important for the social sciences as for the more advanced scientists. In his own words:

> The ultimate problem in the social sciences is similar to that of the physical sciences but is infinitely more complex. The ultimate problem is the problem of understanding the functioning of the elementary units of which the systems are built up. The elementary units in the physical sciences are particles. There are only a few kinds of them [this was written before the current menagerie of particles had been discovered]. It took us a long time to find some of the laws and we haven't got the laws of some of the particles yet. The elementary units

of the social sciences are men [and women] and the corresponding ultimate problem is to understand the individual human being. (1955:49–50.)

Bridgman's position is plainly reductionist. If I am interpreting him correctly, he is not denying that social phenomena can be explained in its own terms. Rather, he is saying that these complex social phenomena can be *more fully* understood if their explanations maintain consistency with what we know about the more elementary units. As reasonable as this seems, there has, nevertheless, been a long history of opposition to this approach. This has been particularly true for criminology because most criminologists operate within departments of sociology, a discipline that is largely antagonistic to reductionism of any kind. Let us briefly explore this history.

When scientists write about the methodologies of their discipline, they typically refer to hierarchically arranged "levels of analysis." These levels serve to organize knowledge of a field of inquiry along manageable lines, albeit often artificially discrete ones. When the term "reductionism" is used in the social and behavioral sciences, it is often used disparagingly to mean that an inappropriate (lower) unit of analysis has been used to explore, describe, and explain a particular research question. It is a mistake, however, to confuse a detailed analysis of a segment of a larger system with the straw man image of reductionism held by some social scientists, although there are indeed some research questions not amenable to reductionist explanations.

When examining the phenomenon of crime, for instance, one level of analysis might be "society." We could ask a question like "Why is society A more criminogenic than society B?" To ask such a question is to seek a reply from the sociologist (or perhaps the political scientist, the historian, or the economist), because it is couched in broad "macro" terms. A psychologist may also attempt to answer such a question by appealing to the vocabulary of psychology. He or she could do so by indicating that society A produces a different kind of mind-set as it relates to conformity/ nonconformity than society B. In doing so, the psychologist has "reduced" the explanation of a question couched in terms of one unit of analysis (whole societies) to a lower unit of analysis (individual mind-sets). A sociologist may consider this inappropriate; the psychologist would beg to differ.

The social scientist need not utilize the vocabulary of psychology to answer the question as posed, for it does not inquire about "mind-sets."

But the psychologist must *necessarily* use the vocabulary of the social scientist because he or she must delineate the nature of the social milieu producing the mind-sets so that the question and its answer maintain consistency. That is, the psychological explanation of the phenomenon requires not only the use of psychological terms but also of specifically sociological, political, economic, and historical terms that do not occur in the psychological vocabulary. But note that by asserting the social milieu of society A produces individuals who tend more than individuals in society B to be competitive, aggressive, hedonistic, or whatever, and that folks possessing such traits tend to be more criminal than those who do not, the psychologist has added a useful dimension to the answer to the question. He or she has decidedly not detracted from the social scientist's explanation as long as the cultural conditions conducive to the development of the enumerated character traits are acknowledged.

A biologist or chemist, on the other hand, could not reply to the question if limited to the vocabulary of biology and chemistry. There are biochemical explanations for why some people are more competitive, aggressive, or hedonistic than others, thereby reducing psychological units of analysis (individuals) to biochemical units of analysis (the molecular goings on within those individuals). But any such biochemical explanation for individual differences says nothing about why such traits translate into criminal behavior more in society A than society B. After all, one can be competitive, aggressive, and hedonistic, and be perfectly law-abiding.

Crime *rates* are an emergent property of sociocultural systems that cannot be deduced from molecular analysis of individuals within them. To assert that they can, a biochemist would have to show that properties of the whole (society) can be deduced from biochemical properties of its constituent parts (individuals). In other words, the biochemist must possess a suitable theory making it possible to analyze the form and nature of the whole as having been derived from the properties of biochemical units of analysis. No such theory exists. Thus, the phenomenon which is to be explained (why society A is more criminogenic than society B) can be adequately explained sociologically, adequately explained psychologically given the proviso that sociocultural variables are acknowledged, and not explained at all by biochemistry. The line separating sociology and psychology is fuzzy with regard to this question, but the line separating sociology and biochemistry is clear and sharp.

Because discipline lines are sharp with regard to some questions, it does not mean that cross-disciplinary lines of communication are closed with regard to other questions. I have always considered the social and behavioral sciences as being continuous with biology in the same way that biology is continuous with chemistry, and chemistry with physics. Others like to draw sharp lines and erect high fences between "their" science and its neighbors regardless of the form in which a particular research question is posed.

The drawers of sharp lines invoke the notion of emergence; the notion that wholes constitute higher levels of organization, the properties of which are not considered predictable from properties found at lower levels of organization. What constitutes a "whole" depends, of course, on the discipline—one science's emergence is another's reductionism. At one time or another, representatives of each science on August Comte's "hierarchy of science" ladder, from chemistry to sociology, conscious of the emergent nature of the phenomena they study, have attempted to disassociate their science from the "reductionism" of the more basic sciences.

In the nineteenth century, chemist Benjamine Brodie made a case for limiting chemical explanations to simple qualitative and gravimetric changes in chemical compounds because there are emergent properties of those compounds that he considered not predictable a priori from their constituent parts (Harre, 1967:290). Brodie wanted an "atomless" chemistry, and the overwhelming majority of the London Chemical Society of the 1870s were in sympathy with him. But where would chemistry be today without its concepts of valence, covalence, ionic bonding, and the periodic table of atomic weights, all derived from physics?

For instance, the constituent properties of ordinary table salt was once an issue in chemistry. Today, we know that salt is a compound of chlorine, a deadly poison, and sodium, a substance that explodes on contact with water. A Swedish chemist named Svante Arrehenius posited these constituents for salt in his doctoral dissertation, which was twice turned down because his committee just "knew" that salt could not be composed of such a deadly combination. Arrehenius's committee considered salt an irreducible "whole" simply because they were ignorant of the properties of its constituent parts. Arrehenius's dissertation elucidated the process of ionic bonding (an ion is an electrically charged atom), and he went on to win the Nobel prize. Today, chemists know that to characterize any phenomenon in their discipline as irreducibly emergent is to admit their ignorance.

Biology, too, attempted in its earlier days to maintain autonomy from chemistry. As late as the 1940s, J. H. Woodger (1948) argued that biological phenomena should not be reduced to the concepts of physics and chemistry, and that biologists should use biological facts to explain other biological facts (sociologists will recognize the Durkheimian ring to that statement). Life, the subject matter of biology, assuredly is an emergent property, and the step from the inorganic to the organic is the most momentous discontinuity in all of science. Life is certainly something more than the arrangement of self-duplicating amino acids around the symmetry of the carbon atom, and to describe it requires a specific biological vocabulary not found in physics or chemistry.

However, the decoding of the "language of life" by Watson and Crick was not achieved by adhering to the various doctrines of biological ontological autonomy, but rather by an exploration of the physical and chemical properties of the DNA molecule. As was the case with Arrehenius, Watson and Crick's reductionism landed them a Nobel prize. Science seems to advance most fruitfully by exploring constituent parts rather than exploring emergent wholes.

Psychology, a step from life in general to human life and all that it implies, especially the behaviorist tradition, has attempted to disassociate itself from biology. It is asserted that behavior can best be examined and explained in its own right with reference to stimulus-response connections and contingencies of reinforcement. Although B. F. Skinner was the strongest modern advocate of this position, he has himself used the biological evolutionary model to explain the basics behind the acquisition of operant behaviors (1966). He realized that the ease or difficulty of acquiring operant behaviors, and the selection of what stimuli we will pay attention to, has its roots in the biological traits of the species.

Nevertheless, within behaviorism as a whole, concepts such as desire, motivation, intelligence, consciousness, and so on, were relegated to the realm of metaphysics. But we are all aware that we do think, learn, desire. If we are to comprehend these mechanisms, psychology soon found out, we must open up the "black box," so to speak, and explore the biophysiology of these concepts. One only has to compare psychology textbooks of today with those of 10–20 years ago to see the major shift that has taken place in psychology with respect to integrating biology into psychological theories. Indeed, a recent special edition of the *Journal of*

*Personality* (58(1), 1990) dealt entirely with the biological foundations of personality. Throughout the issue were papers calling for a more biologically informed psychology of personality. Psychology is a more exact science today than it was in the heyday of radical environmentalism because of its marriage to biology, just as biology and chemistry became more exact when they hitched themselves to physics. In other words, reductionism, while not the only game in town, continues to be the major path to scientific knowledge.

At the top of the hierarchy of science ladder sits the sociologist, who, with apparent acrophobia, disdains to look down. Alone among the sciences, sociology has decided that the path of least resistance lies in ignoring the basic sciences and clings to discipline parochialism. Jeffery (1979:8) points out that "Some of the biggest names in political science, economics, anthropology, psychology, and psychiatry are now involved in biological issues. Only sociology stands out as an opponent of biological systems." I wonder if we shall ever see a special issue of a major sociological journal calling for a more biologically informed sociology?

It can be asserted with confidence that by and large sociology still reveres Durkheim's dictum that we should seek explanations for social facts, such as crime, in other social facts, and nowhere else. On the whole, the discipline still adheres to Dennis Wrong's (1968) "oversocialized, disembodied and desexualized conception of man." Irwin Deutscher (1967:247) exemplified this position in stating that it would be just as absurd to reduce the problem of criminal behavior to psychological explanations as it would be to reduce it to the level of subatomic particles. It would be absurd indeed to attempt to exclude the power of social forces in any psychological (or biochemical) explanation for crime, but the opposite is just as absurd if one wants a more complete picture, a picture that others outside the discipline can recognize. If social science in general, and criminology in particular, is to become more than a set of *ad hoc* systems of moral philosophy, we must file Durkheim's dictum in the historical files alongside Woodger's biological dictum.

While the deductive pyramid of reductionism, a pyramid in which each level incorporates the findings of the level beneath it, appears to be the ideal method of science at present, it is not without its pitfalls. There are radical lovers of reductionism just as there are radical lovers of wholism.

Figure 1.1 presents the reductionist/emergence ladder indicating the direction of causation implied by radical reductionism as it applies to human behavior. A radical reductionist sees a chain of causal events running up the ladder from molecules to human behavior, even to complex social organizations. One such reductionist, biologist Philip Applewhite, has stated emphatically: "Our behavior is controlled by molecules—by nothing else" (1981:1). Applewhite's claim is made on the basis that we are composed of molecules, that there is no "we" apart from the molecules that compose us, and so our behavior is the result of some molecules moving around other molecules.

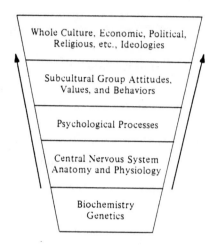

Figure 1.1.   The Reductionist/Emergence Ladder indicating the Reductionist Causal Direction for Human Behavior

This sort of thinking is every bit as nonviable as the radical environmentalist's claim that our behavior is controlled by our experiences—and by nothing else. Applewhite's own "we are composed of" argument can be used against itself, for molecules are themselves "composed of." He stops his reductionism at the molecular level because he is a molecular biologist. Were he a physicist, he might have pointed out that molecules are an emergent property composed of two or more atoms (which are themselves "composed of") held together by physical forces. Were a subatomic physicist so inclined, he or she might make the ridiculous statement that our behavior is controlled by non-material cosmic forces—and by nothing else.[2]

Applewhite's argument implies that the DNA molecule is a directions operative that functions in the same rigidly determined way regardless of the organism's experience. But recent work in genetics has shown that many genes are "switched on" in response to important environmental experiences (Kandel, 1983), and that functional connections between brain nerve cells are not "automatic" but rather are made in response to environmental impulses (Kalil, 1989). Alterations in structure and function resulting from experience may even occur, Applewhite's assertion notwithstanding, at the molecular level (Goelet et al., 1986).

Perhaps it is valid for some purposes to assert that behavior is "nothing but" the result of orchestra of chemical voices in the brain telling us what to do, but no amount of neurochemical knowledge can tell us *what* someone is thinking, the process of creating a poem, or why it was created. To attempt to explain the writing of a poem by brain chemistry is analogous to explaining a Rubenstein performance by analyzing the physics of piano strings. Even a definitive description of the neurochemical bases of some complex behavior would be insufficient to understand that behavior without it being augmented by a description at the functional level of analysis. Any phenomenon is a singular unit or whole *and* a part of a larger totality. The biosocial perspective recognizes this imbeddedness and interrelatedness, and it recognizes the necessity of elucidating the nature of both parts and wholes and how they affect one another. I believe that this is the perspective that will eventually breed a criminology worthy of the honorific title "scientific."

Scientific criminology, according to Jefferey (1977, 1990), should be an interdisciplinary science integrating the insights provided by chemistry, biology, psychology, and sociology, and their interstitial disciplines such as biochemistry, psychobiology, and sociobiology. If we do not start looking down the ladder to other sciences (after all, ladders are for climbing up and down depending on what part of the house needs painting), Ellis (1977) sees "the decline and fall" of sociology. This belief was echoed by Alice Rossi, elder stateswoman of sociology and a first-rate scientist who has become comfortable with the biological literature, in her 1983 presidential address to the American Sociological Association. While she was speaking of parental and gender roles specifically, her comments can be generalized to other interests in sociology. She writes:

> Hence, sociological units of analysis such as roles, groups, networks, and classes divert attention from the fact that the subjects of our work are male and female animals with genes, glands, bone and flesh occupying an ecological niche of a particular kind in a tiny fragment of time. And human sexual dimorphism emerged from a long prehistory of mammalian and primate evolution. Theories that neglect these characteristics of sex and gender carry a

high risk of eventual irrelevance against the mounting evidence of sexual dimorphism from the biological and neurosciences (1984:1).

While I cannot agree with Jefferey (1977:284) that criminologists should have dropped the major sociological theories of crime twenty (now thirty plus) years ago in favor of biopsychological explanations, I do believe that criminological theory does run Rossi's "high risk of eventual irrelevance" by failing to note the evidence relevant to criminal behavior accumulating among the basic sciences. To note the evidence, of course, requires more than a nodding acquaintance with the phenomena of disciplines other than our own. This, according to Wilson and Herrnstein (1985:80), appears to be the biggest stumbling block against criminology being the kind of interdisciplinary science that Jefferey envisions. People have a tendency to disparage what they don't understand (think of all the clever anti-statistics arguments you have heard issued by colleagues who have limited exposure in this area).

### Ideological Issues and Biosocial Explanations

One behavioral biologist has written: "No one in today's behavioral sciences doubts that biology is making, and is destined to continue to make, a massive, profound impact on these sciences" (Konner, 1982:11). He is quite wrong. Many, perhaps most, behavioral scientists still malign biological explanations of any of the phenomenon they study. In fact, for many such scientists the impingement of biology represents their worst professional nightmare.

Much of the animosity directed at any attempt to explain crime and delinquency in biosocial terms may have more to do with ideology and ethical concerns than with discipline loyalty. Opponents envision the ghosts of the likes of Lombrosso, Spencer, the eugenicists, and the social Darwinists, along with Hitler's hordes of racial purists, marching silently between the lines. Criminology's parent discipline, sociology, led the fight against the purveyors of "bad seed," "survival of the fittest," and laissez-faire "let the poor starve" philosophies that found their theoretical sustenance in the biology of the period. Sociology became the self-appointed conscience of science and took on an advocacy role on the part of the oppressed and underprivileged in society akin to the role of the ACLU in law. Because sociologists tend to view criminals as basically "normal folk" who have fallen afoul of unjust social conditions, they view biological explanations of criminality as diverting attention from the ideological agenda of ameliorating social conditions they see as unjust. Much good has come from their stance, and they are to be applauded for taking it. Such advocacy should and must continue, but it should not be confused with science. Neither should the scientific and social justice agendas be considered antagonists. "Ignorance of biological processes," writes Rossi (1987:65), "may doom efforts at social change because we misidentify the targets for change, and hence our means to achieve the change we desire."

In light of Alice Rossi's 1984 ASA presidential address calling for the integration of biological thinking into sociological theories, it is interesting that the first president of the ASA (then the American Sociological Society), Lester Ward, was a biologist who became a sociologist. It was he who led the fight against the fad of biological analogizing among social thinkers such as Herbert Spencer, Walter Bagehot, and William Graham Sumner, and it was he who so thoroughly discredited the primitive behavioral biology of his time that most sociologists since have dismissed as reductionist and irrelevant.

But as sociologist Michael Teitelbaum (1976:17) has pointed out: "The pendulum swung to the other extreme—from facile arguments by analogy to facile dismissal of theory and evidence." Sociological criminology is still fighting the same battles against the same old foes. In continued efforts to further assail long discredited arguments, "bad seed," "criminal atavism," and the Juke and Kallikak families are still trotted out under the heading of "biological theories" in many modern criminology textbooks. A typical example is presented by Farley (1990). After presenting Lombroso, Sheldon's body typing, and the XYY "supermale" theory as examples of biological theories of crime, he concludes that "biological theories explain little, if any, criminal or delinquent behavior" (1990:217).

In company with many other sociologists, Farley ignores the fact that today's biology is light years more advanced than the primitive state it was in during the nineteenth century. The subfield of genetics, for instance, is advancing at a dizzying pace. Geneticists can identify individuals by their DNA, they can sequence DNA to identify chemical components, they can do genetic "engineering," they have identified marker genes (genes that are associated with the presence or absence of some characteristic) on every chromosome, and they are in the process of mapping each and every gene in the human genome. This is a far cry from feeling cranial bumps and measuring foreheads. Those who hurl the gauntlet at Lombroso and his like are fighting battles in wars long ago won: what modern chemist quotes Brodie, or what modern geologist resurrects Bishop Ussher as a straw man to buttress a favored theory? The evidence confronting the detractors of biosocial theory is strong, and rather than meeting it head on with their own data, they string together clotheslines of faded cliches, *ad hominem* arguments, selected anecdotes, and straw men.

For instance, take a typical statement regarding the study of crime and intelligence. Platt and Takagi, stressing the "long and notorious history of biologically oriented theory in criminology" (1985:55), make the statement that "intelligence, as measured by paper and pencil tests, is a reification, a mechanistic construct which assumes that cognitive ability is a fixed attribute" (1985:60). This is an excellent example of a straw man, for I have not seen one instance in the professional literature (at least not in the literature spanning the last twenty years) of anyone asserting that intelligence is a fixed attribute. Neither, I warrant, have Platt or Tagaki.

Other critics of biosocial theory—or any other kind of theory that addresses attributes of individuals, for that matter—stress the ameliorative nihilism and philosophy of "blaming the victim" they presume would be the result of uncovering any biological cause of crime and delinquency. One such critic writes: "Suppose, for example, we could convince ourselves that inner-city violence was the product of 'bad genes' among the urban poor. We could then attribute such violence to the natural deficiencies of the poor rather than to their poverty in the midst of plenty. In short, we could blame the poor themselves for their violence" (Farley, 1990:217).

Contained in these three sentences are a number of unfounded assumptions. The first assumption is that if we uncover a biological basis for some problematic behavior that nothing can be done about it. Wilson and Herrnstein (1985:468–469) point out that the first step toward any control or reversal of any problem area for which there is a known genetic susceptibility is to look for such predisposing factors early in life. If such a susceptibility exists but is not looked for or is denied, then indeed nothing can be done. It is highly unlikely that there are any genes coding specifically for antisocial violence, but there may be identifiable genes that code for certain physiological processes that make violence more likely in certain situations.

The second assumption is that the only "true" cause of violence has been uncovered ("poverty in the midst of plenty"), and therefore it is an exercise in futility to search for spurious causes within a discredited theoretical framework. This unicausal parochialism has already been addressed and will not be elaborated further here.

The third assumption is that relative deprivation causes violence in a completely prescribed fashion, and since this is so, we falsely attribute blame for violence to those who commit it. This is radical environmental determinism at its worst. According to this line of thought, people are pawns of the environmental winds that blow them hither and thither, so we cannot afford them the human dignity of either praise or blame. Criminals and delinquents are as nonviolent and morally upright as the rest of us: they are simply bankrupt members of the bourgeoisie. Since violence is a function of financial rather than characterological deficits, it would be eliminated if the wealth were more equitably distributed. Perhaps some of it would be, but even in utopia there would be violent people whose violence needs explaining.

Closely allied with Farley's concern is the genuine concern that any kind of biological theory of crime and delinquency can be used to "justify all kinds of persecution, oppression, and exploitation" (Radzinowicz and King, 1977:23). However, powerful groups who engage in such despicable behavior have never had to wait for scientists to justify it for them. Gordon (1980) points out that genocidal behavior has almost always been directed at groups who are intellectually superior to their oppressors; e.g., the Jews in Germany, the Armenians in Turkey, the Ibos in Nigeria, and the slaughter of intellectuals in the Central African Republic, Bangladesh, and Cambodia. I believe that it can be demonstrated that radical environmentalism has done more damage to humanity than any claims or "racial superiority" buttressed by dishonest science has. As Wilson (1978:301) has indicated, the belief of the unlimited malleability of humans has served as support for the most reactionary and inhumane of social doctrines (e.g., communist attempts to build the "new Russian/Chinese/Cambodian man"). Shared knowledge, dispassionately analyzed and discussed, and free of ideological censorship, is the true goal of liberalism and of science.

### Conclusion

It is taken as a given that many aspects of crime and criminology, such as criminal definitions, differential rates, and cross-cultural comparisons, can be adequately explained in social, economic, and political terms. But when the focus is on the individual criminal, especially the chronic violent criminal, we must go beyond these broad macro explanations to encompass the biology of the person. This is a position gathering momentum within criminology (Fishbein, 1990). People differ constitutionally, and differences in constitution mean that certain circumstances will more easily activate criminal behavior among those who are biologically predisposed to it than they will for others not so predisposed. Conversely, some people are protected from the influences of a criminogenic milieu by constitutions that predisposes them to prosocial behavior. Of course, there is no one-to-one relationship between biological mechanisms and the behavior of human beings, but an understanding of these mechanisms will aid us in the interpretation and elucidation of that behavior.

To say that some forms of criminal activity may have a biological basis does not discount environmental input. This is decidedly not a book pitting nature against nurture. Rather, it looks at nature *via* nurture. It is interesting that nature-via-nurture questions excite biological scientists more than they do social scientists. As Rossi (1977:7) put it: " . . . researchers in the biological sciences have gone further in incorporating social variables into their research than the social sciences have gone in incorporating physiological variables into theirs, with the ironic consequence that there is more evidence to support the importance of social variables in the biological literature than there is evidence to reject the evidence of physiological variables in the sociological literature." If we continue to defer to the biological sciences in the study of human behavior, we may wake up one day to find that the rest of the scientific community regards us with the same smug condescension that is today reserved for "scientific" creationists.

## ENDNOTES

1. Since sociobiology's stated aim is to understand ultimate phylogenetic causes rather than proximate ontogenetic causes, this should not be construed as a harsh criticism of sociobiology. Marxists, for instance, also posit ultimate causes when they attribute blame for all kinds of pathologies on the capitalist mode of production.
2. Applewhite (1981:228) remarks that anti-reductionists are fond of saying that "reductionists learn more and more about less and less until they end up knowing everything about nothing." In response, he states: "It could be said of anti-reductionists that they learn less and less about more and more until they know nothing about everything." There is a certain

tongue-in-cheek truth in both charge and countercharge. This observation points to the value of interstitial disciplines such as biochemistry and psychobiology, since such disciplines are interested in marrying reductionist phenomena to holistic phenomena.

# Chapter Two

# THE "NATURE" OF INTELLIGENCE

## What is Intelligence?

The following discussion restricts the term "intelligence" to phenotypic intelligence. This restriction explicitly recognizes that the measurable trait to be discussed is the result of variable genotypes interacting with variable environments to produce phenotypes expressing variable traits. The role played by the environment in accounting for variance in IQ scores is recognized, but an exploration of environmental variables is deferred to the next chapter.

There is a vast literature seeking to come to grips with a definition of intelligence. It would seem that intelligence, like pornography, is easier to recognize than to define. But then, all verbal definitions of meaningful concepts (love, truth, justice) are notoriously open to criticism. We fight about verbal definitions of important concepts because they encompass a multitude of sub-concepts (they would hardly be important if they didn't). All is not chaos, though. Most definitions do contain elements about which there is general consensus. "Love is the recognition of special value in the loved·one"; "truth is speaking in a manner consistent with the facts"; "justice consists of impartial adjustments of conflicting claims," are definitions about which there would be very little argument. Nevertheless, they are horribly simple, and whole books—lots of them—have been written that seek to elucidate the "essence" of those concepts.

It is not appropriate to attempt to review the literature debating the "essence" of intelligence in a work devoted to linking intellectual imbalance and love deprivation to violent delinquency. But we do need a definition from which to proceed further. To obtain one, I will take the easy way out and resort to a head count of experts.

Snyderman and Rothman (1988) surveyed 1,020 Ph.D.'s identified as experts in developmental and educational psychology, educational sociology, behavioral genetics, and a number of other fields in which intelligence issues are frequently examined. These experts were asked to check all behavior descriptions that they considered to be important elements of the concept of intelligence. Snyderman and Rothman (1988:56) placed their responses into three categories: (1) those for which there was virtual unanimity—"abstract thinking of reasoning," checked by 99.3 percent of the respondents, "problem-solving ability," 97.7 percent, and capacity to acquire knowledge," 96 percent; (2) those checked by the majority—e.g., "memory," 80.5 percent, "adaptation to one's environment," 77.2 percent, and "mental speed," 71.7 percent; (3) those rarely (less than 25 percent) checked—e.g., "achievement motivation," 18.9 percent, and "goal directedness," 24 percent.

The authors of the study warn that these descriptions should not be taken as a rigorous definition of intelligence. Nevertheless, the listed elements provide a basis for formulating one. The enumeration of indicators or elements of intelligence suffices to say that most intelligence theorists have not argued overly much with the general substance of the definition offered by the "dean" of intelligence, David Wechsler, who defined it as:

> The aggregate of global capacity of the individual to act purposefully, to think rationally, and to deal effectively with his [sic] environment. It is aggregate or global because it is composed of elements or abilities (features) which, although not entirely independent, are qualitatively differentiable. (quoted in Matarazzo, 1976:79.)

Intelligence is thus a complex web of intellectual behavior that is both general (global) and specific to the various situations requiring cognitive evaluation of incoming information so that a variety of academic, moral, ethical, and other sundry problems and concerns can be satisfactorily resolved. Since intelligence is intellectual *behavior,* a person's readiness to engage in it, and the degree to which it will probably result in positive outcomes, can be measured, albeit imperfectly, via IQ tests. If we can measure intelligence, we can measure (also imperfectly) other types of behavior and observe how intelligence influences that behavior.

Some theorists balk at the use of the term "intelligence" in conjunction with IQ tests. For instance, Simmons (1978:267) suggests that IQ be thought of as "a broad set of verbal and problem-solving skills which are better labeled academic aptitudes or scholastic readiness." But "intelligence" is a convenient umbrella label for the bundle of skills Simmons enumerates, and is a label that professionals and lay persons alike readily recognize as appropriately encompassing those skills. Young (1975:71) points out that the litmus test of IQ testing is empirical and not universal agreement on the appropriateness of the label: "They could have called it the Idiocy Test for all the difference it would have made."

I use the terms "intelligence" and "IQ" interchangeably with the knowledge that IQ is an operational definition of intelligence. IQ tests no more capture the "essence" of the concept of intelligence (whatever that abstraction means) than the readings corresponding to the height of a column of mercury in a sphygmomanometer captures the "essence" of the concept of arterial blood pressure. I do not wish to imply that I subscribe to the position that the operationalization of a concept *is* the concept. However, it is only by operationalizing a concept that we can make reliable predictions from concept to concept, and often we cannot know very much about a concept apart from the way we measure it. We can, for instance, predict different health outcomes for individuals A and B if we know that their typical blood pressure readings are 190/110 and 115/75, respectively. Likewise, we can predict different life outcomes for individuals with IQs of 120 and 80. Our predictions based on IQ levels will not be as accurate as our health predictions based on blood pressure, for many more variables impact on "life outcomes" than on cardiovascular health. Nevertheless, our predictions will be more accurate with knowledge of IQ than without such knowledge.

Intellectual behavior is phenotypical behavior, the outcome of genotypes interacting with all sorts of physical and social stimuli. As with all forms of human behavior, genes influence intelligence. Genes do not, however, determine intelligence in any completely prescribed way, as a misinterpretation of the term "quotient" may lead one to believe.[1] Genes place constraints on the extent to which one's intellectual behavior is responsive to environmental stimuli and on the extent to which that behavior can be shaped by such stimuli. Because the major defining characteristic of human beings is the cognitive ability to plan, execute, monitor, and evaluate what we are doing, intelligence can be seen as a "master" behavior that directs and guides all other forms of human activity, including delinquent and criminal activity.

### IQ and Test Bias

To what extent is IQ under the influence of genetic inheritance? This is one of those questions that a lot of us would rather not be asked. Neuroscientist Michael Gazzaniga (1988:53) recognizes this when he writes: "That intelligence is largely inherited is an idea most people accept privately but won't acknowledge publicly."[2] I suspect that Gazzaniga is correct. Nevertheless, and whatever their private thoughts may be, the strict environmentalists' answer to the question posed in the opening sentence is "hardly at all." This position is exemplified by the Staff Writers of *Science News:* "IQ variations are almost completely a result of environmental differences and the cultural bias of the tests themselves" (quoted in Walsh, 1981:166). Similarly, Braginsky and Braginsky (1973:178) state with certitude that "by now, we all know that a cultural bias in IQ tests favors middle-class white persons." Few contemporary environmentalists would be so adamant as this since their argument has now been decisively rejected by the community of experts sampled by Snyderman and Rothman, (1988). However, if IQ tests *are* biased, then the argument that IQ is irrelevant to the explanation of delinquency is accurate. Let us explore the substance of this argument in terms of the reliability and validity of IQ tests.

Intelligence tests are designed to predict individual performances on tasks of an intellectual nature, tasks such as those enumerated by the professionals surveyed by Snyderman and Rothman (1988). The more reliable and valid a measuring instrument is, the more accurate our predictions based on the trait the instrument purports to measure will be. The reliability of IQ tests, whether determined by test-retest, split-half, Cronbach's alpha, or any other method, typically yield reliability coefficients between .94 and .97 (Anastasi, 1976:251). Such coefficients are impressive. Of the 120 or so scales contained in Robinson and Shaver's (1973) *Measures of Social Psychological Attitudes,* none come close to matching the reliability of IQ tests. Clearly, IQ tests are the most reliable of all "pencil and paper" measures of human attributes.

While reliability is a necessary requisite for an instrument to be used for making predictions, it is not sufficient. Such an instrument must also be valid. The discussion of validity will be limited to criterion-related validity, a type of validity that comes closer than any other to what is normally meant by "valid" (Zeller and Carmines, 1980:79). A validity coefficient is usually expressed as a correlation between performance on a test and some criterion performance. The correlation between an index of immigrant assimiliation and the taking of U.S. citizenship is a measure of the validity of the assimilation index, and the correlation between college entrance exams and GPA is a validation of the usefulness of the entrance exams.

In the technical sense, to say that a test is biased for or against a particular group is to say that it predicts accurately for one group but not for another. If, for instance, IQ scores accurately predicted task performance for whites but not for blacks, the test from which the scores were derived would have to be considered biased. Technically speaking, with both the predictor variable (IQ) and the criterion variable (task performance) standardized, a test is biased if the regression slopes are significantly different across tested groups (in the bivariate case the standardized slope equals the correlation coefficient).

Test bias is illustrated in Figure 2.1. In this illustration we see that IQ scores predict scores on the criterion variable differently for group A, whose mean IQ is 95, and group B, whose mean is 105. The slope of group A indicates that we would predict a score on the criterion variable of 35 for an individual with an IQ of 115. We would predict a score of 60 for an individual in group B with an identical IQ score, clearly an indication of test bias.

Figure 2.1    Regression of IQ on a Criterion Score Predicting Different Outcome for Different Groups (Bias).

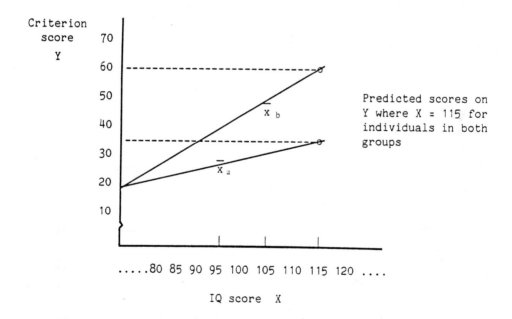

The lack of test bias is illustrated in Figure 2.2. Although the means on both IQ and the criterion variable of group A are below the means for Group B, IQ predicts scores on the criterion variable equally well. For example, we can predict a score of 50 on the criterion variable for individuals in both groups with IQ scores of 102. Because group A scored lower on the instrument we call an IQ test does *not* mean that the instrument is biased against that group. As long as IQ tests predict performance on some criterion variable across racial and SES lines equally well, they are not invalidated because individuals score differently on them.

Figure 2.2    Regression of IQ on a Criterion Score Predicting Equally
            well for Both Groups (Non-bias)

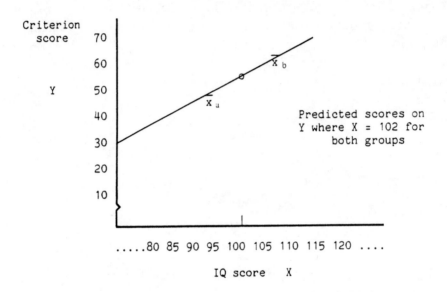

Which of these figures accurately reflects the situation as it relates to criterion validity of IQ tests? That is, do IQ tests predict socially significant criterion performances such as school achievement less accurately for blacks and lower SES children than for white middle-class children? In three articles in the same issue of *Sociology of Education* (Guterman, 1979; Gordon and Rudert, 1979; Eckland, 1979), all authors came to the same conclusion—IQ tests are not biased against blacks or lower SES individuals. The Gordon and Rudert study is particularly sophisticated in terms of its statistical analyses. In their analysis of individual test items, although black and lower SES children missed more items, the *rankings* of relative item difficulty (in terms of percentage of children missing them) were almost identical for both races and across social classes. In fact, item difficulty levels correlate between .95 and .98 between black and white subjects (Snyderman and Rothman, 1988:113). Scores on IQ tests predicted educational attainment equally for all subjects tested and was substantially more powerful a predictor than either SES or race. In other words, black children with high IQ's show evidence of greater educational attainment than white middle-class children with low IQ's.

While some may still refuse to believe that IQ tests are unbiased, the psychometric literature provides no evidence in the form of reliability, predictive validity, factor structure, race x item interaction, and so on, that they are. We must learn to live with these findings and to incorporate them into our thinking rather than condemn them. I recall studies some years back that indicated that the taller a person in the business world is, the more money he or she tends to make. These findings struck me as eminently unfair, but it certainly did not lead me to question the reliability or validity of yardsticks. Some people are tall, some are short, and some people score higher on IQ tests than others. To blame the instruments that measure these differences for the differences is rather like shooting the messenger. Test score differences are the result of environmental circumstances interacting with genetic endowment, not of the instruments that reveal deficits in either or both.[3]

When most sociologists speak of IQ test bias, they do not mean that the tests are biased in terms of the reliability and validity of the tests, although they sometimes confuse these technical aspects with what they really mean. What is most often meant by test bias is that lower SES and black children are less likely to have the kinds of intellectual experiences that prepare them for some kinds of items found on IQ tests. To the extent that IQ tests measure the store of general knowledge one has acquired ("Who wrote Hamlet?" "What is the capital of Turkey?"), the question of cultural bias warrants attention. But it has been found that lower SES children show the same deficiencies on tests designed to test problem-solving abilities, such as the Davis-Eell game tests, which have no basis in abilities unique to one class (Guterman, 1979). Black children have also been shown in many studies to be *more* deficient on the performance section of IQ tests relative to whites than they are on the verbal section (Steelman and Doby, 1983). The performance section of the IQ test is not a "knowledge-based" test and was specifically designed to compensate for the lack of verbal ability in children from culturally deprived homes.

Certain critics of IQ tests maintain that the tests are biased because they do not take into account the motivation of the test takers (Block and

Dworkin, 1976; Simons, 1978). It cannot be denied that to some unknown extent that motivation to do well impacts on the performance of any test, and that to some (also unknown) extent IQ tests measure motivation. (Recall that motivation was not considered a particularly important element of IQ among Snyderman and Rothman's [1988] expert respondents.) Block and Dworkin (1976:455) claim that this observation casts doubt on the "purity" of IQ tests as measures of intelligence. They seem to forget that IQ tests are not meant to be measures of "pure" intelligence, and that their value lies in their ability to predict future outcomes. We cannot judge the reliability or validity of IQ tests by claiming that test takers are differentially motivated anymore than one can judge the reliability of a parachute if one refuses to jump.

Because this is essentially a book about delinquency, the issue of the differential motivation of IQ test takers is somewhat more important in the present context than it may be in other contexts. Simons (1978:270) doubts the ability of IQ tests to predict delinquency because "The delinquent is often described as an unmotivated student who does little schoolwork and receives failing grades. . . . [I]f these students are not motivated to do academic work on any other day of the school year, why should they be motivated to the best of their ability on the day the IQ tests are administered?" One may counter this by observing that if test takers are not motivated to do well in either academic work or testing situations, they are not likely to be motivated to perform other behaviors that will afford them a stake in conformity. The motivational component of IQ tests, while diluting their purity as tests of intelligence, may actually increase their criterion-related validity.

Attempts have been made to "prove" that IQ tests are culturally biased by designing tests that measure one's knowledge of the cultural content of the black subculture such as the Dove Counterbalance General Intelligence Test, which has come to be known as the Chitling Test. Because blacks score higher on such tests, it "proves" to detractors of IQ tests that IQ tests measure nothing but the cultural content of white middle-class society in the same way that the Chitling Test measures the content of the black subculture. Sometimes these tests are offered "tongue in cheek," sometimes not. Whatever the spirit in which they are offered, the concept of such a test is naive at best and deliberately misleading at worst. It has been pointed out by Kaplan (1985:473) that there is no body of evidence that the test successfully predicts performance on any important criterion for either black or white subjects. The Chitling Test, and others like it, such as the BITCH test, merely measure knowledge of the slang and idiosyncrasies of a particular subculture. They do not measure the ability to reason, evaluate, synthesize, or any of the other cognitive abilities that are needed to be successful in the larger culture. Standard IQ tests do measure such abilities.

Nettler (1982:97) summarizes the issue of cultural bias by stating that it is irrelevant "because one gets similar results from so-called 'culture-free' tests," and more importantly, "because the skills measured by mental tests are those which have general applicability for the guidance of lives around the world." Similarly, Brody (1985:382) summarizes a large number of studies designed to explore test bias in relation to black/white differences by writing: "It is quite clear that black-white differences in intelligence are not a function of type of items or tests. As far as is known, it is pervasive and exists on virtually all measures that are generally assumed to be measures of general intelligence." Further, blacks do relatively worse on nonverbal (the manipulation of symbols and objects) tests than on verbal tests than do whites: "If cultural bias is to creep into a test, it presumably has a better opportunity to do so through language than through abstract symbols, yet blacks do better on language tests" [than on nonverbal tests] (Snyderman and Rothman, 1988:114).

This does not lead us to the conclusion that blacks are *innately* less intelligent than whites; i.e., that the difference between the mean IQ scores of blacks and whites are attributable to genetic differences between the races. It is possible, even if 100 percent of the variance in IQ *within* each racial population is attributable to genetics, that the *difference* between the two populations could be attributable to environmental variability. Phenotypic behavior is the result of genotypes interacting with environments in ways known and unknown. Until such time as both races experience identical environments in a color-blind society we can say nothing definitive about the origins of black/white differences in measured intelligence.

### The Heritability of IQ

At the other end of the scale from the environmentalist "test-bias" claimants we have hereditarian psychologists such as Jensen (1969) and Eysenck (1970) who assert that about 80 percent of the variation in intelligence is attributable to genetic variation. We also have behavioral geneticists stating that "differences in family background that affect IQ are largely the result of genetic differences among parents, which affect their own status attainment and which are passed on genetically to their offspring" (Scarr and Weinberg, 1978:691). Scarr and Weinberg are saying, in effect, that social class is inherited genetically (at least in an open society) via its connection with IQ.

Scarr and Weinberg's assertions were made on the basis of two separate studies (1976; 1978) they conducted of adopted children. The 1976 study was particularly interesting because they studied black or racially mixed children who were adopted into white homes. In this study, the correlation between the children's IQ's and their adoptive fathers and mothers were .27 and .23, respectively. The correlations between the children's IQ's and their biological fathers and mothers, on the other hand, were .39 and .34, respectively. Squaring these correlations, we find that the children shared more than twice the IQ variance with their biological parents than they did with their adoptive parents. Scarr and Weinberg's 1978 study showed an even larger discrepancy between the correlations between children and their adoptive and biological parents than were found in their 1976 study. These and other such adoption studies (see Vandenberg and Volger, 1985, for a review) indicate that genetic relationship accounts for more IQ variance than does shared familial relationship. There are no adoption studies that have drawn the opposite conclusion.

On the nurture side of the IQ debate, the Scarr and Weinberg (1976) study found that the black and racially mixed adoptees—tested at a mean of 57.25 months after adoption—had a mean IQ of 105.8. This mean is greater than the population mean of 100, but less than the mean (113.8) of the natural children of the adoptive parents. The earlier the children were adopted, the greater were their IQ scores ($r = -.36$). This finding should be recalled when we discuss the importance of infancy and early childhood experience on IQ in the next chapter. The mean IQ scores of the adoptive parents were in the high average to superior range (mother's $\overline{X} = 118.2$, father's $\overline{X} = 120.8$). The IQ means of the adopted children reflect the benefit of being raised within relatively high IQ family environments.

Claims of genetic transmission rest to a large extent on the concept of heritability, a quantification of the extent to which a given trait in under the influence of genetic endowment. More precisely, heritability is a quantification of *variation* in a population trait that is assumed to be accounted for by genetic factors. If some magic potion were to raise everyone's IQ by 25 points, there would be no change in heritability because, since everyone's IQ had been uniformly raised, there would be no change in the variation existing in the population.

When assessing the heritability of human traits such as IQ, we are considering what geneticists call *broad* heritability. *Narrow* heritability deals only with the sum of the additive genetic factors at discrete chromosomal loci. Broad heritability is more complicated, since it involves the additive genetic variance, effects of dominance at heterozygous loci, and the variance due to interaction among different loci (Hartle, 1981:177). Broad heritability thus yields a somewhat higher estimate than narrow heritability.

To measure the heritability of a trait requires that we hold either genetic or environmental conditions constant. If we hold either condition constant, we can assess the effects of the other on the phenotypical trait in question. This strategy is only imperfectly possible when dealing with human populations. For instance, correlating IQ scores of monozygotic twins reared apart provides us with a measure of the effects of genetics, and the correlation between non-biological siblings raised together from an early age provides us with an estimate of environmental effects. One problem with such a strategy is the assumption that all environmental factors are captured by examining a common family of rearing. It ignores specific environmental influences that may impact on only one of a twin pair. Nevertheless, it is often the only strategy available to IQ researchers.

In 1963, Erlenmeyer-Kimling and Jarvik reviewed 52 studies using interclass correlations between mono- and dyzygotic twins to explore the heritability of IQ. They found that as genotypical similarity increases between matched pairs of individuals, so do the similarities of their IQ scores. That is, the IQ correlations between pairs of monozygotic twins, who are genetically identical, were larger than the correlations between dizygotic twins, who only share half of their genetic inheritance. The correlations between biological siblings were larger than the correlations between adopted siblings, and so on. Based on this and other similar studies, Mednick, Higgins, and Kirschenbaum (1975:287) state that genetic factors account for about 75 percent of the variation in intelligence.

One of the problems with the Erlenmeyer-Kimling and Jarvik data, a problem for which they were hardly responsible, was the inclusion of the highly impressive correlations reported from studies conducted by Cyril Burt. Unfortunately, it has been demonstrated that Burt's data were fraudulent (Kamin, 1974). More recent evidence suggests that the 75 percent heritability figure cited by Mednick and his colleagues is wrong, and that the contribution of our genes to our intelligence is less impressive. A 1980 review of the literature by behavioral geneticists Ploman and DeFries (1980) indicates that individual differences in IQ are less heritable than previously believed. They state that older data indicated a heritability coefficient of about .70, but "the newer data suggest a heritability closer to .50" (1980:15).

In a later summary of 111 studies of the genetics of IQ conducted between the years of 1963 and 1980, Bouchard and McGue (1981) report weighted average correlations between various familial relationships and IQ. As was the case in the earlier Erlenmeyer-Kimling and Jarvik review, the pattern of these correlations are consistent with that which would be predicted on the basis of broad polygenetic inheritance, although they were less strong. The greater the degree of genetic sharing among familial pairs, the higher the correlation between the paired IQ's. A similar, but smaller, effect is seen for increasing similarities in environment. Figure 2.3 shows the pattern of correlations found, as well as the pattern predicted from a strict polygenetic theory of broad IQ inheritance.

As we see, monozygotic twins reared together showed the highest average correlation (.86), followed by monozygotic twins reared apart (.72). A strict theory of polygenetic inheritance would predict a correlation of 1.00 in both cases, since monozygotic twin are genetically identical. The difference between the two correlations provides a rough estimate of environmental effects. Because monozygotic twins reared together share identical genes *and* the same family environment, the lack of a perfect correlation (taking measurement error into consideration) indicates that the term "environment" means more than simply sharing the same parents and the same home. Individuals obviously experience environmental influences specific to themselves that appear to influence IQ.

Similarly, a strict polygenetic theory of inheritance for IQ would predict a zero correlation between adopted child and parent. But when in fact the average weighted correlation is .19. The departure of these correlations from the correlations predicted by a strictly hereditarian position, as well as the differences in IQ between twins reared together and twins reared apart, underscore the contribution of family environmental differences, as well as different experiences specific to the individual, to IQ levels. Nevertheless, and as the authors point out, the magnitude of the correlations as well as the pattern of biological relationship/IQ correlations "would be difficult to explain on the basis

Figure 2.3    Weighted Average Correlations Between IQ and Degree of
   Relatedness and Expected Correlations from Strict Polygenetic Theory
   of IQ Inheritance.  Adapted from Bouchard and McGue, Science, 1981,
   p. 1057.

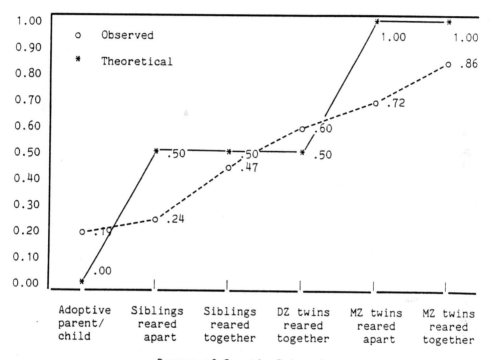

Degree of Genetic Relatedness

of any strictly environmental hypothesis" (1981:1056). To put it otherwise, the fact that IQ scores across 111 studies are most similar among genetically identical twins and least similar among genetically unrelated persons strongly supports the position that the abilities measured by IQ tests are to a rather large extent hereditary.

Bouchard and McGue did not compute a heritability coefficient from the reported data. However, one can be easily computed using the weighted averaged correlations for monozygotic pairs reared together and dizygotic pairs reared together (r = .60) by $h^2$ = 2(rmz − rdz), yielding 2(.86 − .60) = .52.[4] This heritability coefficient conforms to the earlier estimate by Plomin and DeFries' (1980) to the effect that newer data suggest a heritability for IQ of about .50. What this means practically is that about half of the variance in population intelligence is attributable to genetic variation. Even if we correct the coefficient for measurement error, we would attain a maximum $h^2$ of no more than .60. This would mean that at least forty percent of the variance in IQ is attributable to environmental conditions.

### Heritability in Different Environments

Despite the fact that the coefficient of heritability just computed is based on weighted average correlations derived from a large number of studies, it is nevertheless a gross estimation of the extent to which IQ is a genetically inherited trait. The problem of its impreciseness lies in the concept of heritability itself. Heritability is a population statistic, indicating the proportion of the total variation in a particular trait that is genetically determined *in the population as a whole,* and says nothing about how much of the variance in individual intelligence is attributable to genetic factors. As a population statistic it is subject to sampling error, and other sources of variation having nothing to do with genetic variation. The strict determination of heritability requires that all elements of the population possessing the trait, whether the trait in question is the height of sunflowers or the IQ's of delinquents, be exposed to absolutely identical environments. It follows then that heritability coefficients change as the environment changes. For instance, mean height in Japan was less before WW II than it is today. The Japanese are a taller people today, not because of a change in the gene pool, but rather because their diets have improved appreciably. As geneticist Eldon Gardner puts it: "The coefficient of heritability is not a constant but only indicates the proportion of variance caused by differences in additive gene effects in a particular population at a particular time" (1972:412).

Unfortunately for those of us who would like to see a more precise measure of heritability for IQ across all races and classes of the human family, the major heritability studies, according to Jensen (1969:64–65), "have been based on samples of white European and North American samples, and our knowledge of intelligence in different racial and cultural groups within these populations is nil." This is precisely the problem Jensen himself must confront, but appears to discount, when he supposes that differences between white and black IQ scores are attributable to genetic differences. (To be fair to Jensen, he only hypothesized, not asserted, that racial differences may be attributable to genetics.)

The importance of Jensen's observation is that the more similar the environments experienced by genetically heterogeneous organisms, the more individual differences can be attributed to genetics, and the less similar the environments the less individual differences can be attributed to genetics. Any observed variability among phenotypes can only be attributed to the factor that varies. For instance, if we take a barrel of genetically heterogeneous rose seeds that have been thoroughly mixed and shuffled, take a random sample of those seeds and plant them in identically nourishing environments, any differences among them would be *entirely* attributable to genetics and $h^2$ would be 1.0. Similarly, if we take a sample of genetically homogeneous seeds and plant them in diverse environments, observed phenotypical differences among them would be one hundred percent attributable to environmental conditions and $h^2$ would be zero. In the first instance, environment is a constant, and in the second instance, genetic material is constant.

On the other hand, if we take a genetically heterogeneous sample of seeds and plant them in a wide range of diversely nourishing environments, we have considerable difficulty in trying to decompose the variance in individual differences into genetic and environmental components. This is the situation with which we are confronted when we try to apportion IQ variation into genetic and environmental components among samples of genetically heterogeneous people living within diverse environments. In other words, the heritability coefficients reported within fairly homogeneous white environments may not be adequate to express the genetic contribution to IQ among more culturally disadvantaged groups.

A purely genetic model (posited for heuristic purposes only) for the determination of IQ would predict equal heritability across all races and classes regardless of the magnitude of differences in mean IQ scores across the same groups. A model which takes environmental as well as genotypical variability into account would predict low heritability in the most disadvantaged environments, high heritability in advantageous environments, and moderate heritability in environments falling somewhere between the extremes.

Sandra Scarr-Salapatek (1973) devised a study to test these competing models. She reasoned that only with optimal environments for development would genetic differences account for almost all of the variance in IQ, and that the restricting environments of lower SES children would suppress the expression of genotypical potential. Why would this be so;

genes are genes aren't they? Recall that genes are protein molecules of *potential* that are "more or less" realized in a given environment. As we have seen, certain environments allow for the full expression of genes for a given trait, others serve to suppress the trait. Examples of biosocial variables that could serve to suppress the full expression of a gene-based trait such as intellectual performance are low birth weight, lack of prenatal and neonatal medical care, deficient tactile stimulation during periods of active neuronal growth, malnutrition, abusive parenting, maternal drug use during pregnancy which could result in the loss of infant brain neurons, and a generally stimuli-deprived home life. Although not limited to lower SES and black families, these deficiencies are more prevalent among those groups (Bouchard, Jr., and Segal, 1985). Children whose genes are more fully expressed suffer few if any of these biosocial deprivations.

Scarr-Salapatek divided her sample of 992 mono- and dizygotic twin pairs into "advantaged" and "disadvantaged" groups for each race based on a median split on social class. She found that there was greater phenotypic variability of intelligence among children in the advantaged groups of both races: "One can see that the percentage of total variance attributable to genetic sources was always higher in the advantaged groups of both races" (1973:223). For instance, the heritability coefficient for verbal intelligence was .343 among disadvantaged black children and .723 for advantaged black children. Combining the advantaged and disadvantaged children, she calculated a heritability of .522, a figure which is in accord with the coefficient I calculated from the Bouchard and McGue (1981) data. These figures also suggest that black and white heritibilities are identical.

Scarr-Salapatek's findings are fully in accord with current behavioral genetics theory. The findings indicate that in an advantaged environment genetic differences among children are expressed more fully. Conversely, a child from a deprived environment with the raw genetic potential for scoring in the above average range in intelligence will tend to produce IQ scores more like those of a child with less raw potential, but who enjoys a richer environment.

A later study by Fischbein (1980) among white twins produced almost identical results. Dividing his sample into three categories based on social class, he found that the heritabilities of IQ increased with increase in SES. In the lowest SES group, he found interclass correlations of .61 and .51 for mono- and dizygotic twins, respectively. These correlations yield a h$^2$ of .30 for the lower SES twins. The h$^2$ for twins in the highest SES group was .78. These coefficients are practically identical to those reported by Scarr-Salapatek. Fischbein's and Scarr-Salapatek's studies showed unequivocally that human heritability for IQ is high in advantaged environments and low in disadvantaged environments.

It is also a reasonable assumption that *environmental* variation will be greater among disadvantaged groups than among advantaged groups. That is, the range of events experienced in disadvantaged environments is probably much greater than in the comfortable "standard" experiences of higher SES groups. If the experiences of higher SES groups are more homogeneous, it follows statistically that there is less environmental variance and thus a higher heritability coefficient. Conversely, the greater environmental variability within lower SES groups leads to a decrease in the heritability coefficient. In other words, change the environment and the genetic contribution to phenotypical IQ variability changes.

What might all this discussion of the vicissitudes of heritability have to do with the discussion of delinquency? It was noted earlier that the Japanese have become a taller people because of an improved diet. Because the Japanese diet has more or less improved uniformly throughout the country (the environment has become more homogeneous), it has had the effect of increasing the heritability of height among the Japanese. We would expect the same increase in the heritability of IQ as the environment becomes more favorable for the development of IQ for all people. The fear has been expressed that such a situation would raise the specter of a hereditary meritocracy and a permanent underclass based on IQ (Herrnstein, 1973). A Norwegian study of 8,389 twin pairs found that the heritability of educational attainment has increased dramatically with the equalization of educational opportunities in Norway. For individuals born before 1940, family background accounted for 47 percent of the variance in educational attainment, with genetic factors accounting for another 41 percent. For males born between 1940 and 1961, family background accounted for only 8 to 10 percent of the variance, and genetic factors accounted for 67 to 74 percent. Changes in the family background/genetic ratio was less dramatic for females, suggesting perhaps that opportunities had become less "equal" for them (Heath et al., 1985).

The lesson from the Norwegian study is that the closer we come to optimizing the environment for everyone, the more people are differentiated by their genes. The corollary of this, according to Herrnstein

(1973), is that sooner or later people will sort themselves into classes based solely on merit (IQ). Those with the lowest IQ's will find themselves locked into a permanent underclass. There is evidence that this has already occurred to some extent in the black community. According to Harvard's Glenn Loury (1987), programs such as Affirmative Action have skimmed the brightest blacks from the community and left the rest behind to live in abominable ghetto conditions. To the extent that the observed bifurcation of the black community is a function of division by IQ, we can expect the continuation of high levels of crime and delinquency within that community. Such is the paradox of Affirmative Action and other "special favors" programs aimed at ameliorating the plight of blacks. "Improving the environment" must go beyond civil rights-type programs to encompass those factors that most impact on IQ in a society that is becoming increasingly based on merit.

## Conclusion

Because genes appear to account for more of the variance in intelligence than environment, it does not mean that the genetic contribution is more important than the environmental contribution. Hydrogen contributes twice as much as oxygen to rain, and the length of the garden on which it falls may contribute twice as much to the garden's area as its width. Heredity and environment are to intelligence as hydrogen and oxygen are to rain, and length and width are to area. None of these pairings "contribute" anything in isolation from the wholes they constitute: IQ, rain, or area.

Thus, heredity and environment are not mutually exclusive categories, although they are often assumed to be. This assumption, according to Jencks (1980), is derived from a narrow physiological view of how genes affect behavior. Genes do affect some behaviors directly via the physiological functioning of ribosomes, but most non-trivial human behavior that is under genetic control is mediated by the environment in reactive and active ways (Plomin, DeFries, and Loehlin, 1976). For instance, when individuals with different genes seek out different environments (I'm assuming that some polygenetic trait such as temperament leads to seeking different environments) and their experiences within those environments affect future behavior, are the effects attributable to heredity or environment? The importance of such observations have been well-stated by Jencks (1980), who has demonstrated rather elegantly that non-genetic variation $(1 - h^2)$ does not provide a measure of the upper limit of the possible explanatory power of environmental variables, nor on the effects of creating new and better environments.

I think that the most sensible stance on this emotional nature/nurture controversy was best stated over thirty years ago:

> The genetic endowment in respect to any one trait has been compared to a rubber band and the trait itself is stretched by outside forces. Different people initially may have been given different lengths of unstretched endowment, but the natural forces of the environment may have stretched their expression to equal length, or led to differences in attained length sometimes corresponding to their innate differences and at other times in reverse of the relation. (Stern, 1956:53.)

We may conclude that intelligence, as measured by IQ tests, is to some imprecisely known extent a rather highly heritable trait. But to assert this is not to assert that one's wits are inevitably determined at conception. It merely means that within a hypothetically uniform environment people's wits would still vary, although not to the same extent that they do in the real world of highly heterogeneous environments.

## ENDNOTES

1. It is often wrongly thought that the term "quotient" in "intelligence quotient" is used to refer to one's "quota" or share of intelligence. Such an interpretation leads one to think of IQ as being a person's unchanging allotment of mental acuity which is granted to him or her at birth by virtue of genetic inheritance. It does not mean this at all. The term "quotient" simply refers to the numerical ratio between a test score and a measurement on which the score might be expected to depend. The term is derived from the Stanford-Binet test in which a child's IQ score is the quotient of its tested mental age divided by its chronological age.

2. Jensen and Eysenck, as well as other IQ hereditarians, have suffered vicious verbal and even physical attacks from radical environmentalists in the academic community for having the temerity to publish unpopular findings. However, Banton and Harwood (1975:113), a sociologist and a biologist, respectively, have written: "Readers will have noticed that hereditarians such as Jensen and Eysenck allow a significant place to environmental factors and are much less extreme in their views than some of their scientifically illiterate supporters." Banton and Harwood might also have added that Jensen and Eysenck are also less extreme than some of their scientifically illiterate detractors, even those in academia.

3. Another form of bias—intercept bias—does seem to exist when the criterion variable is earned income and the predictor variable is IQ. Intercept bias exists when we observe identical regression slopes across groups but different

intercepts. Banton and Harwood (1975:107) point to studies in which it has been shown that blacks make significantly less income than whites matched on IQ. This means that predictions for blacks and whites based on their respective slopes would be equally accurate, but since the Y intercept for blacks is below that for whites, the predicted income for blacks based on any value of X (IQ) would be consistently lower. However, this has nothing to do with the validity of IQ tests because they are designed to predict intellectual performance, not how well one is paid for performing.

4. A more precise measure of heritability is $h^2 = 2(rmz - rdz)/1 - \sigma e$. That is, we divide the numerator by 1 minus the percentage of variance due to measurement error. This has the effect of increasing the heritability coefficient. If we assume the error variance across all 111 studies is constant at the .073 value reported by Scarr-Salapatek (1971), we obtain a coefficient of $.52/.927 = .561$. This formula is specific to determining heritability using human twins. It is a variation of the more general formula: a ratio of phenotypic variance to genotypic variance, which is more readily ascertained with non-human organisms (Hartle, 1981).

# Chapter Three

# THE "NURTURE" OF INTELLIGENCE

## The Malleability of IQ

If IQ is linked to crime and delinquency and if we accept the influence of genes on IQ, what are the implications for public policy? That is, if we accept that IQ scores that fall within a certain range increases the probability of antisocial behavior, does it mean that nothing can be done to prevent such behavior? No it does not. It would only do so if IQ scores and the cognitive abilities they operationalize were fixed and imutable entities, which they are not.

There is very little doubt that intelligence, in addition to being a highly heritable trait, is a malleable one. The greatest period of malleability is during early childhood. Benjamine Wolman, author of the "bible" of intelligence, *Handbook of Intelligence*, writes: "In one area, intelligence and mental health are closely related—namely, in early childhood deprivation" (1985:685). He goes on to cite various authors who unite in their belief that if children are not loved and accepted, they will develop inadequate self-love, inadequate self-esteem, inadequate cognitive skills, and hostile attitudes toward other people. This view is echoed in Watters and Stinnett's (1971:91) review of the relevant literature: "Consensus existed among the studies reviewed that academic achievement, leadership, and creative thinking of children was positively related to warm, accepting, understanding, and autonomy-granting parent-child relationships." I prefer to use the term *love* to encompass these parent-child relationships.

Curiously, the best and most solid evidence for environmental influence on intelligence comes from genetic research: "The findings of greatest social significance to emerge from human behavioral genetic research to date involve nurture, not nature," write two researchers in that area (Plomin and Daniels, 1987:1). Since any human phenotypic trait is the result of hereditary and environment and since the best modern estimates of the percentage of IQ variance attributable to genetics are between 50 and 60 percent, it follows that between 40 and 50 percent of the variance (and perhaps more in certain environments) has to be attributed to environmental factors minus measurement error. Yet, no researcher has been able to empirically account for such a proportion. Plomin and DeFries have stated that they know of "no specific environmental influences nor combination of them that account for as much as 10 percent of the variance in IQ" (1980:22). Likewise, Fincher (1982:72) points out that "the environmental contributions to intelligence—nutrition, loving care and attention and intellectual stimulation—have been harder [than the genetic contribution] to prove scientifically."

It is more difficult to get a firm handle on environmental influences because the variables we refer to when we speak of the "environment" are a legion, encompassing all that we can subsume under the physical, psychological, and social worlds. What is more, these variables interact and permutate in a multitude of ways, and many have transactional effects: miseries multiply and advantages accumulate. Any attempt to account for them all would be a monumental, perhaps even impossible, task. It would require constant monitoring of children's environmental experiences almost from the moment of conception and would necessarily entail a major intrusion into the lives of their families. Even if such close scrutiny were possible and desirable and even if it did not contaminate the study by influencing parental behavior, we would still not obtain an adequate accounting of environmental influence.

Such an accounting would require a control group of genetically identical infants (to hold genetic influences constant) exposed to different environmental influences beyond their common prenatal and perinatal experiences. That is, it would require a large sample of monozygotic twins separated at birth and raised in quite different environments, such as different racial and SES households and a variety of family constellations. Given the rarity of such occasions, as well as the thicket of environmental influences to be constantly monitored, it is probably true that we will never be able to empirically account for the percentage of variance in IQ that genetic research informs us is attributable to the environment. We can, however, explore environmental influences on IQ by examining how certain environments lead to increases or decreases in intellectual functioning.

One of the earliest studies of the tragic consequences of deprived environments on intellectual capacity is Spitz's (1945) work with institutionalized infants in the 1940s. Spitz was concerned with the high mortality rates of infants in "foundling homes." Abnormally high numbers of infants were dying of no apparent organic causes in these institutions, despite adequate standards of hygiene and nutrition. In an effort to determine the cause, Spitz compared conditions in a foundling home with those existing in a nursery in a penal institution for delinquent girls. While the conditions (medical care, hygiene, nutrition) in the foundling home were superior to those in the penal institute, there was significantly less illness and death among infants in the penal institute.

Spitz compared the two sets of infants, all of whom were less than one-year old, on six indices of development: perception, body mastery, social relations, memory, relations to inanimate objects, and intelligence. These measures yield a general "developmental quotient" (DQ). Initially, Spitz found the infants from the foundling home to have superior average DQ's (124 versus 101). He attributed the relatively low scores of the penal infants to their "psychically defective" delinquent mothers. However, while the DQ's of the nursery children improved normally over time, the DQ's of the foundling home children declined the longer they were institutionalized. Upon retesting the children one year later, Spitz found that the penal infants averaged 105, while the average DQ of the foundling children had plummeted to 72. But the real tragedy of the story is that within two years after the start of the study 37% of the foundling children were dead, while all of the penal children were still alive five years later.

Given all the apparent advantages of the foundling home infants, why such tragic consequences? For Spitz, the answer was obvious. The penal children were cared for by their own mothers, "psychically defective" as they may have been. Their mothers kissed, cuddled, stroked, talked to, fed, played with them; in short, they loved them. The foundling home children had no opportunity to develop this kind of relationship with caregivers. Despite the greater technical efficiency of the professional nursing staff of the foundling home, nurses simply did not have the time, even if they had the inclination, to develop this kind of bond with all children in their care.

If the lack of tender loving care can kill and have adverse effects on intellectual development, a remarkable long-term study by Harold Skeels (1966) bears testimony to the curative property of love. Skeels randomly divided a number of institutionalized "mentally retarded" two-year-old children into two groups. One group of children was placed in the care of individual surrogate mothers, who were themselves classified as mentally deficient and who were institutionalized. The other group remained behind in the orphanage. As was the case with the Spitz study, Skeels observed dramatic results. Over the years of testing the IQ's of the two groups of children, it was found that those in the care of surrogate mothers showed an average increase of 28 points, while those still institutionalized showed an average decrease of 30 points.

Thirty years later, Skeels decided to trace his subjects to determine what became of them. He found that all those who were placed in the care of surrogate mothers were self-supporting members of the community. The mean IQ of this group was 92. Such IQ levels hardly qualify for membership in MENSA, but they are within the normal range and a long way from mental retardation. His search for the unfortunate members of the control group left behind in the institution found that they were all either dead or still institutionalized. Such evidence strongly supports the importance of love in the developmental scheme of things and has led Michael Young (1975:30) to state that "love is biochemistry's chief assistant" in what he calls "the full glandular development of the infant."

### Recent Studies on IQ Decrement/Increment

One of the major bones of contention among IQ researchers is whether racial differences in IQ are genetic in origin or can be traced to environmental circumstances. Arthur Jensen, the man who is most responsible for resurrecting and refueling the race/IQ controversy (1969) and who favors a genetic explanation for racial differences, has himself provided evidence for the tremendous importance of the environment with respect to IQ. In a test of the "cumulative deficit hypothesis"; i.e., the hypothesis that an increasing decrement in IQ scores relative to population norms is found among children in deprived environments, Jensen (1977) compared IQ scores of 1,300 black and white children living in a low socioeconomic region of rural Georgia with the IQ scores of black and white children in Berkeley, California. He found that IQ scores decreased among the rural Georgian black children an average of 1.42 points per year, or about 15 IQ points between the ages of 6 and 16 years. There was no corresponding decrement for either the Georgian white children or the Berkeley black children.

Jensen attempted to partially rescue his genetic hypothesis for black/white IQ differences by citing studies showing that "California blacks have a somewhat larger admixture of Caucasian ancestry than do blacks in Georgia."[1] But like the scientist he undoubtedly is, he let the data speak for themselves. He concluded: "The present results on Georgia blacks, when viewed in connection with the contrasting results for California blacks, would seem to favor an environmental interpretation of the progressive IQ decrement. If the progressive IQ decrement were a genetic racial effect, it would have shown up in the California blacks as well" (1977:190). Such a conclusion is particularly heartening given its source.

The opposite phenomenon, IQ increment, has been demonstrated by Strickland (1971) based on data from the Milwaukee Project. This project concentrated its efforts on the black infants of forty mothers who had IQ's typically in the seventies and who were living in slums of Milwaukee. Half of these infants were placed in an experimental group and half in a control group. The project team then launched into a comprehensive program of intervention in the lives of the experimental group of infants. Teachers visited the home for several hours each day exposing the infants to a wide range of stimuli and instructing the mothers on proper infant care techniques. When the children were older, they were picked up and taken to educational centers, where they received individual attention from specially trained teachers.

The results of all this special treatment were quite gratifying. The average IQ of the experimental group at 42 months was 33 points higher than that of the control group, and at 63 months the mean IQ of the experimental group was 124 compared to the control group mean of 94. Many other IQ researchers found these results to be too good to be true. Indeed, Clarke and Clarke (1976) indicate that the mean IQ scores of the experimental group had faded to 106 shortly after the children entered regular schools. Brody (1985:366) states that this is typical of the so-called "fading effect" often found among Head Start children who initially tend to show rather large IQ gains. Brody feels that large reported gains reflect such things as "test-wiseness" and not true gains in ability.[2]

Nevertheless, despite the fading effect, clearly something is happening when we see an experimental group outscoring a matched control group by such a wide margin. We can attribute part of the tendency to score high on the tests administered to these children to "test-wiseness." But both groups were tested with the same frequency, so the difference between the group means, even given the instability of the reported IQ gains, have to be attributed to the experimental group's exposure to their stimuli-enriched environment. To use Stern's "rubber band" metaphor, it is probable that children in both the control and experimental groups started the experiment with identically small lengths of IQ potential, and that the experimental group had theirs stretched beyond the level they would have attained had they not experienced environmental enrichment.

### IQ and the Plastic Infant Brain

To explore how childhood experiences translate into differential IQ levels, it is necessary to look briefly at the development of the human infant brain. All living organisms, from the lowly amoebae on up to Einstein, carry on the various functions of living driven by electrochemical processes governed by their genetic endowment. Having genes that "fix" responses of an organism to its environment is very advantageous to organisms going about the business of living, feeding, and reproducing in relatively static environments. Evolution within such an environment produces specialized genes that "hard-wire" the organism's central nervous system to produce the appropriate response to the relatively limited range of stimuli it will confront.

Such genetic hard wiring, however, is disadvantageous to organisms that inhabit highly variable environments and who must frequently adapt to new conditions. In such animals the genetic endowment must be less specialized, less rigid, and less fixed. If fact, the genes must surrender much of their control of behavioral traits to a more open, plastic, and complex system of control. As we go up the phylogenetic scale to human beings, we observe greater and greater freedom from the fixed patterns of responses that dominate organisms at the lower end of the scale. The system that allows us this freedom is the "plastic" (malleable) human brain (Rose, 1976; Witleson, 1987).

It is this brain plasticity that makes for the almost limitless variability in human beings, of the uniqueness and irreplaceability of us all. Each of us have different experiences and learn different things, giving us all a unique set of characteristics and emotions with which to confront the world. Human beings have operated successfully in a bewildering variety of physical and cultural environments, from the simple caves of the ice age to the immense complexity of urban life in the nuclear age. The plastic brain not only allows us to adapt to changing conditions but also to create many of the conditions to which we must adapt. Certainly, the brain has a specificity about it that determines the common characteristics of the species. It is this combination of the brain's specificity—determined by the common genetic material of the species—and plasticity—

indicating our intimate relationship with the environment—that simultaneously makes us similar to everyone else in some respects and unlike any other person in other respects. The important thing for our present purposes is that experience, especially during infancy and early childhood, can produce long-lasting effects in the brain's biochemistry and physiology and thus on intelligence.

The human infant comes into this world full of potentialities that require experience to actualize them. These experiences are perceived, processed, and acted upon via an intricate electrochemical maze of interactions among roughly 10 billion units of communication we call brain cells or neurons. The brain's neurons are surrounded by the more numerous but non-communicating glial cells that function to insulate, support, and nourish the neurons. Projecting out from the body of the neuron are axons which transmit information from one cell to another in the form of electrochemical signals, of constant strength but varying frequencies, at infinitesimal synaptic junctions.

The information is transmitted from neuron to neuron via neurotransmitter chemicals and is received by dendrites. This neuron-axon-dendrite-neuron transmission can be viewed simplistically as a kind of communication relay system of the brain. Each piece of communicated information is received only by the neurons for which it was intended. This fine information differentiation is accomplished by neuroreceptors. There are thousands of receptors, each specialized for chemically receiving particular transmitters. For instance, the endorphins can kill pain, cause euphoria, or sedate the individual, depending on where in the brain circuitry the endorphins are operating and on the type of receptor they bind with. Somehow the brain knows where to secrete the substance in response to the immediate needs of the organism. Each one of our billions of neurons can make perhaps as many as 3,000 connections with other neurons.

The neurons in the infant's brain, with their attendant structures, are largely unorganized and undifferentiated at birth. "From a single collection of immature, undifferentiated cells" writes neuroscientist Ronald Kalil, "emerges an organ so structurally complex that most other natural or human-crafted systems seem simple by comparison" (1989:76). Certainly, the architecture of the brain follows the genetic blueprint of the species, but like everything that develops organically, the environment influences the final form. We can view the infant's neurons as a computer relay board slowly being assembled into a fully integrated mechanism, partly by chemically coded specifications and partly by the guiding hand of the environment. The intimacy of gene/environment interaction is a central feature of brain development, governing cortical thickness, the amount of neurotransmitter chemicals, and most importantly, the brain's neuronal pathways (Joseph, 1982). As T. N. Wiesel (1982:592) put it in his Nobel prize lecture, "such sensitivity of the nervous system to the effects of experience may represent the fundamental mechanism by which the organism adapts to its environment during the period of growth and development."[3]

Except for those pathways or connections governing reflexive behavior, the human infant's brain at birth is not ready "wired" to function independently in its environment almost immediately as are the less plastic brains of the lower animals. The human infant cannot within hours or days start to walk or swing from trees. It is true that the potential to do all the things that human beings do is contained in the infant's genes at birth, but the genes are "switched on" at appropriate developmental junctures in response to environmental experiences. Within hours or days of birth, most non-human mammals are developmentally at the stage that it will take human infants about one year to reach (Bruner, 1972).

Intelligence and adaptability are crucial parts of the human repertory, requiring a cortex much larger relative to body size than is necessary for other animals. By the end of the first year of life the human infant's brain will have almost tripled its birth weight (Bruner, 1972). If humans were developmentally equal to non-human mammals at birth, the size of the human head would be too large to pass through the birth canal. One evolutionary strategy to accommodate the increasing human cranium would have been to increase the size of the female pelvis. Evolution may have tried this tactic at one time, but had to discard it. The disadvantage of such a strategy would be that the mobility of the female would be considerably constrained. The loss of the ability to move fairly speedily across the open savanna would have proved disastrous in the presence of so many predators. The strategy that evolution finally settled upon was that human infants would be born at an earlier and earlier stage of development (Omenn and Motulsky, 1972), a strategy that assured a greater role for the external environment in human development than is true for the development of any other species.

The evolutionary compromise reached to accommodate both increasing brain size of the human infant and the continuing need for the speedy mobility of their mothers leads many authorities to posit a dual human gestation period: uterogestation (gestation in the womb) and exterogestation (gestation after birth). The period of exterogestation encompasses the period between birth and the beginning of crawling—about ten months (Montagu, 1981).

Although interuterine experiences can have an influence on the infant's subsequent development, the experiences it has during the ten months or so after birth is of greater importance. The infant is safe and secure in its sac of amniotic fluid during uterogestation, and one infant's experience during this period is very much like every other infant's unless the mother is in particularly poor health, is malnourished, takes drugs, uses alcohol and tobacco to excess, or is extremely stressed. Unfortunately, these adverse prenatal conditions tend to negatively correlate with SES and may account for different constitutions of infants who have endured such prenatal environments. Children may thus be "constitutionally" different, meaning physiologically different, without the differences being attributable to genetic inheritance: "constitutional differences are the products of *genetic materials* meeting *perinatal environments* (Nettler, 1982:88, emphasis original).

Exterogestation environments are obviously more diverse, but as Montagu points out (concerning the two gestation periods) "a continuing symbiotic relationship between mother and child in the exterogestation period is designed to endure in an unbroken continuum until the infant's brain weight has more than doubled." Montagu goes on to expand on this by stating that love is the cement of this relationship: "It is, in a very real and not in the least paradoxical sense, even more necessary to love than it is to live, for without love there can be no healthy growth or development, no real life. The neotenous principle for human beings—indeed, the evolutionary imperative—is to live as if to live and love were one" (1981:93).

It is most pleasant to realize that the selection for intelligence and plasticity in humans made the selection for love so necessary: we're smart because we love and love because we're smart. Both are necessary for humans to be the kind of beings we are. Without love, intelligence would make for the never-ending oppression of the dull by the bright. Luckily, evolution has selected for both love and intelligence, each feeding the other in mutually beneficial ways.

The negative side of this pleasant thought is that because we are so plastic, so subject to environmental influences, our programming can go

awry. What if infants do not experience Montagu's "continuing symbiotic relationship?" A human infant is not only at the mercy of adults in
terms of its physical survival. The human infant can be molded and
cultivated into a decent and caring adult, or its development can be
distorted horribly in a way than no non-human animal can have its
nature altered by experiences that occur within its species. If animals
exhibit psychotic, neurotic, or psychopathic-like behavior it is because
they have experienced the influence of human beings. Their instinct-
driven behavior protects them from extreme deviations in their normal
habitats. For better or for worse, humans have no strong instincts that can
override their experiences and protect their development into adjusted
adulthood. I have written elsewhere (Walsh, 1991) of the many physical,
psychological, and social disabilities associated with early love deprivation.

Applying Montagu's "neotenous principle" to the infant at the neurophysiological level, it means that the neonate's plastic undifferentiated
brain must be organized for love—a quite literal "wiring" of the neuronal
pathways. An analogy to show what I mean by the process of neuronal
"wiring" may prove useful here. Imagine a small circle of newly planted
rose bushes. If we could peer through the surface soil and observe their
roots, we would see that they are sparse and widely separated. This is
roughly the spatial patterning of the axons and dendrites (the "roots")
within the neonate's brain. Viewing the same cluster of bushes ten months
later (assuming adequate nurturing) we would discover that the roots
had branched out like hundreds of tiny fingers to contact the roots of
neighboring bushes. Further time would reveal an even greater mass of
intertwined roots, their number and density varying positively with the
quality of environmental conditions. The patterning of neuronal growth
in an infant newly planted on this earth is similarly dependent of the
quality of environmental conditions.

Unlike the roots of the rose bushes, the touchings of the neuronal
"roots" are of great importance; they establish functional pathways between
neurons. Intelligence can be viewed neurophysiologically as a function
of the density and complexity of synaptic connections, the strength of
these connections, and the speed with which they are made. Reaction-
time tests—tests which measure neuronal firing patterns in response to
audio and visual stimuli via the EEG—find strong positive relationships
between reaction time and IQ (Fincher, 1982:70). The density and complexity of structure and interconnective speed and strength are governed

by both our genetic inheritance and our experiences, especially our early experiences (see Walsh, 1983, or Pardes, 1986, for brief reviews).

During the period of intensely active development, the human infant's brain makes many more neuronal connections than it will ultimately use, for there is much competition going on in the brain for synaptic space. Many connections will be pruned because of disuse; others will be firmly established because of frequent use (Purves and Lichtman, 1980). Thus, interneuronal communication becomes habitual the more often the electrochemical synapses governing a particular response are activated. The process of forming and maintaining new synapses is known as synaptogenesis. The process is rather like the establishment of a trail in the wilderness. The more often the trail is trodden, the more distinct it becomes from its surroundings and the more functional it becomes.

In a series of brilliant works for which he received the prestigious Laskar Award for Medicine in 1983, Eric Kandel (1983) demonstrated the process of synaptic habituation in his laboratory. He used four-pound marine snails called *Aplysia Californica* because of the exceptionally large size of their neurons and because their synapses are virtually identical with those of human beings. Kandel subjected his snails to a variety of stimuli and was able to observe and photograph changes at the synapses produced by the stimuli. Kandel's work unequivocally demonstrated how environmental input regulates gene expression in the brain and how it modifies brain function by altering synaptic strength. Such findings strongly suggest that the relationship between biological and social processes is more intimate than was heretofore realized. Kandel's work also strengthened the notion held by many neuroscientists that emotions, such as love and hate, are related to specific areas of the brain rather than being diffused across the entire brain.

From this and similar research, psychophysiologist Gary Lynch (cited in Baskin, 1985) has developed a neurophysiological theory of long-term memory, the ability called upon in tests of verbal intelligence. He theorizes that an experience with strong emotional content is accompanied by especially strong neuronal stimulation. The strength of the stimulation results in the neurons involved becoming more sensitive and responsive to similar stimuli for weeks or months. If the emotional experience is repeated, the synapses are not only more receptive, they also become further sensitized. Lynch calls this phenomenon *long-term potentiation.* His work suggests that in the process of long-term potentiation an enzyme called calpain works on the neuronal membrane to expose additional receptors at the synapse. More active receptors means more information transfer and a possible reshaping of the dendritic branching and the creation of new synapses.

If the information being transmitted by either word or deed is negative, "you're not worthwhile or lovable," "the world is a cold, harsh, and abusive place," the developmental long-term potentiation consequences are obvious. Later communications, even if they are positive, will tend to be relayed along the same negative track as though some mischievous switchman were stationed at a critical neurological junction ready to derail any train of pleasurable thought or feeling.

As indicated, synaptic connections can also be pruned by disuse, just like a trail can again disappear if no longer trodden. Well-trodden pathways laid down during infancy and childhood tend to be more resistant to pruning than pathways laid down later in life. To give an example of the strength of early learning in contrast with later learning, it is well known that very young children can learn two languages simultaneously with very little effort. They can continue to be comfortable with both languages throughout their lives, with neither language being contaminated by the accent of the other. Anyone who has tried to learn a foreign language in adulthood knows how difficult it is and how it's almost impossible to speak it without an accent. Children have this ability because their young brains are physiologically more receptive.

The resistance to synaptic pruning of pathways laid down during early life is both good and bad, depending on whether the trail leads to love or to some pathology. We know that physical and emotional abuse, or any other manifestation of love deprivation, can have severely negative effects on childhood development, including intellectual development. For instance, Hoffman-Plotkin and Twentyman (1984) report a mean IQ difference of 20 IQ points between abused and non-abused preschool children. Elmer's (1977) study of abused children found that 30 percent of them had central nervous system damage, and that 57 percent had IQ scores of 80 or less. In comparing abused/neglected and non-abused/neglected school children, Salzinger et al. (1984) found three times as many (27% versus 9%) abused and neglected children than non-abused/neglected children were two years below grade level in verbal ability, and eleven times as many (33% versus 3%) were behind to the same extent in math ability. These are the children who will drop out, associate with delinquent peers, and become delinquents themselves.

## Tactile and Other Stimuli and Intelligence

Responses require stimuli, and stimuli for the infant originate in a very limited environment. The more stimuli experienced by the infant, the greater the number, complexity, and speed of the interneuronal connections. The less the stimuli experienced, the fewer will be the functional neuronal connections and the weaker they will be (Goldman-Rakic, 1987). It has been repeatedly shown in animal studies that organisms raised in stimuli-enriched environments develop greater cortical density and generate greater quantities of essential neurotransmitters than organisms raised in less stimulating conditions. For instance, Rosenzweig, Bennett and Diamond (1973) conducted a series of 16 experiments over a period of 9 years assessing neurological consequences of raising rats in stimuli-enriched and stimuli-impoverished environments. In 14 of the 16 experiments they found that rats raised in stimuli-enriched environments had significantly ($p < .01$) greater cortex weight and significantly greater quantities of a number of neurotransmitters than rats raised in stimuli-impoverished environments. This biophysical brain enrichment of stimuli-enriched rats resulted in greater ability of such rats across a number of learning tasks.

Evidence of the same phenomenon among human infants is provided by Rice (1977). Knowing that premature infants are at greater risk for physical, neurological, and social handicaps, as well as at greater risk for parental abuse, Rice explored the effects a daily dose of tactile stimulation would have on these infants. Fifteen premature infants were assigned to an experimental group and fourteen premature infants were assigned to a control group. The experimental infants were given a full-body nude massage by their mothers for fifteen minutes four times a day for one month. Following the massage, the infants were rocked and cuddled for an additional five minutes. The infants in the control group were provided with the usual hospital care, with the massages being the only difference in otherwise identical treatment for the two groups.

Although there were no differences between the groups on the variables of interest measured at the onset of the experiment, comparing them after a period of four months, it was found that the experimental infants were significantly superior to the control infants in weight gain, mental development, and most markedly in neurological development. Rice also provided evidence that the mothers and infants in the experimental group became more attached to one another than did the mothers and infants in the control group. Plentiful tactile stimuli is thus reflected in neural structure and chemistry, as well as a more secure love bond between mother and infant.

Scarr-Salapatek and Williams (1973) provide similar evidence. They report a significant difference of 10 IQ points between an experimental and control group of black low birth weight infants tested at age one. As was the case with the Rice (1977) study, the only difference between the randomly assigned groups was additional tactile and visual stimulation given to the experimental group beyond hospital norms. Many developmental differences favoring the experimental group were apparent after only six weeks of treatment.

Another important study pointing to the importance of environmental stimulation in conjunction with adequate nutrition for neural development during the critical period of brain growth was conducted by Lewin (1975). He studied a number of very young children whom he cross-classified into four groups on the basis of the amount of stimuli they received and nutritional adequacy: (1) malnourished children from stimuli-enriched environments, (2) malnourished children from stimuli-deprived environments, (3) well-nourished children from stimuli-enriched environments, and (4) well-nourished children from stimuli-deprived environments.

Having established these categories, Lewin administered various tests of intellectual development to each child. His results clearly showed that both malnourishment and stimuli deprivation have deleterious effects on intellectual development. Well-nourished children growing up in stimulating environments averaged 71.4 points on Lewin's intellectual tests, while well-nourished children from stimuli-deprived environments averaged 60.5. This latter group of children actually averaged less on the tests than malnourished children who were fortunate enough to live in stimuli-enriched homes, whose group average was 62.7. Predictably, the children who scored lowest on the tests, an average of only 52.9, were children suffering a combination of malnutrition and a stimuli-poor environment.

Adequate nourishment and adequate stimulation are not mutually exclusive variables in terms of brain development. Malnourishment results in lethargic and apathetic behavior in the infant, which in turn results diminished interest in it on the part of the caregiver, meaning that he or she will be less disposed to providing the infant with the vital stimuli it needs. The synergistic effects of malnourishment and deprivation of stimuli are aptly demonstrated in Lewin's study.

If a condition of malnourishment occurs in an adult, very little brain damage results because the body will take nourishment from other organs to satisfy the voracious appetite of the brain. For an infant, however, a protein-deficient diet has terrible consequences. Protein is essential for the myelination of the neuronal pathways. Myelin is a fatty substance that coats the axons and acts as a kind of insulator. Myelin acts like the rubber insulation around an electrical wire, in that it prevents the nerve impulses from "short-circuiting" and paying attention to irrelevant stimuli. Myelin also prevents neuronal fatigue, maximizes conduction velocity, and maximizes the possible rate of neuronal firing (Konner, 1982:163).

An infant's brain at birth is relatively low in myelin, the vast proportion being laid down in the first two years of life, and not fully established until age four (Dobbing, 1973). The lethargic and apathetic behaviors characteristic of unfortunate individuals suffering with pellagra and kwashiorkor—the diseases of malnutrition—are traced at the neural level to the inadequate myelination of the brain. A number of studies have shown that severe malnutrition during infancy is related to a number of adverse neurochemical consequences, including decreased myelination, reduced cell numbers, and lower DNA measures (Bouchard, Jr., and Segal, 1985:403). The lower IQ levels of children from poverty-stricken homes to a significant extent may be attributable in large part to their inadequate protein-deficient diets during infancy and early childhood. For instance, Hertzig et al. (1972) found that school children who were malnourished during their first two years of life had a mean full-scale IQ 8.27 points less than a comparison group of children who had been adequately nourished.

As we have seen, stimulation is also important for neural development. The particular stimuli with which we are concerned are acts of cutaneous stimulation—affectionate touching, kissing, cuddling—tactile assurances for the infant that it is loved and secure. These manifestations of mother love are not merely mutually satisfying psychological experiences; they are neurophysiologically critical during the sensitive period in which the neural pathways are being laid down. The importance of tactile stimulation to infant development demonstrated by Rice, among others, was stressed by Anna Freud long ago. She writes:

> In the beginning, being stroked, cuddled, and soothed by touch libidinizes the various parts of the child's body, helps to build up a healthy body image and body ego, increases its cathexis with narcissistic libido, and simultaneously promotes the development of object love by cementing the bond between child and mother. There is no doubt that, at this period, the surface of the skin in its role as erotogenic zone fulfills a multiple function in the child's growth. (1965:199.)

The effects of tactile stimulation on the structure of the brain can be appreciated in the understanding that the skin is almost an extension of the brain, formed as it is from the same layer of tissue during the embryonic stage of life (Taylor, 1979:136). It has also been established that the nerve fibers connecting the skin to the central nervous system are better developed than are the fibers of any other organ (Casler, 1973). The intimate connection between the skin and the brain has been attested to by many neuroscientists who find that even light stimuli deprivation during the stage of active cell growth results in reduced neural metabolism, reduced dendritic growth, and the atrophy of neuron-nourishing glial cells (Rutter, 1972:57). It is therefore of the utmost importance that infants be exposed to multiple stimuli, especially loving tactile stimulation, during this critical period. The more stimuli the infant receives, the more his or her neural machinery is honed and oiled to deal with all kinds of future emotional and intellectual problems. The brain doesn't get another chance.

Apart from its affect on dendritic growth, tactile stimuli appears also to increase the rate of myelination. It has been shown experimentally that animals who are petted and loved up have significantly greater amounts of the material (cholesterol and the enzyme cholinesterase) necessary for myelin formation than animals who are not (Denenberg, 1981). The more the nerve fibers of the brain are used, the more rapidly they become myelinated. The increased mylination results in greater ability to function in the environment, as determined by greater curiosity, problem-solving ability, dominance, and general liveliness among petted animals.

The importance of tactile stimulation is made palpable by the fact that the infant can only experience and express love or its absence through its body. It has no psychological referents by which to interpret the multitude of emotional states it is experiencing. A lack of intimate bodily contact between mother and child has to be interpreted as abandonment, since, in a very real sense, the infant can only "think" with its skin. The infant's contact comfort experienced during times of duress from its mother's sensitive responses tells it that everything's okay: "She's there for me," "I'm safe," "All's right in my world."

Ashley Montagu summarizes the relationship between tactile stimulation and human development for us when he writes: "The kind of tactuality experienced during infancy and childhood not only produces the appropriate changes in the brain, but also effects the growth and development of the end-organs in the skin. The tactually deprived individual will suffer from a feedback deficiency between skin and brain that may seriously affect his development as a human being" (1978:208).

### Accounting for Environmental IQ Variance

If a liberal estimate of the variance in IQ accounted for by genetics is about .60, it follows that at least .40 of the variance is accounted for by the environment. I attempted to account for as much of this variance as possible using the variables included in this study. I entered love deprivation, birth order, number of siblings, SES, broken home, family size, and birth status (legitimate/illegitimate) into a multiple regression equation using backward elimination of variables. Only those variables attaining significance at < .05 are retained. (The theoretical importance of each of these variables are discussed at appropriate points in this book.)

Table 3.1 shows that I was able to account for 19.1 percent of the variance in IQ with those variables retained at < .05. Race is the most important variable in the model. With the other variables in the model held constant, whites have an IQ mean 11.94 points higher than blacks. Race is included as an "environmental" variable because I consider it to be a concise and convenient index of all the disabilities suffered by blacks in this country: low birth weight, anoxia (respiratory distress at birth), lack of prenatal medical attention, inadequate pre and postnatal nutrition, and so forth. These disabilities are not unique to blacks, but they are all found more frequently among them (Bouchard, Jr., and Segal, 1985). What is unique about the black experience is the sense of powerlessness, alienation, incomplete assimilation into American culture, institutionalized racism, and even the paternalism of social science "do-gooders" (Baratz and Baratz, 1982). All these environmental disabilities can impact on black IQ in subtle and insidious ways that are not captured simply by holding constant the other variables in the model.

One could argue that I have misspecified my model by including race

TABLE 3.1

Environmental Variables Regressed on Full-Scale IQ

| Variable | b | s.e. | $\beta$ | t | sig. |
|---|---|---|---|---|---|
| Race (white/black) | -11.94 | 1.62 | -.319 | -7.38 | .0000 |
| Socioeconomic Status | .33 | .05 | .271 | 6.29 | .0000 |
| Love Deprivation | -1.19 | .43 | -.118 | -2.76 | .0060 |
| Number of Siblings | .66 | .25 | .113 | 2.59 | .0099 |
| (Constant) | 85.07 | 2.12 | | 40.08 | .0000 |

Adj. R Squared = .191,  F = 28.57,  p = .0000

as an environmental variable, and by doing so I have confounded genetic and environmental influences. If race is "really" a genetic rather than an environmental variable in the IQ context, then the observed difference in black/white IQ is a function of genetic differences, plus unmeasured environmental differences, and plus measurement error. This is not a proposition that I am willing to accept in the absence of any definitive evidence at present that the IQ is biologically related to race, or even that blacks constitute a genetically distinct race.[4]

SES is the next most important variable accounting for IQ variation. However, the model assumes that SES variation accounts for variation in IQ rather than the other way around. As we saw in the last chapter, this assumption may be untenable. I am more open to the idea that SES differences may have a genetic basis than I am that race differences have. Even so, it is indisputable that the disabilities of class have negative influences on IQ that compound any genetic influences.

Assuming that just forty percent of the variance in IQ is accounted for by the environment, we may ask what improvement in IQ scores would we theoretically expect if delinquents who are one standard deviation below the SES mean had been placed at an early age into families who are one standard deviation above the SES mean? SES scores in the sample range between 9 and 52 with a mean of 26.3 and a standard deviation of 11.5. We may take this as a rough approximation of the range of environments experienced by delinquents.

The sample IQ standard deviation is 14.6; squaring this yields a variance of 213. Forty percent of 213 is 85, which is taken as the

IQ variance accounted for by non-genetic factors. A change of two standard deviations in SES would, therefore, result in $\sqrt{85} \times 2 = 18.44$ IQ points. Delinquents who are one standard deviation below the mean on SES have a mean IQ of 87.8. Adding the assumed increment due to an improved SES environment would theoretically yield an IQ mean of 106.24.

Empirically, the SES mean IQ of delinquents who are one standard deviation above the SES mean is 100.3, giving us a difference between the upper and lower SES delinquents of $100.3 - 87.8 = 12.5$ IQ points. It is clear that an improvement in the environment would result in an improvement in IQ scores. The difference between the theoretically predicted improvement and what we observe using this sample is an indication that SES measures provide only a very crude approximation of environment advantage/disadvantage.

The variance accounted for by love deprivation is disappointingly low given the stress placed on this variable in the developmental literature. But we must consider the gross inadequacy of our love deprivation measure, which is, at best, a minimal estimate of the damage that boys in the sample may have suffered. The theoretical literature stresses abuse, neglect, and lack of stimulation during early infancy as being of the utmost importance. We have only incidents of negative parental behavior reported by social workers and juvenile probation officials subsequent to the child's first encounter with the authorities. Even then we have no assurances that every such behavior was discovered and reported. Nevertheless, love deprivation, inadequately measured as it is, exerts an independent influence on intellectual functioning. A more precise and comprehensive measure would doubtless reveal a more robust effect on IQ.

The only other variable to have an independent impact on IQ is number of siblings. The literature generally reports low negative correlations with IQ for this variable (Scarr and Weinberg, 1978). We note that in the present sample, with other independents held constant, the relationship is positive. No adequate explanation for this reversal from the expected can be offered other than it may be reflective of differences in sample composition (delinquents versus non-delinquents).

## Conclusion

Intelligence is not a fixed attribute. Evidence from genetics, neurophysiology, psychology, and sociology points to the many ways that the organism's environment interacts with genetic endowment to increase or decrease intelligence as measured by IQ tests. Intelligence is a function of the way the brain operates, and the way the brain operates depends of its structure and its neurotransmitter patterns. The brain develops continuously for a number of years after birth, with most of the basic connections being made at certain critical developmental junctures during infancy and childhood. The brain's physical structure, size, number of cells, degree of myelination, and its neuronal pathways establishes itself in intimate interaction with the outside world.

It appears that neuronal metabolism is highly influenced by nutrition and infancy and early childhood stimulation, especially tactile stimulation. This observation paves the way for developing intervention strategies, especially for lower SES children. Prenatal and perinatal care and education among the poor in this country is primitive compared to what is available in other industrialized democracies; we now rank twentieth in infant mortality in the world. Malnutrition and improper medical care for mothers can leave their children vulnerable to poor brain development and, hence, to a level of intellectual functioning which will leave them severely disadvantaged in the struggle to become productive, law-abiding members of society. We can be doing so much more than we currently are to raise intellectual functioning among the disadvantaged classes. Indeed, if we are serious about our desire to tackle the problem of delinquency and the issues of injustice and inequality in general, we must do more. Possible intervention strategies will be addressed more fully in the final chapter.

## ENDNOTES

1. Jensen's claim that California blacks may have a greater degree of white genes than Georgia blacks, and that this white "blood" may account for the higher IQs of California blacks, is not supported by the evidence. Scarr, Pakstis, Katz, and Barker (1977) used blood group and serum-protein markers to estimate the degree of European/African ancestry among 181 pairs of black twins. They found that higher degrees of European ancestry did not result in higher IQs among their sample.

2. This is analogous to physical strength training. A person with limited natural potential can train his or herself beyond the strength level of someone with more potential but who is not trained. In strength training there tends to be rather dramatic early "training effects" as muscles adapt to the various movements. If training is discontinued, the same fading effects noted for IQ

scores are noted in strength gains, but there always remains residual benefits and the trained person will be somewhat stronger than he/she would have otherwise been.

3. Not all structures of the human brain are plastic. For instance, the paleomammalian or "primitive" brain (the brainstem, medulla, pons) is hard-wired. In fact, for the first few weeks of life the human infant operates exclusively from this "reflexive" brain (Lipsitt, 1979). Other areas, such as the visual cortex, only temporarily exhibit the molecular characteristics of plasticity. After so-called critical periods are passed, these structures are no longer malleable because the mature organism has to respond consistently to important stimuli. Structures such as the hippocampus and the cerebral cortex, seats of emotion and learning, retain a lifelong ability to alter their neuronal connections (Kalil, 1989).

4. There are problems with considering blacks to be a race genetically distinct from whites, although they do constitute a fairly endogamous reproductive group. The most obvious is that American blacks are a hybrid people *socially* classified as a race on the basis of skin color. Biological testing has shown that American blacks as a group have about 80% African and 20% European Ancestry. The range of degree of African ancestry is between 40% and 95% (Scarr, Pakstis, Katz, and Barker, 1977). As indicated in endnote 1, no relationship between degree of African/European ancestry and IQ has been found to exist.

## Chapter Four

# INTELLECTUAL IMBALANCE:
# THE WECHSLER P > V TEST

### The Wechsler IQ Subtests

Having looked at the nature and nurture of IQ, this chapter examines the two major components of IQ, how they reflect cognitive styles, and how they influence behavior.

The most popular IQ test for juveniles in use today is the Revised Wechsler Intelligence Scale for Children (WISC–R). The WISC–R is divided into verbal and performance subtests, providing measures of verbal IQ (VIQ) and performance IQ (PIQ). Chase et al. (1984) and Duara et al. (1984), using positron emission tomography (PET), have shown that the neurological processes engaged when subjects are administered these different IQ subscales are lateralized to opposite hemispheres of the brain.[1] Glucose metabolism rates vary with the type of test being administered. VIQ-related tasks are associated with metabolic activity in the left hemisphere (the left parasylvian area), and PIQ-related brain activity is mainly localized to the right posterior parietal area. The Chase et al. study found strong significant positive correlations between full-scale IQ ($r = .68$), VIQ ($r = .61$), and PIQ ($r = .56$) and overall cerebral metabolism. The Grady et al. study reported a non-significant correlation of .37 between full-scale IQ and metabolism. These studies suggest that high IQ individuals have more efficient neurometabolic systems, a suggestion previously made from studies correlating IQ with electroencephalograph data (Fincher, 1981; Corning, Steffy, and Chaprin, 1982).

The Wisc-R subscale tests alternate VIQ and PIQ subtests, and they are administered in the following order:

|  | Verbal Scale |  | Performance Scale |
|---|---|---|---|
| 1. | Information | 2. | Picture completion |
| 3. | Similarities | 4. | Picture arrangement |
| 5. | Arithmetic | 6. | Block design |
| 7. | Vocabulary | 8. | Object assembly |
| 9. | Comprehension | 10. | Coding (or mazes) |

Taking all ten subtests as a whole, we can see that they are operationalizations of global intelligence; that is, they measure an individual's capacity to think rationally, act purposefully, and to deal effectively with his or her environment. They attempt to measure such things as long- and short-term memory, concentration, computational skills, verbal abstractions, awareness of and openness to one's culture and its norms, manual dexterity, visual/spatial acuity, and adaptability. The extent to which the subtests measure the same thing (global intelligence) can be gauged by the average correlation found between them, reported by Anastasi (1975:253) to be .783. In other words, individuals who score well on the verbal test tend to score well on the performance test also.

However, the average proportion of variance in one subtest left unexplained by the other (approximately 39%) indicates that there is certainly no one-to-one relationship between them. They are measuring somewhat different domains of intelligence, with the performance scale providing a fairer assessment for juveniles whose family backgrounds do not promote verbal skills. It is important to note that both subscales contribute about equally to an individual's full-scale IQ score. The average correlation between FIQ and VIQ is .933, and between FIQ and PIQ it is .927 (Anastasi, 1976:259).

Most sociological studies linking IQ to crime and delinquency have viewed IQ as a unitary phenomenon. That is, such studies have correlated *full-scale* IQ with various measures of crime and delinquency. Such a conceptualization of IQ may obscure as much about the IQ/delinquency relationship as it reveals. Full-scale IQ (FIQ) is a composite of the two subtest scores; the mean of the VIQ and PIQ scores yield the subject's FIQ. For example, if an individual has a VIQ score of 100 and a PIQ score of 90, his or her FIQ is given as $(100 + 90)/2 = 95$. The reason why the use of FIQ might distort the IQ/delinquency relationship is that offenders tend to show a greater deficit in VIQ than they do in PIQ relative to general population norms. Combining the two subscales to obtain FIQ has the effect of making the overall IQ mean scores for the general and delinquent populations somewhat more equal than they would otherwise be (Herrnstein, 1989:3), and thus probably leads to the underestimation of the effects of cognitive variables on delinquency.

### Verbal IQ and Neuronal Development

What I am getting at is that these different but overlapping measures of intelligence may correlate differently with delinquency, and that combining the two subtest scores may obscure the picture, especially when examining different types of delinquent activity. For instance, crimes which take some degree of forethought, such as burglary and various types of fraud, may be more successfully executed by offenders with the kinds of cognitive skills tested on the verbal scale. For instance, Walsh (1987) found that property offense scores increased with *increased* VIQ within a sample of offenders. On the other hand, offenders lacking verbal skills may be less prone to offenses requiring cognitive skills, but may be more prone to violent and impulsive crimes and perhaps more able to carry them out due to relatively superior visual-spatial abilities.

Low VIQ boys may be viewed as being more prone to violence and aggression because they lack verbal skills that mediate between a stimulus and a response. Joseph (1982) has noted that the motor areas of the cortex mature earlier than other areas, making for speedy non-cognitively mediated responses to stimuli on the part of infants and young children. As children mature, there is increasing communication between the verbal and visual-spatial hemispheres of the brain, and they slow down their responses to stimuli while the left brain processes and interprets motor behavior initiated by the right brain. Initially, this is a post hoc process, but through the processes of language acquisition and socialization, the child eventually is able to *foresee* its response before he or she reacts rather than interpreting action after the fact. In Joseph's (1982) neuropsychological theory of the origin of thought, he sees an ever-increasing engagement of the left hemisphere in the processing, organization and, when needed, inhibition, of emotional transmissions received from the right brain.

The efficiency with which the verbal qualities of the left hemisphere performs its interpretive and inhibitory task varies considerably from person to person. This variability appears to be greatly influenced by early environmental experience. Joseph (1982:11–13) points out that there is stiff competition within the infant's rapidly branching neurons for synaptic connections. We have already seen that functional connections between neurons are greatly influenced by experience and are made stronger and more secure the more frequently they are made — they "dig in," so to speak, and fend off competing connections. The established patterns of neuronal connections function as "memory tapes," playing over and over in the head until they become a sort of "life script" that governs our interactions with others.

Children who have strong visual-spatial capabilities relative to their verbal capabilities may tend to retain some of the unmediated rapidity of response to stimuli that is characteristic of the immature brain. As such children grow older they retain their childhood priorities for instant pleasure and self-gratification without having developed the "self-talk" necessary to generate a sense of discipline, responsibility, and a recognition of the rights of others. When we have a young child that processes information this way, we have a "brat" who slaps playmates and steals their candy. When we have a juvenile or young adult using similar cognitive processes, we have a delinquent or a criminal who steals, assaults, robs, and rapes. The cognitive *processes* of the immature child and the delinquent or criminal are the same, but the *content* of those cognitions becomes much more threatening as the person becomes older, stronger, and more ambitious in the pursuit of self-gratification.

Lacking an adequate measure of the internal speech that mediates stimulus and response, cognitively immature individuals are prone to act impulsively in response to frustration and to real or imagined insults. Impulsiveness, the failure to inhibit motor activity, presages violence, as well as the inability for sustained intellectual activity. Bonnie Camp (1977) tested these assumptions among a group of aggressive (teachers' evaluations) and normal grade school boys. She found that the aggressive boys performed more poorly in terms of verbal ability, reading achievement, impulsivity, ability to inhibit responses, and response modulation following verbal commands. She matched the two groups according to PIQ scores, so this variable, unfortunately for our purposes, could not be tested for significance of difference. She did find, however, that aggressive boys evidenced faster response times, a trait that is useful when being tested for PIQ. Camp (1977:145) concluded that her findings were "consistent with the formulation that young aggressive boys fail to use verbal mediational activity in many situations in which it would be appropriate, and when it does occur, covert mediational activity may fail to achieve functional control over behavior." In other words, low VIQ constitutes a cognitive deficit which involves a failure to modulate dominant motor impulses.

Consistent with the neurological thesis of brain maturation is a study conducted by Huesmann, Eron, and Yarmel (1988). These researchers studied 600 subjects over a 22-year period. They found that although most children tested at age eight showed less and less aggressive behavior over the years as they learned appropriate coping strategies, children with low IQ's remained aggressive at about the same rate throughout the period of the study. The authors suggested that low IQ makes it difficult for children to learn alternative methods of coping with frustration, and that "low IQ must exert most of its effect on aggression before age 8, as it does not predict changes in aggression after that time" (1988:239). They also found IQ to be negatively related to harsh physical and psychological punishment and parental rejection.

Some further evidence that IQ, particularly VIQ, functions as a barrier to criminal activity is offered by Kandel et al. (1988). She and her colleagues examined data from 1,400 males in a Danish birth cohort. The cohort was divided into high and low risk for criminal activity based on father's criminality. The risk for serious criminal activity was 5.6 times greater for cohort members whose fathers had serious criminal histories than for members whose fathers had no criminal history. The high and low risk group members were further divided into categories based on whether or not subjects had a criminal record. It was reasoned that if high-risk subjects were to resist criminal involvement, they would be seen to have a higher mean IQ than members of the other three (high-risk/criminal, low-risk/criminal, and low-risk/non-criminal) groups. The high-risk/non-criminal group did have a statistically significant higher mean IQ than the other three groups. These findings indicate that high IQ insulates against delinquent behavior even among those who, due to home environment, were otherwise at high risk.

Other researchers have linked low VIQ to levels of interpersonal maturity using the I-level ("I" for "interpersonal maturity") system (Andrew, 1980). This system proposes that cognitive and personality integration follows a sequential pattern in normal human development and sets up seven I-levels. Level 1 is the most basic and level 7 is considered the ideal. It has been found that delin uents generally fall into levels 2 through 5, with level 5 so rarely found among delinquents that only levels 2 through 4 are usually used to assess delinquent subjects (Austin, 1981:187). There are also 9 subtypes within the 3 primary types (2, 3, and 4) used with delinquent population.

As might be expected, interpersonal maturity varied positively with VIQ in Andrew's (1980) study. Level 2 subjects, subjects in which the only system of cognitive reference appear to be themselves and their personal needs, had a mean VIQ of 78.7. Level 3 subjects, those who have internalized some social rules but who use them to manipulate, had a mean VIQ of 90.4. Level 4 subjects, who tend to be neurotic and acting-out because of conflicts between personal needs and social rules that have been more strongly internalized than other I-level subjects, had a VIQ mean of 98.4. These VIQ differences were partly mediated by age, with younger children naturally being more cognitively immature. However, the significant effect remained so when controlling for age ($F = 12.84$, $p < .001$).

The main determinants of I-level appear to be verbal intelligence, so much so that Austin (1975) has suggested that the I-level system measures intelligence plus "moral orientation" more so than social maturity. Intellectual maturity is probably a necessary, if not sufficient, prerequisite for moral maturity. Moral orientation, of course, means moral reasoning, and moral reasoning involves making decisions about what is acceptable and what is unacceptable behavior. A deficit in moral orientation also means a mental fixation on egocentric thinking and short-run hedonism, patterns of thought more congruent with infantile and early childhood brain development than that of the mature adult (Joseph, 1982). What this suggests is that juveniles with a deficit in left-brain VIQ relative to right-brain PIQ have a tendency to act out rather than think out in a variety of situations. In a sense, then, violent and aggressive behavior is a form of visual/spatial ability that is unregulated by verbal ability among individuals lacking in internal moral standards of conduct.

## PIQ and P > V Discrepancy

More important than simple verbal and performance IQ scores in the exploration of delinquent behavior is the discrepancy between these two subtest scores. As Wechsler put it: "The most outstanding feature of the sociopath's test profile is the systematic high score on the performance as compared to the verbal part of the scale" (1958:176). Individuals who exhibit a significant PIQ > VIQ discrepancy, then, may be psychopathic (sociopathic), although we have been warned not to make such a diagnosis on the basis of P > V discrepancy alone because there is more than one path to both intellectual imbalance and psychopathy (Matarazzo, 1972).[2] The present study, lacking diagnostic information independent of the P > V profile, does not claim that juveniles having significant P > V discrepancy are psychopathic.

The P > V definition of psychopathy places individuals on a continuum of lesser or greater psychopathy rather than into discreet categories defined as psychopathic or non-psychopathic. A person with a P > V discrepancy of 25 points is considered more psychopathic than one with 12 points. Although Joan McCord argues for a discrete definition of

psychopathy, she acknowledges that "dimensional definitions of psychopathy have been supported on the grounds that aggression, capacity for
love, scope of conscience, impulsiveness, and willingness to violate norms
appear to be continuous variables" (1983:359). The continuous definition
of psychopathy implies that the degree of P > V imbalance should vary
positively with both degree of love deprivation and degree of violence.

Numerous studies have been conducted to test Weschler's contention
that significant P > V discrepancy is a marker of psychopathy. While
some studies have supported it and others have not, the weight of the
evidence is clearly supportive. A perusal of this literature shows that a
number of sample and methodological differences exist between supportive and non-supportive studies. Generally speaking, non-supportive
studies tend to have low sample N's, tend to be based on samples of less
serious delinquents, tend to dichotomize dependent (delinquency/crime)
and independent (P > V) variables and, as a consequence of the latter, to
use less powerful non-parametric statistics. Nevertheless, Miller (1987:120)
has stated: "This PIQ > VIQ relationship [with crime and delinquency]
was found across studies, despite variations in age, sex, race, setting, and
form of Wechsler scale administered, as well as differences in criteria for
delinquency."

To determine if the proportion of boys in our sample who show
significant intellectual imbalance, as measured by P/V discrepancy, differ significantly from the proportion of boys in the general population
with the same profile, I take what Kaufman (1976) calls the "normative
approach." That is, the incidence of imbalance in Kaufman's normative
sample (N = 2200) can be compared with the incidence in the present
sample. For his male-only sample (N = 1100), Kaufman found that a
discrepancy score of 12 points in either direction (V > P or P > V) was
necessary for significance at < .05. The normative sample found that 18
percent of the boys had a V > P profile, 16 percent a P > V profile, and
66 percent to be intellectually balanced (V = P).

As is readily seen from Table 4.1, this sample of delinquents differs
considerably from Kaufman's normative sample of boys in the various
P/V categories. While most boys (57.3%) are P = V, only 7.2% are V > P,
and 35.5% are P > V. Thus, the delinquent boys are underrepresented
by a factor of about 2.5 in the V > P category and are overrepresented by
a factor of about 2.2 in the P > V category. Another way of putting it is
that although the proportion of V > P and P > V boys is about equal in
the normative sample, P > V boys are about five times more likely than

V > P boys to appear in a delinquent sample. These percentages closely resemble those found by other researchers using delinquent samples. For instance, among a sample of 74 delinquents, Andrew (1977) found 11.3% in the V > P category, 55.6% in the P = V category, and 33.8% in the P > V category. The respective percentages in each category found by Tarter, Hegedus, Winsten, and Alterman (1985) were 7.9, 63.4, and 28.7 (N = 101).

TABLE 4.1

Chi-Square Goodness-of-Fit Test: P/V Discrepancy Scores of Delinquent Boys and General Population

| Category | Observed | | Expected | | Residual |
|----------|----------|------|----------|------|----------|
|          | N        | %    | N        | %    |          |
| V > P    | 37       | (7.2)  | 92.00    | (18.0) | -55.00   |
| P = V    | 294      | (57.3) | 339.00   | (66.0) | -45.00   |
| P > V    | 182      | (35.5) | 82.00    | (16.0) | 100.00   |
| Total    | 513      | (100)  |          |      |          |

$$X^2 = 160.805, \quad df = 2, \quad p < .0001$$

In addition to the highly significant goodness-of-fit chi-square for P/V categories, we can further assess the difference between the delinquent sample and population norm in terms of mean discrepancy differences. The literature consistently finds significant different P > V means between delinquents and the population norm. For instance, Andrew (1974) reports a P > V mean of 6.76 among 112 delinquents, and Loro and Woodward (1976) report a mean P > V of 8.92 among 80 delinquents. The mean P > V discrepancy in the present sample is 7.15, with a standard deviation of 13.31. The population mean P > V discrepancy has been standardized to 0 with a standard deviation of 10 (Matarazzo and Herman, 1985). Applying the single-sample z test for difference between population and sample means, I obtained a highly significant z of 16.19.

The departure from "normalcy" is further seen when we compare the correlation between PIQ and VIQ among these juvenile delinquents

(.601) with the average correlation between the two subtests within non-delinquent samples of .783 as reported by Anastasi (1976:253). The totality of the preceding evidence strongly indicates that a V > P profile can be considered a marker predictive of good behavior in the general population, and a P > V profile to be a marker predictive of delinquent behavior in the general population.

It was noted earlier that Andrew (1980) found VIQ to be related to interpersonal maturity using the I-level system. In an earlier study of hers among 122 probationers (Andrew, 1974), she found that interpersonal maturity was even more closely related to P > V than to VIQ. The most mature probationers (I-level 4) had a mean P > V discrepancy of 4.41 points, the I-level 3 probationers had a mean discrepancy of 7.33 points, and the I-level 2's had a mean of 17.78. It is clear that low verbal intelligence alone cannot account for interpersonal immaturity, and that a high PIQ relative to an individual's VIQ also plays an important part.

## Is P > V Artifactual?

A number of explanations contend for the observed discrepancy between VIQ and PIQ. The most obvious is that because delinquents have lower overall IQ's and because they tend to come from the lower socioeconomic classes of society, the discrepancy may be a function of lower overall intelligence (FIQ), of low VIQ, or of low SES. Yochelson and Samenow (1976:98) suggest that it is the tradition of "not talking" that lower-class delinquents bring with them to the testing situation that deflates VIQ scores relative to PIQ scores. Empirical studies, however, suggest the opposite; i.e., elevated PIQ rather than deflated VIQ is most responsible for the P > V profile. Haynes and Bensch (1981) found among a sample of 90 delinquents that recidivists and non-recidivists did not differ significantly on VIQ, but that recidivists had a significantly higher PIQ (97.0 versus 90.3) than non-recidivists. Similarly, Moffitt and Silva (1988) found that while delinquents had significantly lower FIQ and VIQ means than non-delinquents in a birth cohort of New Zealand juveniles, they did not differ significantly on PIQ.

Since the present sample is overwhelmingly composed of boys from the lower end of the social class strata and since lower class is related to lower overall IQ, it behooves us to determine if the excess PIQ is an artifact of (1) low FIQ, (2) low VIQ, (3) or SES. To explore these possibilities I performed a median split (Md = 6) on P > V and performed t-tests on FIQ, VIQ, and SES. I also performed a t-test on PIQ to see if P > V is more a function of elevated PIQ than of a deficit in any of these other areas.

The first t-test presented in Table 4.2 shows that P > V boys actually have a significantly higher mean FIQ than the low P > V boys. Thus, P > V discrepancy does not appear to be a function of overall lower intelligence. The second t-test shows that high P > V boys have a significantly lower VIQ than low P > V boys (a 4-point difference between means). However, from the third t-test we see that there is a much larger difference between the PIQ means of the two groups, with the high P/V boys showing a mean PIQ 17 points greater than the low P/V boys. We can readily see from the respective eta squared values that PIQ excess is more important than VIQ deficit in accounting for P > V imbalance. In other words, we see that P > V grouping explains 14.6 times more of the variance in PIQ (29.2%) than it does in VIQ (2.0%). The zero-order correlations between PIQ and P > V in its original undichotimized metric (r = .57) and between VIQ and P > V (r = −.30) further reinforce the above. Similar findings by Andrew (1977:102) led her to conclude that high PIQ is the "active ingredient" in significant P > V discrepancies; and in Barnett, Zimmer, and McCormack's (1989:18) study of 1,792 prison inmates they concluded that "the P > V discrepancy appears to be the result of a comparatively elevated performance score . . . rather than a depressed verbal score."[3] Finally, we observe almost identical social class means for the two groups. It appears that excess PIQ is indeed the active ingredient in P > V intellectual imbalance rather than a deficit in VIQ, and we must also conclude that P > V imbalance in not an artifact of social class.

Further indicative that significant P > V is not an artifact of lower overall intelligence are the results shown in Table 4.3. The number of boys who are intellectually imbalanced at the .05 level in either direction becomes progressively larger from the lowest to the highest FIQ categories. All the 18 boys in the lowest FIQ category are intellectually balanced, 80.4 percent in the next lowest category are balanced, 62.2 in the next lowest, and 49.1 percent in each of the normal and above normal FIQ boys are intellectually balanced. The boys in the highest FIQ category have the greatest percentage of V > P imbalanced cases, and the boys in the normal FIQ category the greatest percentage of P > V imbalanced cases. It is also noted that the mean P > V (−5.17) is lowest in the lowest FIQ category and highest in the 91-110 FIQ category. These findings conform to those found by Matarazzo and Herman (1985) among a

TABLE 4.2

Comparing High and Low P > V Boys on FIQ, VIQ, PIQ and Social Class

| Category | N | $\overline{X}$ | s | t | df | sig. | Eta$^2$ |
|---|---|---|---|---|---|---|---|
| Full-Scale IQ | | | | | | | |
| Low P>V | 260 | 90.57 | 16.1 | -4.83 | 467.9 | .0000 | .044 |
| High P>V | 253 | 96.51 | 11.4 | | | | |
| Verbal IQ | | | | | | | |
| Low P>V | 260 | 92.53 | 15.6 | 3.28 | 474.1 | .0001 | .020 |
| High P>V | 253 | 88.57 | 11.4 | | | | |
| Performance IQ | | | | | | | |
| Low P>V | 260 | 89.11 | 15.3 | -14.39 | 486.1 | .0000 | .292 |
| High P>V | 253 | 106.43 | 11.8 | | | | |
| Social Class | | | | | | | |
| Low P>V | 240 | 26.62 | 11.5 | 0.00 | 467 | .997 | .000 |
| High P>V | 229 | 26.71 | 11.6 | | | | |

Note: df adjusted for significant inequality of variance.

normative sample of 1,880 youngsters using a cutting point of 13 rather than 12 discrepancy points.[4]

## Intellectual Imbalance and the Autonomic Nervous System

If significant P > V is not an artifact of the variables just examined, the question remains: What does account for it? Since VIQ and PIQ are highly correlated, it is difficult to envision significant intellectual imbalance being a genetically coded trait, although McFie's (1973) research leads him to suggest that perhaps it is. Brain lesions are sometimes used to explain deficits in intellectual functioning. For instance, Matazarro and Herman (1985:928) state that "an accumulating literature strongly suggests that dysfunction in the left hemisphere of the brain is, on the average, differentially associated with a lower Verbal IQ, whereas a dysfunction in the right hemisphere is, on the average, associated with a

TABLE 4.3

Numbers and Percentages of Cases in V > P, V = P, and P > V in Various FIQ Categories, and Mean P > V Discrepancy Scores

FIQ Category

|  | low – 65 | | 67 – 79 | | 80 – 90 | | 91 – 110 | | 111 – high | | Total | |
|---|---|---|---|---|---|---|---|---|---|---|---|---|
|  | N | % | N | % | N | % | N | % | N | % | N | % |
| V > P | 0 | (0.0) | 1 | (1.8) | 6 | (5.0) | 21 | (7.9) | 9 | (16.4) | 37 | (7.2) |
| V = P | 18 | (100) | 45 | (80.4) | 74 | (62.2) | 130 | (49.1) | 27 | (49.1) | 294 | (57.3) |
| P > V | 0 | (0.0) | 10 | (17.9) | 39 | (32.8) | 114 | (43.0) | 19 | (34.5) | 182 | (35.5) |
| Totals | 18 | (100) | 56 | (100) | 119 | (100) | 265 | (100) | 55 | (100) | 513 | (100) |

$X^2 = 41.9$, df = 8, p = .0001

| $\bar{X}$ P>V | -5.17 | 1.23 | 7.76 | 9.32 | 5.69 | 7.18 |
|---|---|---|---|---|---|---|

$F_{(4,508)} = 9.15$, p = .0001

relatively lower Performance IQ." In other words, abuse suffered by a child which results in damage to the central nervous system may reveal itself in the form of significantly different VIQ and PIQ scores.

Flor-Henry (1978:157) has pointed out that the right hemisphere of the brain (where visual-spatial skills are represented) is less vulnerable to damage than the larger and less well-irrigated left hemisphere (where verbal skills are represented). Thus, if structural damage to the central nervous system is to be invoked as an explanation for intellectual imbalance, it is more likely to be in the form of VIQ decrement than in PIQ increment. Moreover, research suggests that PIQ is less heritable than VIQ.[5] If this is indeed the case, the implication is that PIQ scores are more subject to environmental influences (other than brain lesions due to blows and falls) than VIQ.

It has been shown in this and other studies that intellectual imbalance appears to be more a function of elevated PIQ than low VIQ. Although the high P > V group of boys were shown in Table 4.3 to have significantly lower VIQ than low P > V boys, and thus providing us with an indication that some left hemisphere damage may be involved, the high P > V boys have a mean PIQ higher than even the mean of the general population (106.43 versus 100). This difference in PIQ between the high P > V boys and the general population is statistically significant (z = 6.82, p < .0001). This suggests that a different mechanism, perhaps in conjunction with left hemisphere damage, is needed to explain elevated PIQ scores among high P > V delinquent boys.

One such mechanism is differential functioning of the autonomic nervous system (ANS). The ANS is the collective term for the efferent nerves that activate the major visceral organs of the body. The autonomic nerves are divided into two groups: the sympathetic and parasympathetic branches. The sympathetic system is often referred to as the adrenergic system because it activates and mobilizes the major organs of the body to aid the individual to cope with some emergency or stressful situation (the "fight or flight" reaction). The sympathetic branch is a regulator of our emotional life, guiding our pleasurable arousal and our avoidance of pain. The parasympathetic system operates as a counterbalance—a cholinergic system—that functions to return the body to a chemical balance when the emergency situation has passed.

Individuals differ in the functioning of their ANS's. While most have ANS's that function within a normal range, some have hyperactive ANS's and some have hyporeactive (underreactive) ANS's. Hyporeactivity of the ANS has been related to criminal and delinquent behavior and has been considered to be a physiological marker of psychopathy. Hare and Quinn (1971), for instance, found significant differences between psychopaths and non-psychopaths in various indicators of ANS arousal such as electrodermal, cardiac, and vasomotor activity. Schalling (1978) found significantly lower levels of stress-related catecholamines in the urine of psychopaths awaiting criminal sentencing—tested at two weeks, one week, and immediately prior to sentencing—than in the urine of non-psychopaths awaiting the same anxiety-generating experience. Summing up the literature on crime and ANS functioning, Mednick and Finello (1983:8) state that across a wide variety of studies and national settings, "the antisocial individual consistently evidences a relatively unresponsive ANS."

Mednick (1979:50–51) offers a theory based on ANS responsiveness of how children learn to inhibit aggression. Succinctly stated:

1. A child contemplates aggressive action.
2. Because of previous punishment he suffers fear.

3. He inhibits the aggressive response.
4. His fear begins to dissipate, to be reduced.

The progression of this process requires a censuring agent, which can be the individual's own conscience or some outside agent, and an ANS that responds quickly, both in terms of generating the fear response and in terms of quickly returning to equilibrium. An individual who inhibits the contemplated aggression (perhaps by using verbal skills in self-talk) is reinforced by the reduction of ANS upheaval as it switches from the "fight or flight" sympathetic branch of the ANS to the parasympathetic branch, which acts to restore visceral homeostasis. The fast recovery of the ANS reinforces the individual's aggression-inhibiting behavior. And, as Mednick (1979:50) points out: "We know that fear reduction is the most powerful, naturally occurring reinforcement that psychologists have discovered."

An individual whose ANS is relatively unresponsive to fear is less likely to inhibit the aggressive action because the contemplated aggression does not evoke fear and anxiety. It is instructive to note that the experiencing of sanctions and the possible fear and anxiety they may provoke is a left hemisphere function (Buikhuisen, 1988:177), the area that is relatively non-responsive in serious delinquents. If such an individual does experience fear, slow recovery does not provide the aggression-inhibiting reinforcement that individuals with fast-reacting ANS's experience. In other words, people differ in their readiness to be conditioned—to internalize rules—and in the mechanisms governing this readiness to condition and to develop a conscience is the ANS (Eysenck, 1977).

This general line of thinking has been supported in a number of studies. For instance, Eaker, Allen, and Gray (1983) factor-analyzed various measures among a sample of delinquents and found that high anxiety loaded highly with lack of aggression and having good verbal skills. Valliant and his colleagues (1984) examined a group of dangerous and non-dangerous inmates in a Canadian psychiatric hospital. Although both groups did not differ in terms of overall psychopathology, the non-dangerous offenders were significantly more anxious and "sensitive" than the dangerous offenders. Among a non-offender sample of children, Kagan, Reznick, and Snidman (1987) found that behaviorally inhibited children had significantly higher levels of the stress hormone cortisol than behaviorally uninhibited children based on both home and laboratory measures. The Mednick (1979) article lists a number of other studies relating various physiological measures of ANS arousal and recovery among psychopaths and non-psychopaths.

A hyporeactive ANS may be related to elevated PIQ scores because most of the subtests measuring PIQ are tests of short-term memory, and short-term memory is more affected by anxiety than is long-term memory (Frank, 1983:74). It follows that boys who are relatively unaffected by anxiety should score well on such tests relative to their scores on VIQ.[6] The possible neurological process by which anxiety intrudes on short-term memory has been stated by Keiser (1976:306): "[A]n interference hypothesis might suggest that when affective processes are generally underreactive there will be less distortion of immediate memory traces within the same anatomical structures, for example, the hippocample circuits that are thought to play a role in short-term memory systems." Thus, the lack of anxiety and fear (ANS arousal) that characterizes psychopathic behavior may also account for a tendency to score highly on PIQ relative to VIQ scores.

The preceding discussion linking violence to ANS hyporeactivity may seem quite puzzling. Aggressive and violent behavior requires the powerful *arousal* of the sympathetic branch of the ANS. How, therefore, is it that individuals with ANS's slow to arouse are more violent than those with ANS's that are fast to arouse? It appears that violent individuals, especially violent psychopaths, are hyperarousable under certain conditions of personal threat or affront. Mawson and Mawson (1977) have developed a sophisticated neuropharmacological theory that attempts to reconcile the low arousal/high arousal theories of violence propensity among psychopaths. The theory involves fluctuations in the relative dominance of two neurotransmitters systems. The norepinephrine and dopamine-based system is responsible for sympathetic ANS arousal and behavioral activation, the acetylcholine and serotonin-based system being responsible for parasympathetic ANS activation and behavioral inhibition.

The Mawsons assert that attention should be focused on the character of the oscillations of the pharmacological and physiological systems rather than arguing whether low or high arousal most characterizes violent individuals. The Mawsons provide plentiful evidence that violent individuals are *both* hypo- and hyperarousable, depending on the situation. In other words, they possess very labile ANS's. They are hypoarousable to relatively mild stimuli (such as taking an IQ test or awaiting the inevitable), but hyperarousable when confronted with physical challenges and threats.

A number of animal studies support the Mawson and Mawson notion that serotonin modulates violence and generally inhibits behavioral responses to emotional stimuli (van Praag et al., 1987). Similar findings among humans are reported by Virkunen et al. (1989), who found that low serotonergic activity significantly differentiated recidivist from non-recidivist violent offenders and compulsive fire setters.

The Mawsons conclude their article by writing: "[N]either the present theory nor the low-arousal theory explains what is, perhaps, the major distinguishing characteristic of the psychopath: namely, his lack of affect and the inability to form close, personal relationships" (1977:65). The remainder of this chapter attempts to link this lack of love experiences among many delinquents to ANS functioning.

### Conditioning the Autonomic Nervous System

While the mechanisms underlying ANS functioning are primarily hereditary, the ANS is remarkably open to classical conditioning (DiCara, 1970). One such mechanism that may permanently alter the way the ANS functions is prolonged and protracted stress. We have seen how the sympathetic and parasympathetic divisions of the ANS work antagonistically—the sympathetic system revving up the individual's physiochemical processes, and the parasympathetic system restoring it to equilibrium. Hans Selye (1956, 1970) has examined these processes in detail, focusing on the consequences to the system of repeated exposure to stress. He has termed his general theoretical model the *general adaptation syndrome.* He posits that the ANS and endocrinal systems react to stress in three general stages. The first, or the *alarm reaction,* stage includes all the processes we associate with ANS upheaval leading to increased alertness and vigor. The second, or *resistance,* stage centers on attempts to "de-stress" the part of the body under primary stress, e.g., the heart, and also leads to a general decrement of arousal. If this latter process is unsuccessful in returning the body's internal system to equilibrium, the organism may succumb to the third, or *exhaustion,* stage. Experiencing this stage may result in death or a marked change in the organism's physiochemical system.

The process of physiochemical adjustment to constant stressful arousal has been frequently demonstrated in laboratories. For instance, Solomon (1980) has shown that repeated stressful stimuli, in the form of electric shocks administered to laboratory animals, has a steadily decreasing effect on autonomic responses as the ANS struggles to avoid Selye's exhaustion stage. Over a period of time, the administration of negative stimuli has little or no effect on an animal's ANS, indicating that it has accepted the stimuli as "normal" and nothing to be particularly fearful about. The violent individual's ANS may be similarly unreactive to fear and anxiety for the same reasons: frequent exposure to a cruel, brutal, and loveless environment.

Psychiatrist Wouter Buikhuisen (1982) suggests that this is indeed the case. After writing at some length about child abuse, he states:

> After some time he [the abused child] feels rejected and no longer loved by his parents. The continuous stress he is experiencing makes it necessary to look for defense mechanisms. To avoid being hurt, he develops a kind of flat emotionality, a so-called indifference with its physiological pendant: low reactivity of the autonomic nervous system. (1982:214.)

Empirical evidence linking ANS functioning to negative childhood experience and to delinquency is provided by Wadsworth (1976). He found that slow pulse rates (bpm) among 5,362 young boys, an indicator of an underreactive ANS, were predictive of later violent and sexual delinquent behavior. Boys with slow pulse rates were also shown to have been victims of childhood emotional stress at a significantly higher rate than boys with normal pulse rates. Other studies have confirmed these findings. Farrington (1987) found that convicted violent youths had significantly lower pulse rates than a control group of non-offenders ($p < .05$). Similarly, Venables (1987) found that "antisocial" youths had a lower pulse rate mean that "prosocial" youths ($p < .02$). Wadsworth (1976:246) makes the connection between ANS reactivity and childhood stress as follows: "Certainly from the published work it would be reasonable to speculate that children who in early life lived in surroundings of stress and emotional disturbances are more likely to develop some kind of mechanism for handling the effects of stress, and this may be reflected in later autonomic reactions to stressful stimuli."

There have been a number of animal experiments that help us to understand and link the line of thought presented by Wadsworth (1976) to the Mawson and Mawson (1977) theory of ANS lability. It has been shown that the stress-responsive adrenal cortices of rats unstressed during infancy weighed more than the cortices of rats subjected to stress during infancy. This suggested to Konner (1982:392) that the cortices of stressed rats had been "toughened," and would help to explain why stressed rats remained relatively calm when faced with fearful situations in adulthood. However, Levine and his colleagues (1967) have shown that rats subjected to stresses during infancy are not uniformly unresponsive to stress. Rats stressed during infancy were shown to secrete less of the stress hormone corticosterone when mildly stressed as adults, but when confronted with severe stress they secreted significantly *more* corticosterone. So, early stresses and emotional deprivation do appear to produce ANS's that are both hyporeactive to mild stressors and hyperreactive to severe stressors. We can readily see how such lability of ANS functioning can be productive of violence. Such a person would be more ready, because of his relative lack of fear, to put himself in a potentially violent situation. Once in such a situation, he would be more aggressively responsive when his hormonal resources were called upon.

Another possible mechanism accounting for the elevated PIQ scores of abused children relative to VIQ, one that perhaps augments it rather than contends with it, is DeLozier's (1982:98) "frozen watchfulness" hypothesis. DeLozier suggests that an abused child's efforts to avoid punishment favors development of the visual/spatial skills of the right hemisphere. If frequently abused children are to avoid as much punishment as possible, they must become sensitive to environmental cues that punishment is imminent. They may develop exceptional (relatively speaking) visual/spatial skills and the ability to associate these cues to verbal cues. The frequent interpretation of verbal and visual cues as threatening may explain the abused child's tendency to respond to verbal, as well as nonverbal, stimuli in aggressive and violent ways as the child grows older.

To reiterate: fear and anxiety serves to inhibit aggressive and violent behavior and also interferes with short-term memory, skills tested in many of the subtests of the WISC–R performance scale. Most boys will have ANS's that are in the normal range of reactivity and will not have any significant P/V discrepancy. Boys who generate fear and anxiety relatively easily will tend to inhibit aggression and violence and will tend to have a low PIQ score relative to their VIQ score. Boys who do not generate fear and anxiety so easily will tend to be both more violent and aggressive and to score significantly higher on the PIQ subscale than on the VIQ subscale. To the extent that emotional stress has a muting effect on ANS responsiveness to mildly threatening situations, boys who are intellectually imbalanced in the direction of P > V would be expected to be both more violent and more love deprived.

This pattern of expectations is revealed in Table 4.4. The Scheffe multiple comparison test shows P > V boys to be significantly more violent than the V > P boys, although the difference between the P > V and P = V boys does not attain statistical significance. The P > V boys are also shown to have been significantly more love deprived than either the V > P or V = P boys. The correlation ratios (etas) are fairly weak, but if we enter P/V discrepancy scores in ungrouped form, thereby making finer discriminations, we obtain higher correlations (r). The correlation between violence and P/V discrepancy is .21, and between P/V discrepancy and love deprivation it is .254. The latter correlation offers some support for Wadsworth's (1976) contention vis-à-vis the relationship between childhood emotional stress and ANS functioning.

TABLE 4.4

Violence and Love Deprivation Means Within
Each P/V Profile

| N | Category | Violence Mean | Love Deprivation Mean |
|---|---|---|---|
| 37 | V > P (a) | 46.65c | 19.73c |
| 294 | V = P (b) | 54.57 | 22.31c |
| 182 | P > V (c) | 77.41a | 27.35ab |
| | Grand mean | 62.10 | 23.14 |
| | F ratio | 6.97 | 10.26 |
| | sig. | 0.001 | 0.0001 |
| | eta | .16 | .20 |

*Conclusion*

The different but overlapping cognitive abilities measured by the verbal and performance IQ tests tell us a lot about differential propensities to commit violent crimes. There is very little doubt that intellectual imbalance is a predictor of both prosocial and antisocial behavior. V > P imbalanced juveniles are greatly underrepresented among juvenile delinquents, and P > V imbalanced juveniles are greatly overrepresented. Consistent with other studies, elevated PIQ rather than low VIQ appears to be most responsible for the P > V profile.

These findings perhaps explain why some researchers have reported little or no relationship between IQ and various measures of criminality and delinquency. If VIQ is negatively related to delinquency and PIQ is positively related to delinquency, the opposing effects are likely to cancel each other out when they are combined as FIQ. Low VIQ combined with relatively high PIQ, as well as the relative lack of anxiety such a profile suggests, also explains why delinquents are typically youths who do poorly at school, are noisy, restless, disruptive, easily bored, geared to action, and are relatively impervious to punishment threats.

It is acknowledged that intellectual imbalance may be to some extent heritable. This possibility has not been subjected to the tests employed by behavioral geneticists, to the best of my knowledge. It is believed that the suggestions of Wadsworth (1976) and the other theorists mentioned here relating to ANS conditioning offers the most plausible biosocial explanation presently available for the development of intellectual imbalance. The proposition maintains an internal consistency among its various components and it is certainly worthy of further research.

## ENDNOTES

1.  Positron emission tomography is similar to the more familiar CAT scan. Rather than revealing the anatomy of the brain, the PET scan reveals metabolic functioning by injecting subjects with radioactive isotopes of glucose. As the glucose is metabolized, the computer reveals a colorized biochemical map of the brain's metabolism as the brain converts the glucose into energy.

2.  Some criminologists (e.g., Gibbons, 1973) disparage the concept of psychopathy as a pejorative label that is of no diagnostic use. They decry the fact that the label is often affixed based on behavior, forgetting that behavior is a criterion-related validation of the label. The psychopathic label is only correctly applied on the basis of psychological and physiological assessment, any manifestations of psychopathic behavior serving only as a validation of the label. It has been shown that psychopaths can be distinguished from non-psychopaths on a number of physiological, psychological, and sociological variables (see Walsh, 1988:13–16).

3.  The difference between VIQ and PIQ among the P > V intellectually imbalanced in this prison sample was particularly striking, with the mean VIQ being 89.9 and the mean PIQ being 112.1. If these two means are combined to obtain a

FIQ mean of 101, we would conclude that IQ and criminal behavior are unrelated. Such a conclusion would be grossly misleading.

Just as striking was the finding that only 17 individuals (less than one percent of the sample) were V > P imbalanced. These findings suggest that as offenders become older their intellectual profiles further sort them into antisocial and prosocial categories.

4. Matarazzo and Herman used 13 rather than 12 as the cutting point because they found 13 discrepancy points to be significant at the .01 level, whereas I follow Kaufman's cutting point of 12 for significance at the .05 level.

5. In an analysis of the Weschler subtests, Vandenberg and Volger (1985:43) report heritability coefficients for the various VIQ and PIQ subtests. Averaged across all subtests, the heritability coefficient for the VIQ subtests is .632, and for the PIQ subtests it is .405.

6. The anxiety inherent in testing for PIQ may also partly explain the relatively good behavior of V > P boys. They have a significantly lower PIQ mean relative to the mean for the rest of the sample (92 versus 98.1, t = −2.19, p < .02). In other words, low PIQ scores, the unrepresentativeness of V > P boys in delinquent samples, and the relatively low violence mean of those who are represented, may be partially a function of an overreactive ANS. However, their superior VIQ mean (111.4 versus 88.9 for the rest, t = 10.49) characterizes them more than does their deficit in PIQ. The V > P boys were not significantly different from the rest of the sample on social class.

# Chapter Five

# THE IQ/DELINQUENCY RELATIONSHIP

## A Brief History of IQ in Delinquency Research

The study of IQ as it relates to crime and delinquency has had a checkered career in criminology. Until the 1930's, it was a widely accepted and "common sense" notion that delinquents and criminals had lower than average intelligence, as this concept is operationalized by IQ tests. For instance, writing in 1914, Harry Goddard stated with certitude that: "It can no longer be denied that the greatest single cause of delinquency and crime is low-grade mentality, much of it within the limits of feeble-mindedness" (quoted in Shulman, 1959:75). After the 1930's and despite literature reviews consistently reporting that offenders IQ's averaged 10 to 12 IQ points below the population mean, criminologists began to disparage IQ as an explanatory variable (Wilson and Herrnstein, 1985:154). Few criminological textbooks devote any space to the subject, and even the 1,179-page *Handbook of Criminology* (Glasser, 1974) has only two minor references to it (in terms of prison classification and malnutrition).

Not only was it often asserted after the 1930's that IQ bore no significant relationship to crime, some even held it "taboo" to attempt to link IQ with crime (see Gordon, 1980, for an essay on the alleged attempts of criminologists to turn the IQ/crime relationship into a taboo topic). For instance, Sagarin (1980:16), citing the usual bête noire's of IQ research such as Jensen and Shockly, admonishes researchers in the area of IQ and crime: "Go slowly, this is ground fraught with potential danger."

Notwithstanding Sagarin's warning, the issue of the link between IQ and crime and delinquency is enjoying something of a renaissance in criminology today, with many of its foremost scholars reasserting the cogency of the link. Herrnstein (1980:48) has stated that despite the bad press the IQ/crime link received during the 1930's through the 1970's, it nevertheless operated as a "silent partner in standard sociological and economic explanations of many aspects of society." And as Wilson and Herrnstein (1985:159) exclaim in their definitive *Crime and Human Nature:*

"[C]riminology acted rashly when, in the 1930's, it virtually ceased considering IQ a significant correlate of criminal behavior, for it was just at that moment in the evolution of mental testing that the tests were beginning to yield solid data on the cognitive predispositions toward offending."

Regardless of improvements of mental testing procedures, we are still confronted with Sagarin's warning. The danger to which he refers revolves around the relationship of IQ to race and SES. There is no real argument with the frequent finding that blacks and individuals of lower socioeconomic class tend to score significantly lower on IQ tests than middle-class whites (Hirshi and Hindelang, 1977:573). Since blacks and lower-class individuals tend to be more involved with crime and delinquency than their middle-class counterparts (Wolfgang, Figlio, and Sellin, 1977) and since these same groups tend to have lower IQ's, the danger is that their higher crime rates may be explained in terms of lower class and/or black "feeblemindedness." Furthermore, because intelligence (or whatever else we choose to call the cluster of cognitive skills measured by IQ tests) is to some extent a heritable trait, the implication is that very little can be done about black and lower SES crime. Linking crime and delinquency to IQ also locates one of the causes of these phenomena within the personal makeup of those who engage in it. This is, of course, anathema in a discipline which has a real tendency to claim that the responsibility for crime lies with everything and everybody—except the criminal.

### Differences in Delinquent and General Population IQ

It is well known that delinquents score significantly lower than non-delinquents on IQ tests (Wilson and Herrnstein, 1985:155). This is the case for the present sample of delinquents. How can one test the IQ/delinquency connection when delinquency is a constant in the data? First, since IQ is a normally distributed variable with a known mean and standard deviation, we can compare the mean of the present sample with the known population mean. Second, we can explore the effects of different IQ levels on delinquency within the sample.

The population IQ has been standardized to a mean of 100 with a standard deviation of 15. The mean full-scale IQ for the delinquent sample is 93.7, s = 14.6. The significance of difference between the population and sample means is $z = -9.51$. The delinquent sample IQ mean is therefore significantly lower than the mean IQ of the general population. This difference must be considered a conservative estimate.

The actual gap is probably somewhat larger since the samples used to generate population IQ norms most likely included an unknown proportion of offenders. Note that as high as this z statistic is, it is substantially lower than the z of 16.19 assessing the significance of difference between the delinquent sample and the general population in terms of P > V.

It would be instructive to compare the proportion of delinquent boys in each of the seven IQ categories utilized by psychologists to determine which categories' frequencies depart most strikingly from the expected frequency. A goodness-of-fit chi-square was performed and the results reported in Table 5.1.

TABLE 5.1

Chi-Square Goodness-of-Fit Test
Full-Scale IQ of Delinquents and General Population

| IQ Category | | Observed | Expected | Residual |
|---|---|---|---|---|
| Defective | low - 65 | 18 | 11.02 | 6.98 |
| Borderline | 66 - 79 | 56 | 34.07 | 21.93 |
| Dull Normal | 80 - 90 | 119 | 83.16 | 35.84 |
| Normal | 91 - 110 | 265 | 256.50 | 8.50 |
| Bright | 111 - 119 | 47 | 83.16 | -36.16 |
| Superior | 120 - 127 | 6 | 34.07 | -28.07 |
| Very Superior | 128 - high | 2 | 11.02 | -9.02 |
| | Total | 513 | | |

$$X^2 = 80.5, \ df = 6, \ p < .0001$$

Table 5.1 shows that the delinquent FIQ distribution does not fit the expected frequency based on population norms. The boys in the dull-normal category are the most overrepresented and the boys in the bright category are the most underrepresented. These figures accord well with those reported by the Cambridge-Somerville Youth Study (McCord and McCord, 1959). Of the 239 delinquent boys in that study, 24.7 percent were in the dull-normal category (23.2 percent in the present study), and 9.6 percent had IQ's of 111 and above (10.7 percent in the present study). Although he does not make such fine discriminations between IQ levels as presented here, West (1982:38) reports that 39.2 percent of his 84 London delinquents had IQ's below 90. This figure roughly corresponds with the 34.1 percent in the present study and with the 33.9 percent in the Cambridge-Somerville study. It appears that the percentage of delinquents with IQ's below normal is remarkably consistent across time and location. IQ level is thus related to delinquency: dull-normal boys being most delinquency prone, and boys in the bright and above categories being the least delinquency prone.[1]

## IQ and Opportunity

The fact that a highly disproportionate number of delinquents fall into the lower IQ categories is particularly important with regard to delinquency because not all IQ gaps mean the same thing. IQ is more an ordinal than an interval-level variable with respect to substantive outcomes. In order to predict "success" in our American culture via school performance, occupational niche, income level, and so forth, the substantive difference between, say, 80 and 100 IQ points is much greater than the substantive difference between 120 and 140 points. The National Association for Mental Retardation has set the borderline for mental retardation at an IQ of 85, up from its previous borderline of 70 (Jensen, 1974:66). This IQ "inflation" is not arbitrary but, rather, a reflection of the fact that most occupations today require at least this level of intellectual functioning for effective performance. The difference between 80 and 100 IQ points is perhaps the difference between being permanently assigned to America's underclass and having the ability to make a go of it, while the gap between 120 and 140 points is a one of diminishing returns. An individual with an IQ of 120 can probably achieve anything that one with an IQ of 140 can, perhaps with just a little extra effort.

Any bivariate distribution of IQ and success as it is defined in American culture would be best described by a sigmoid logistic curve rather than the straight line of ordinary least squares regression. If we examine the hypothetical distribution of IQ and success in American society presented in Figure 5.1, we see that at the low end of the IQ distribution almost all individuals fail to achieve their fair slice of success. On the other hand, almost everyone with an IQ of 120 or above achieve high levels of success. Of course, a high IQ does not *guarantee* success, for IQ is more a prediction of what one probably cannot do than what one will do. According to the hypothetical curve, the threshold levels at which successful outcomes could go in either direction, depending on personal and structural factors having essentially little to do with IQ, is in the 90 to 110 range, the "average" range.

Figure 5.1    Hypothetical Bivariate Distribution of IQ and Success
Fitted to a Logistic Curve

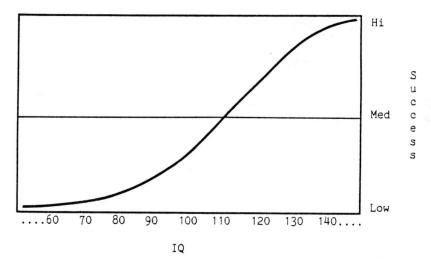

This observation leads to an alternative interpretation of Robert Merton's long-lived anomie theory of criminality. The thrust of Merton's theory is "in discovering how some social structures exert a definite pressure upon certain persons in society to engage in nonconformist rather than conformist conduct" (1938:672). Merton saw American social structure and American social values as exhorting all citizens to strive for certain success goals, while at the same time denying access to legitimate ways of obtaining these goals to significant segments of the population. Crime or delinquency is simply the result of individuals obtaining illegitimately what they have been taught to want. For these people "the 'end justifies the means' doctrine becomes a guiding tenet for action when cultural structure unduly exalts the end and the social organization unduly limits possible recourse to approved means" (1938:681).

As well as the grand tautology inherent in Merton's theory (he poses a cause of crime—lack of legitimate opportunity—and then uses the alleged effects of that cause—crime—as a measure of the opportunities one has not had), he is guilty of reifying social structure. Social structure does not act as a gatekeeper denying access to opportunity, although entrenched discriminatory practices undoubtedly were more prevalent at the time Merton formulated his theory. In today's world, opportunities are offered by individual institutions that have a vested interest in obtaining the best people available to serve their purposes. The gatekeeper denying access to these opportunities is the lack of preparation exhibited by those seeking them. The lack of preparedness, in turn, can be seen as a function of IQ deficiency. Bouchard, Jr., and Segal (1985:408) state that the research evidence from England and the United States leads to the conclusion that "in open societies with high degrees of occupational mobility, individuals with high IQs migrate, relative to their parents, to occupations of higher SES, and individuals with lower IQs migrate to occupations of lower SES." To the extent that this is true, it appears that Merton's conformists, ritualists, retreatists, rebels, and innovators adopt their modes of adaptation more in response to their intellectual capacities than in response to a monolithic "social structure" selectively denying or granting access to opportunities.[2]

### The Spuriousness Argument

While criminologists do not dispute that a significant zero-order correlation exists between IQ and delinquency, many recoil from imputing any causal influence to IQ. One of the most recent and most cited studies of this kind is that of Menard and Morse (1984). These researchers argue that, "The correlation of IQ with delinquency is not because IQ exerts any causal influence on delinquent behavior but because, in certain institutional settings (the schools), it may be selected by the institution as a criterion for differential treatment" (1984:1347). Menard and Morse reject Hirschi and Hindelang's (1977) assertion that the causal influence of IQ operates through its relationship with school performance. Such an assertion, they feel, rescues the influence of IQ on delinquency by specifying a process (school performance) by which it works.

Menard and Morse prefer to think of IQ as having only a spurious relationship to delinquency, and they enumerate variables which they feel demonstrate it to be so. Their specified model includes IQ, the Differential Aptitude Test (DAT), GPA, "perceived negative academic labeling," home and school alienation, and association with delinquent peers. However, to show that a variable is spurious, one has to demonstrate that a control variable precedes the independent variable in time and that the control variable "explains away" the initially observed relationship. In other words, the "independent variable" has only a coincidental relationship with the dependent variable.

None of Menard and Morse's posited control variables precede IQ in time if we consider IQ to be a measure of intellectual ability that children bring with them to the school experience. And surely, none of their control variables are only coincidentally related to IQ. GPA and DAT scores depend greatly on IQ, and any negative labeling ("perceived") has a lot to do with these scores. Just as surely, these test performances relate to school alienation, which relates to having delinquent peers. In a review of the literature on friendship, Berndt (1982) concludes that the most consistent of findings is that like seeks like. Thus, friendship patterns as well as delinquency are "caused" by Menard and Morse's school-related variables, which are themselves strongly linked to IQ. Menard and Morse cannot get around this by simply dropping IQ from their final model as they do in their Figure 5 (1984:1367).

### Association with Delinquent Peers and IQ

Among the strongest correlations reported in the delinquency literature between delinquency and some assumed causal agent is the positive correlation found between delinquency and association with delinquent peers. Delinquent peers are assigned a causal role in an individual's own delinquency, most notably in Edwin Sutherland's differential association theory (Sutherland and Cressey, 1970). In the formulation of this theory, the priority, frequency, duration, and intensity of association with delinquent peers leads to "an excess of definitions favorable to violations of law over definitions unfavorable to violations of law" (Sutherland and Cressey, 1970:75). Despite the popularity and longevity of this theory, it has not gone uncriticized. For instance, Nettler, (1978:265), in addition to describing differential association as "true but trivial," states that it "reduces to the common sense idea [not to mention, tautological idea] that people are apt to behave criminally when they do not respect the law."

In Travis Hirschi's control theory there is no causal influence exerted by delinquent peers, although he agrees that it is a concomitant of delinquency (1977:336). "Birds of a feather flock together," and they flock together to pursue common interests and goals. Association with delinquent peers acts more as a "releaser" of delinquent behavior for those already disposed to it than as a stimulator goading otherwise prosocial juveniles into delinquency. It should not surprise us, then, that tests of differential association theory produce some of the largest zero-order correlations between delinquency and an alleged cause seen in the criminological literature. They should, for the correlation is "built-in" and arises full-blown. Similarly large correlations could be found between priority, frequency, duration, and intensity of association with, say, judo peers. But few would argue that such association was not preceded by a predisposition among members of the judo group toward "definitions favorable to engaging in judo over definitions unfavorable to engaging in judo."

This is, of course, consistent with Berndt's (1982) review of various studies of friendship patterns cited earlier. But what is it that moves people to associate with delinquent peers? Trajanowicz and Morash (1983:90) feel that association with delinquent peers is a function of parental rejection: "Rejected or neglected children who do not find love and affection, as well as support and supervision, at home, often resort to groups outside the family; frequently these groups are of a deviant nature." Hirschi (1977) voices the same opinion in stating that ties to delinquent peers are more reflective of weak attachment to prosocial groups rather than strong attachment to antisocial groups.

IQ should also influence one's choice of companions. Because the basis of differential association theory lies in learning criminal codes and modes of conduct, it would seem that the differential ability to learn any code of conduct should be a vital part of the theory. If we follow Hirschi's thinking, however, it is the learning of prosocial, not antisocial, behavior that is problematic. It has often been said that as far as anti-social behavior is concerned, there is nothing to learn. "What is there to be learned about simple lying, taking things that belong to another, fighting and sex play," asks Glueck (1956:94). He goes on to say: "Do children have to be taught such natural acts? . . . . It is rather non-delinquent behavior that is learned. Unsocialized, untamed and uninstructed, the child resorts to lying, slyness, subterfuge, anger, hatred, theft, aggression, attack and other forms of asocial behaviour in its early attempts of self-expression and ego formation."

I am in total agreement with Glueck's expression and have difficulty envisioning how it could be otherwise. Simple observation, as well as a voluminous child development literature, tells us that we have to learn painful lessons as we gain insight into what constitutes moral behavior and as we come to consider the rights of others. We do not have to learn to be selfish—self-interest runs deep and is original. We learn to value the feelings of others by being decently treated ourselves and by having the intellectual capacity to view the remote, as well as the immediate, consequences of our behavior.

An interesting and sophisticated study conducted by Rowe and Osgood (1984) involving the concepts of differential association and IQ showed that while they found a fairly strong correlation (.51) between self-reported delinquency and association with delinquent peers, most of the correlation was attributable to individual differences. Rowe and Osgood take issue with the simplistic assumption that association with delinquent peers is somehow independent of the propensity for delinquent activity among individuals in the peer group. Rather, they support Hirschi's contention that members of a delinquent peer group would be delinquent regardless of their association with one another. Otherwise stated, the causal order is propensity for delinquency leads to association with delinquent peers, not the other way around. They do not deny, of course, that individual propensities can be intensified in interaction with other like-minded individuals. Johnson (1979:118) has pointed out that the role of delinquent peers is passive (non-causal), but not entirely so. But this observation is not very useful, since any activity is likely to intensify in the company of fellow afficionados. What we would like to know is why some boys congregate with delinquents and others do not.

To attempt to answer this question, Rowe and Osgood studied 168 monozygotic and 97 dizygotic twin pairs. They used the same strategy that behavioral geneticists use to sort out genetic and environmental sources of variance in IQ levels; that is, by comparing interclass correlations between monozygotic and dyzygotic twins. Their objective was to decompose the .51 correlation into (1) a genetic component, (2) a common environmental component, and (3) an individual environmental component. Monozygotic twins have identical genes and share a common family environment. However, it is entirely possible that one twin can have an important experience not shared by the other twin, such as a commitment to a juvenile institution. Unlike many other twin studies, Rowe and Osgood make allowances for this possibility in their calculations.

The results of this apportioning of the phenotypical correlation between delinquency and association with delinquent peers showed that the genetic component (61%) was more than two-and-one-half times more important than the common environment component (23%) and 3.8 times more important than the specific environment component (16%).

For our present purposes, the importance of this study is that Rowe and Osgood emphasize intellectual functioning (school achievement and IQ) as the variables explaining the genetic component of the relationship between association with delinquent peers and delinquency. They state: "When twin partners have different IQs, they can be expected to have dissimilar rates of delinquency and dissimilar degrees of association with delinquent peers" (1984:537). They also indicate that other traits known to have large heritable components, such as impulsivity and temperament, may also aid in the explanation of the observed correlation.

### IQ and Socioeconomic Status

Socioeconomic status is often found to be significantly related to violent delinquency and to IQ. As we have seen, the primary explanation for the relationship between IQ and violence is that violent individuals have poor verbal skills mediating between stimulus and response (Camp, 1977; Heilbrun and Heilbrun, 1985). Table 5.2 examines violence means within 4 categories of VIQ. Also presented are class means and percentages of blacks and whites in those VIQ categories. We see that violence means decrease as we go up the VIQ categories, and that VIQ increases and violence decreases as we go up the SES scale. We also see that blacks are highly overrepresented in the lower VIQ categories.

Using identical cutting points for PIQ, no significant relationship was found between the groupings and violence. But if we compare the boys with PIQ scores of 111 ("bright average") and higher (N = 120) with all others, we find that the high PIQ boys had a significantly higher violence mean (75.3) than the low PIQ boys (58.1), t = −2.34, p = .019. We can conclude, then, that cognitive skills associated with verbal and performance IQ work in opposite directions in terms of violent delinquency: boys with VIQ's of 111 and above were the least violent; boys with PIQ's of 111 or over were the most violent.

Because social class is positively related to IQ and negatively related to violent delinquency, it is a variable frequently alleged to render the IQ/ delinquency relationship spurious. The unspoken assumption of those who make the allegations is that SES influences on IQ are entirely environmental in origin. The ability of class to render the IQ/delinquency relationship spurious depends on differences in IQ between classes being directly a function of differences in SES. The opposite assumption—that class is at least partially a function of IQ—is rarely considered by those who believe controlling for class will falsify the IQ/delinquency relationship.

TABLE 5.2

Violence and SES Means and Percentages of Blacks and Whites
For Various Verbal IQ Categories

| Verbal IQ Category | N | Violence Means | SES Means | Percent Black | Percent White |
|---|---|---|---|---|---|
| A) low - 79 | 115 | 72.56cd | 19.75cd | 41.0 | 18.8 |
| B) 80 - 90 | 169 | 72.85cd | 23.76cd | 33.3 | 32.8 |
| C) 91 - 110 | 179 | 51.10ab | 28.84ab | 25.3 | 36.7 |
| D) 111 - high | 50 | 41.14ab | 30.77ab | 00.0 | 11.7 |
| Totals | 513 | 62.10 | 26.37 | 100.0 | 100.0 |
| F ratio | | 5.17 | 17.35 | $X^2$ = 27.5 | |
| probability | | .002 | .0000 | | .0000 |
| eta | | .17 | .32 | V = | .23 |

abcd = pairs of means that differ from one another at the .05 level
using the Scheffe multiple comparison test.

To the extent that the latter assumption is true and to the extent that
IQ is heritable, statistical controls for class partial out both genetic and
environmental variance (Bouchard, Jr., and Segal, 1985:408). Controlling for class under these conditions would mean that IQ is partially
serving as a control for itself. My assumption is that IQ and SES are
interactive in the sense that each influences the other. Rutter and Madge
(1976:110) stress the interactive nature of the association between IQ and
SES when they assert that it is "in part... a reflection of genetically
determined differences in intelligence influencing social class distribution... but also there is evidence that the association reflects social
influences on intellectual development."

Nevertheless, it has been argued that since performance on IQ tests
varies directly with SES, "the results of these tests are one important
index of the ability of the child to meet middle-class expectations, to do
the kinds of things that bring rewards in the middle-class world" (Cohen,
1955:102–103). In other words, IQ functions as a measure of social class.
Although Cohen is to some extent saying the same thing as Bouchard

and Segal (SES = IQ), he is assuming that IQ is a function of SES and not that SES is a function of IQ. The logic of Cohen's argument is that since lower-class children are less prepared than their middle-class counterparts for the school experience, they perform poorly in school, become alienated from it, drop out, and turn to delinquency.

In specifying a mechanism (school performance) intervening between IQ and delinquency, Cohen has asserted the importance of IQ rather than negated it, as intended. Hirschi and Hindelang point out that given Cohen's belief of the interchangeability of IQ and SES, "IQ should be more strongly related to delinquency than such indirect measures of the ability of the child to meet middle-class expectations as 'father's occupation'" (1977:578). Since in Cohen's view IQ is nothing more than a measure of the *child's* social class, IQ should be more closely linked to delinquency than *parental* social class, an indirect measure of the child's social class. Therefore, IQ should influence delinquency equally across categories of indirect measures of the child's social class (parental SES).

The interchangeability of IQ and SES in Cohen's theory means that researchers who rely on the theory will place subjects into categories based on parental SES when, to maintain consistency with the theory, they should be placed in categories dictated by their own IQ's. Cohen's insistence that IQ operates differently for middle-class boys than it does for lower-class boys, and therefore middle-class delinquency needs different explanations, is rendered untenable by his own theory with respect to the interchangeability of IQ and SES. As Hirschi and Hindelang (1977:578) put it: "Cohen's reliance on a separate mechanism for middle-class boys (Cohen, 1955:162-9) is inexplicable or is, at the very least, theoretically and empirically inelegant."

Hirschi and Hindelang also take issue with Cloward and Ohlin's (1960) suggestion (offered without empirical evidence) that a positive relationship should exist between IQ and delinquency among lower-class boys. According to Cloward and Ohlin, lower-class boys with high IQ's possess the intellectual capacities to obtain illegitimately that which society has denied them legitimately due to the SES of their parents. (Cloward and Ohlin's statement appears to tangentially support my assertion that Merton's modes of adaptation are related to IQ levels.) Note that they do not view IQ as "just another measure of social class" in the manner of Cohen, but rather IQ and SES are two separate but overlapping attributes.

We may perform a test of both Cohen's and Cloward and Ohlin's theoretical speculations with our data, at least in terms of violent delinquency. I first split the sample at the median on SES to obtain two approximately equal subsamples. These two subsamples will be addressed before we discuss the results obtained from a further subsample composed of the top 10 percent of the boys based on SES.

As seen in Table 5.3, the SES means of the two subsamples were quite discrepant, with the boys in the upper 50 percent having a mean more than twice the size of the boys in the lower 50 percent. The essential similarity of the coefficients of variation (C.V.) indicates roughly equal SES variation within each subsample.[3] In terms of Cohen's assertions, the most interesting features are that IQ explains variation in violent delinquency more strongly than does SES in both subsamples, and that IQ explains violence among the upper 50 percent more strongly than it does among the lower 50 percent. Full-scale IQ has no relationship with violence among the lower 50 percent, but a significant *positive* relationship with violence among the upper 50 percent. However, this latter finding does not support Cloward and Ohlin's speculation. They specified that it would be the high IQ *lower*-class boys who would, in response to frustration, be more delinquent.

Among the lower SES 50 percent, the strongest correlation with violence is the negative association with VIQ. This supports the contention that verbal ability functions as a prophylactic against violence regardless of SES. The next strongest association is that between P > V and violence, which is stronger than that between SES and violence. The positive correlation between FIQ and violence among the upper SES 50 percent is almost entirely a function of the positive correlation between violence and PIQ, there being essentially no relationship between VIQ and violence among this group. It should also be noted that within-group parental SES variation has no association with violence among the boys in the upper 50 percent of the distribution.

The comparison of these two subsamples provides us with three findings of interest: (1) IQ is more important than SES in explaining variance in violent delinquency, (2) VIQ and PIQ operate in opposite directions in terms of their influence on violence, and (3) P > V is a very good predictor of violence, its influence increasing with increased SES. This latter observation suggests Cohen was right (although not in the way he supposed) in his suggestion that IQ operates differently in different SES environments.

TABLE 5.3

Correlations Between Violence, IQ Measures, and SES
Means and Coefficients of Variation of the Variables

|  | FIQ | VIQ | PIQ | P>V | SES | Violence |
|---|---|---|---|---|---|---|
| | | Lower 50% of SES Distribution | | | | |
| r | -.046 | -.172b | .018 | .156b | -.146c | 1.000 |
| $\overline{X}$ | 89.9 | 86.6 | 94.7 | 8.1 | 17.8 | 71.9 |
| C.V. | 14.2 | 13.0 | 17.2 | 175.3 | 27.5 | 100.3 |
| | | Upper 50% of SES Distribution | | | | |
| r | .143b | .017 | .278a | .333a | -.034 | 1.000 |
| $\overline{X}$ | 95.7 | 93.5 | 99.0 | 5.7 | 35.6 | 57.3 |
| C.V. | 15.6 | 15.9 | 15.8 | 212.3 | 26.1 | 125.5 |
| | | Top 10% of SES Distribution | | | | |
| r | -.018 | -.363b | .410a | .691a | -.260c | 1.000 |
| $\overline{X}$ | 96.6 | 92.4 | 102.4 | 10.1 | 48.7 | 57.0 |
| C.V. | 8.7 | 9.8 | 10.4 | 119.9 | 5.1 | 97.4 |

a  $p < .001$,  b  $p < .01$,  c  $p < .05$

The most interesting findings are those found among the boys in the approximate top 10 percent of the SES distribution (N = 55). The correlations between VIQ and PIQ and violence are of almost equal magnitude, but in opposite directions. The opposing influences of VIQ and PIQ have the effect of rendering the relationship between FIQ and violence non-existent. If we did not examine VIQ and PIQ separately, we might make the mistake of concluding IQ is not related to violent delinquency, when it is related in very interesting ways. The strength of the relationship between P > V and violence is particularly striking.

The pattern of correlations across the three subsamples supports a central assumption of behavioral geneticists with regard to genetic/environmental interaction. That is, the more advantageous and the more homogeneous the environment, the more genes are able to express themselves. We see that as we move up the SES groupings the stronger the correlations between IQ and violence become. The boys in the top 10 percent of the sample are more environmentally homogeneous in terms of SES and, by definition, enjoy a more advantageous environment. The homogeneity of upper 10 percent boys is seen by the class C.V., which is more than five times smaller than the C.V.'s in the other subsamples. The advantageousness of their environments is seen in the SES mean, which is 2.7 times larger than the mean of the lower 50 percent and 1.4 times larger than the mean of the upper 50 percent.

Taken as a whole, these findings support Hirschi and Hindelang's assertion that IQ is more important than social class in explaining delinquency, and that IQ can explain delinquency across classes (albeit in different ways). It also adds further support to the proposition that IQ is best explored via its two components (VIQ and PIQ) and in terms of P/V discrepancy scores.

## IQ and Race

We saw in Table 5.1 that black delinquents were highly overrepresented in the lower categories of VIQ. This, by no means unique, finding is a source of much vituperation and ad hominem arguments in the literature of the human sciences. To even report such findings opens one up to charges of racism, an intimidating label that is all too cavalierly tossed around these days. As Gordon (1980) points out, it is a rather meaningless epithet that adds nothing to the content of the discourse, because it usually concludes any such discourse. He goes on to assert that a racist is one who holds positive or negative attitudes "in excess of what facts warrant," and that such attitudes are "plainly unscientific and gratuitously invidious" (1980:53). I certainly agree. It is just as plainly unscientific not to honestly report findings, whatever they may be, and to try to get to the bottom of them. "Science," said Percy Bridgman, "is using your wits, no holds barred" (quoted in Levin, 1980:23). To impugn the reporting of findings one does not like by ad hominem arguments is to impugn the integrity of science itself.

In the present sample, the mean FIQ for blacks is 83.3, and for whites it is 95.5. This 12.2 IQ point difference is fairly consistent with differences found in the general population (Banton and Harwood, 1975:100) and is highly statistically significant ($t = 8.1$, $p < .0001$). As I have previously acknowledged, blacks bear terrible crosses that few whites have to hoist, and these crosses have highly detrimental effects on IQ scores. Nevertheless, IQ tests are measuring something more than the effects of this social disability. The range of black IQ scores is $64 - 107 = 43$. The fact that the range within the black subsample is more than 3.5 times as large as the between-group difference of 12.2 indicates that within-group differences are much greater than between-group differences, and, consequently, that the tests are measuring something other than SES and subcultural disabilities. Needless to say, the between-group/within-group disparity would be much greater in a large sample of the general black and white populations.

What happens to the IQ/delinquency relationship when race and class are controlled for? Hirschi and Hindelang (1977:573) state that "since both class and race are frequently used to discount the effects of IQ, this comparison will provide evidence relative to the common argument that IQ effects are merely a by-product of race and class effects." In their review they cite a number of studies that have shown that IQ exerts an independent effect on delinquency rates after class and race have been partialed out. Studies subsequent to the Hirschi and Hindelang review have confirmed this. For instance, Moffitt, Gabrielli, Mednick, and Schulsinger (1981) present findings from two longitudinal birth cohort studies in Denmark. In both samples it was found that IQ was negatively and significantly related to delinquency both before and after social class was partialed out. This study, however, contained few violent offenses and did not simultaneously control for race (Denmark being highly racially homogeneous). We may do this with our data.

From Table 5.4 it is seen that race, PIQ, and P > V are positively related to violence, and that SES and VIQ are negatively related to violence. Full-scale IQ is not significantly related to violence, as one would have predicted from the opposite and significant relationships of VIQ and PIQ to violence. This finding does not dispute vast amounts of research indicating that there is a relationship between FIQ and delinquency. We have seen that the delinquents in this sample are significantly below population norms on IQ. It only means that within a sample composed of boys who are *already* delinquent, there is no significant relationship between FIQ and the frequency and seriousness of their violent activities. The correlations between SES, race, and the various measures of IQ are all significantly related in directions predicted from prior research.

TABLE 5.4

Correlations (r) and Standardized Betas Between Violence, Various IQ Measures, SES, and Race

|  | Correlations with Violence | IQ Correlations with SES | IQ Correlations with Race | Standardized Betas IQ & Violence Controlling for | | |
|  |  |  |  | SES | Race | Race & SES |
|---|---|---|---|---|---|---|
| Class | -.123b |  |  |  |  |  |
| Race | .117b |  |  |  |  |  |
| FIQ | .029 | .306a | -.315a | .072 | .048 | .087 |
| VIQ | -.091c | .352a | -.233a | -.059 | -.069 | -.036 |
| PIQ | .125b | .224a | -.335a | .124b | .149b | .179a |
| P>V | .241a | -.082c | -.163a. | .197a | .231a | .222a |

a  p < .001,  b  p < .01,  c  p < .05     Race: white = 0  black = 1

Instituting controls for either SES or race alone or in conjunction via multiple regression does not change the non-significant effect of FIQ on violence. Controlling for SES diminishes the negative zero-order relationship between VIQ and violence. Simultaneous control of race and SES increases the effects of PIQ on violence, while the same controls slightly diminish the effects of P > V on violence slightly.

VIQ correlates most strongly with SES, and PIQ with race. Because PIQ was designed to compensate the test scores of children from verbally deficient homes, the latter finding may be viewed as somewhat of an anomaly in that white PIQ ($\overline{X}$ = 100.0) exceeds black PIQ ($\overline{X}$ = 85.3) even more than white VIQ ($\overline{X}$ = 92.0) exceeds black VIQ ($\overline{X}$ = 83.2). However, this is a typical finding in black/white comparisons (Steelman and Doby, 1983:103). We also see that whites are most likely to evidence the P > V profile. The .306 correlation between FIQ and SES is lower than the "typical" IQ/SES correlation reported by Rowe and Osgood (1984:537). This lower correlation is doubtless a function of the restricted range of the present sample (see endnote 1).

Since there is a large difference between black and white boys with regard to all IQ measures, it might prove instructive to examine the effects of IQ within separate racial categories. Table 5.5 shows that only PIQ and P > V are significantly related to violence among whites. The IQ effects among blacks are much stronger, particularly the .37 correlation with P > V. Once again, P > V emerges as the component of cognitive functioning that most impacts on violent delinquency for both whites and blacks.

TABLE 5.5

Zero-Order Correlations Between Violence and Various IQ Measures and Standardized Betas Controlling for SES (in Parentheses) For White and Black Samples

|  | Whites | | | |
|---|---|---|---|---|
|  | FIQ | VIQ | PIQ | P>V |
| Violence | .02 (.06) | -.08c (-.04) | .12b (.14b) | .21a (.20a) |
|  | Blacks | | | |
|  | FIQ | VIQ | PIQ | P>V |
| Violence | .20c (.23c) | -.01 (-.01) | .31b (.37b) | .37a (.38a) |

a  p < .001,   b  p < .01,   c  p < .05    Race: white = 0   black = 1

## The Differential Detection Hypothesis

One of the most widely subscribed to arguments against ascribing validity to IQ as a causal agent in delinquency is the differential detection and differential response hypotheses. These arguments go back as least as far as 1926, when they appeared in Carl Murchison's *Criminal Intelligence*. The argument is that brighter delinquents are more difficult to catch, and, if caught, social control agents treat them more leniently (Haskell and Yablonsky, 1974). Not all researchers subscribe to these hypotheses. After reviewing available literature, Hirschi and Hindelang (1977:583) conclude that "the differential ability to avoid detection and the differential official reaction on the basis of IQ arguments are not supported by available evidence."

Vold and Bernard (1986:79) take issue with Hirschi and Hindelang's assertion that there is no empirical support for the differential detection/differential response hypotheses by citing a study by British criminologists Tennent and Garth (1975): "A recent study of 50 delinquents with superior intelligence found that they received more lenient treatment from the courts." (This study dealt with differential response rather than differential detection, but Vold and Bernard chose to cite it as evidence favoring the differential detection hypothesis.) The cited study actually compared bright boys (IQ of 115 and above) with boys in the average range of intelligence (90–105), leaving out boys of below average intelligence (and apparently boys with IQ's between 106 and 114 for some unknown reason). However, despite having similar criminal histories, a fact militating somewhat against the differential detection hypothesis, the bright boys were treated more leniently. It was found that the bright boys realized a mean value per offender of 69 pounds sterling from their delinquent acts as opposed to 1,151 pounds for the boys of average IQ. It would seem that the respective values of the rewards received from offenses go a long way in explaining differences in official reactions, although Tennent and Garth did not test the hypothesis.

One way to test the differential detection hypothesis is to correlate IQ with self-reported delinquency, which would include boys who had and had not committed delinquent acts and who had and had not been detected by the authorities. Hindelang, Hirschi, and Weis (1981:203) indicate that "most studies do find a relation between IQ and self-reported delinquency, although this relation is less robust than that found in official data." There are two possible explanations for the attenuation of the correlation between IQ and delinquency in self-reported as opposed to official data. The first is that brighter delinquents are indeed more successful in avoiding apprehension. The second explanation is the deficiencies that are inherent in self-reported data.

The samples upon which most self-reported studies depend are typically composed of high school students. Since serious delinquents are more likely to drop out of high school than are non-delinquents, these most serious delinquents are excluded from such studies (Hindelang, Hirschi, and Weis, 1981:203; Wilson and Herrnstein, 1985:37), thus excluding a large amount of variation in both delinquency and IQ. Those students who do complete self-reported questionnaires are then asked if they have committed a series of peccadilloes—fighting, talking back, smoking, stealing small items, and so on—rather than "real" delinquency (Nettler, 1978:105). Since almost all boys have done some of these things at one time or another, it is not surprising that IQ, or anything else, correlates only weakly with such behavior. When attempts are made to include serious delinquency items rather than misbehavior in self-report studies, they frequently have to be dropped from the analysis because of extremely low incidence (Wilkinson, Stitt, and Erickson, 1982).

To test the differential detection hypothesis, Moffitt and Silva (1988) developed a rather elegant research design. They compared IQ means of three different groups of New Zealand juveniles from a cohort born between April 1, 1972 and March 31, 1973. The juveniles were divided into (1) self-reported delinquents who had been officially defined as such, (2) self-reported delinquents who were not known to the police, and (3) a non-delinquent group. Delinquency was self-reported and checked against official police records in order to code children into one of the three groups. The mean IQ scores for the two delinquent groups did not significantly differ from one another, meaning that undetected delinquents are no "brighter" than their peers who are known to the police. However, both the detected and the undetected delinquents had significantly lower IQ means than their non-delinquent cohort peers. More precisely, both delinquent groups had significantly lower FIQ and VIQ means than the non-delinquents, but there was no significant difference between delinquents and non-delinquents on PIQ. It would be extremely difficult to perform a more definitive and sophisticated test of the differential detection hypothesis than Moffitt and Silva's. Their findings are clear: delinquents, both detected and undetected, have significantly lower IQ's than non-delinquents, and detected and undetected delinquents do not differ on FIQ, VIQ, or PIQ levels.

## Conclusion

The results presented in this chapter support those who view IQ as having an important effect on violent delinquency. Along with numerous other studies, this one found a statistically significant difference between the mean IQ of the delinquent sample and the mean of the general population. As expected from the discussion in Chapter Four, the effect of IQ on violent delinquency is not a function of full-scale IQ but rather a function of the opposite influences of VIQ and PIQ. High VIQ serves to inhibit violence, while high PIQ (relative to a subject's own VIQ) seems to facilitate it.

Although violence means were found to be lower in the upper 50 percent of the SES distribution, P > V was able to explain more of the variance in violent delinquency than it did in the lower half of the SES distribution. P > V is a consistent predictor of violent delinquency, but the power of its influence varies across SES groupings. Further, the influence of P > V on violent delinquency is not rendered spurious by controlling for SES and race. Until there is strong evidence to the contrary, we must agree with Hirshi and Hindelang (1977) that the cognitive variable measure by IQ tests play a role in the development of violent delinquency independent of race and SES.

This chapter says nothing about the influence of IQ on types of crimes other than violent ones. IQ level may be more a variable determining what kind of crime a person commits rather than whether he or she becomes delinquent. Also, except for those correlations found in the upper groupings of SES, the correlations between the various IQ measures and violent delinquency are weak to moderate. Clearly, variables other than IQ must be considered.

## ENDNOTES

1. The correlation between IQ and delinquency in the general population is doubtless stronger than the correlation reported here among a sample of defined delinquents. In a fairly homoscedastic distribution—one in which the variance in Y remains approximately equal across the range of X values—the error variance around the regression line remains relatively constant. However, in a sample with restricted range on both the predictor and criterion variables,

the total variance, by definition, is less than it is in a sample distribution that includes observations from across the entire population distribution. Since r is the square root of the coefficient of determination, which is the total variance minus the error variance, and that difference divided by the total variance, the effect on the reported strength of association computed on the basis of restricted total variance is obvious (Walsh, 1990:308).

2. As coincidence would have it, the article following Merton's (1938) by Clark and Gist (1938) looked at occupational choice and intelligence and found, as one might expect, that IQ is highly correlated with occupation, and that IQ functioned to funnel people into their various occupations, not "social structure."

3. The coefficient of variation is used rather than the standard deviation because it is more useful in comparing variation between and among groups having different means. It is obtained by multiplying the standard deviation of a distribution by 100 and dividing the product by the distribution mean. The variance within a sample is expressed as a percentage of its mean, and the standard deviations are thus "standardized" across samples making them fully comparable.

## Chapter Six

# LOVE DEPRIVATION AND
# VIOLENT DELINQUENCY

### Love and Human Development

Many giants of the social and behavioral sciences have written eloquently of the positive power of love in human affairs. August Comte, the father of sociology, saw love as the guiding principle of his positivist philosophy (Coser, 1971); Freud saw it as the wellspring of human civilization (1961); Pitirim Sorokin (1954) spent a lifetime exploring its manifold aspects; and Abraham Maslow considered it imperative that we understand love "or else the world is lost to hostility and suspicion" (1954:181). Add to this galaxy of behavioral science stars the insight of Marx and Engels, who wrote: "Love, which first really teaches man to believe in the objective world outside himself, which not only makes man an object, but the object a man" (1956:32).

Although the domains of interest, ideological orientations, meta-theoretical assumptions, methodologies, and personal backgrounds of these theoreticians and clinicians differed widely, they spoke with one voice on the subject of love.[1] Despite the insights provided by these men, modern empirically minded behavioral scientists have been loathe to introduce such a "mystical" and "unmeasurable" variable as love into their work, for the word trips too uneasily on the tongue.[2] If love is as vitally important in human affairs as the likes of Freud, Marx and Maslow have asserted, it is indeed puzzling that so few attempts have been made to explore what kind of human beings are wrought in its absence. Such an exploration would seem particularly important in the area of juvenile delinquency.

Although it is often asserted by sociologists that the family is the nursery of human nature, concepts most evocative of this metaphor such as "bonding," "attachment," and "maternal deprivation," all synonyms for love or its deprivation, have had difficulty finding their niche in sociological criminology. According to Jencks (1987:33), liberal criminologists tend to shy away from imputing causal importance to upbringing:

"Since Americans see upbringing as the responsibility of the family rather than society, the ultimate villains more often turn out to be the mugger's parents (who are also black), not the federal government, capitalism, white racism, or other targets of liberal reform."

Such a circumscribed and ideological approach leads to the ignorance of some potentially useful data provided by the child development literature that could help us to better understand the phenomenon of delinquency (Baltes and Nesselroade, 1984; Sampson and Laub, 1990). For instance, a review of this body of literature by Rutter (1979) identified four "principle syndromes" at its forefront. Three of these four syndromes—conduct disorders, intellectual retardation, and affectionless pychopathy—have obvious applicability to delinquency research. Yet, what are arguably the two most influential textbooks on criminology over the past three decades—Vold and Bernard's *Theoretical Criminology*, and Sutherland and Cressey's *Criminology*—do not even have the terms "love," "affection," "bonding," or any analogous term, in their indices.

Criminological researchers in the first half of the century were much more likely to emphasize love deprivation as an explanation for crime, although they tended to rely primarily on clinical case-study data. Summing up this literature, psychiatrist Abram Blau wrote:

> Just how the characters of the criminal, of the delinquent, and of the child who manifests a behavior disorder are related to love and discipline of the family is disclosed by comprehensive child-guidance studies. Because his need for protection, love, and the good opinion of his guardians is greater than his desire to satisfy his instinctual tensions, the child becomes willing to make social concessions. In every one of the cases I have cited, and in many more that have been studied, the outstanding factor in the child's life was the lack of parental affection . . . he had never found love or understanding in his home. . . . And the more severe the anti-social behavior, the more complete and long-standing the emotional deficiencies are found to be. (1943:265.)

Not all modern criminologists ignore the role of love in the etiology of crime and delinquency. Travis Hirschi (1977:332) makes "attachment" the foundation of his control theory of delinquency. Attachment refers to one's psychological and emotional closeness to others, particularly to one's parents. It implies a reciprocal love relationship within which one feels secure, valued, and respected. The attachment felt within the family constellation is the template for later attachments to individuals and institutions outside the family. The attached child behaves in a way designed to please those whose good opinion he or she values. Behaving in such a way (mutual respect, cooperation, doing well in school and in other prosocial endeavors) leads to the development of Hirschi's other three controls—commitment, involvement, and belief—that are said to militate against delinquent behavior.

If children lack the vital bond of attachment to parents, if there is little love, concern, or respect within the family, they will come to view the world as a cold and heartless place. They will treat it as abusively as they themselves were treated. They will fail to sympathize or empathize with the suffering of others, will not develop a commitment to a prosocial career or be involved in a pattern of prosocial activities, and will tend to develop a set of beliefs more suited to the jungle than to modern society. People who lack sympathy, empathy, and a conscience, people who are unable to form close relationships with others or to conform to a sense of decency are found in abundance in our correctional systems. Buikhuisen et al. (1984:310) characterize criminals as having histories of not being "loved by their parents and often beaten, by father and mother. Being raised under such conditions gives rise to personality traits like lack of self-control, negativism, hostility, trait anxiety, and high scoring on the psychopathic deviate scale of the abridged MMPI."

Among the many variables explored in the Cambridge-Somerville study, none was more strongly linked to delinquency than maternal love:

> Only if the mother was non-loving did high rates of crime appear. Consistently love-oriented discipline, in addition, reduced criminality among boys reared by cruel fathers.
>
> Paternal neglect led to crime, except in those cases where maternal love or consistently love-oriented discipline were present. Neglected sons became criminal at an early age and were convicted in high proportions for every type of crime. (McCord and McCord, 1959:170.)

A prospective study conducted by Matas, Arendt, and Sroufe (1978) showed a strong relationship between maternal attachment and personality outcomes among young children observed over a period of five years. Infants who were judged to be securely attached to their mothers at six months showed less dependency, stronger egos, better behavior, higher self-esteem, less anger, impulsivity, and aggression, and were more persistent in performing various tasks than infants judged to be weakly attached.

The relationship between affection/attachment and personality variables associated with violence is found across cultures. Anthropologist Ronald Rohner studied the effects of the lack of love in 101 cultures over a period of 15 years. He concluded that the need for love is independent of culture and that it is a universal feature of all members of the human species. If we do not receive it, writes Rohner, "pernicious things happen to us" (1975:166), and these pernicious things "have implications permeating throughout both personality and the entire social system" (1975:173).

Developmental neuropsychologist James Prescott (1975), who believes his research has shown that there is a reciprocal relationship between love and violence (the presence of one neurologically inhibits the other), tested his thesis using data from 49 different societies. Using infant behavior ratings and violence ratings from cultural anthropological sources, he divided the sample into cultures who were high or low on both infant physical affection and on violence. He hypothesized that cultures who evidenced high rates of infant affection would have low rates of physical violence, and vice versa. Prescott found that adult physical violence could be accurately predicted from the infant affection variable in 36 of 49 cultures. I computed statistics from Prescott's reported data and found the corrected chi-square value to be 8.38 (p = .0038, Q = .76). He concluded: "I am not aware of any other developmental variable that has such a high degree of predictive validity. Thus, we seem to have a firmly based principle [from the neurological and anthropological data]: Physically affectionate societies are highly unlikely to be physically violent" (1975:13).

Much of Prescott's work exploring the relationship between violence and what he says "psychologists call 'tender loving care'" (1975:11) has been carried out with monkeys raised in love-deprived conditions. Prescott sent five isolation-raised monkeys to the laboratory of Robert Heath to determine if such an experience manifested itself in their neurophysiology. Heath found that it did and concluded: "This was the first evidence that aberrant electrophysiological activity occurs in deep cerebellar nuclei, as well as other deep-brain structures—most pronounced in the limbic system [the "emotional brain"]—in association with severely disturbed behavior resulting from maternal-social deprivation" (quoted in Restak, 1979:150). Commenting on these findings, Restak (1979:151) writes that they "provide a preliminary basis for a psychobiological theory of the origin of human violence which may result from a permanent defect in the pleasure centers secondary to inadequate early mothering. . . . [S]uch people may be suffering at the neuronal level from stunted growth of their pleasure system." A review of the literature on the connection between violence and stunted development of the pleasure centers is contained in Haynie (1980).

Don Gibbons (1970:202), while more attuned to structural than functional explanations of delinquency, states that "scientific candor compels us to conclude that the link between parental rejection and aggressive conduct is one of the more firmly established generalizations concerning delinquency." Gibbons is correct: a number of separate but greatly overlapping factors—physical and psychological abuse, neglect, coldness, absence, and sexual promiscuity and substance abuse on the part of parents—which I collectively call "love deprivation," has consistently been shown across time and national boundaries to be associated with delinquency, especially violent delinquency (Rutter, 1979). As Ashley Montagu put it: "Take almost any violent individual and inquire into his history as a child, and it can be predicted with confidence that he will have had a lacklove childhood, to have suffered a failure of tender, loving care" (1978:178).

The greatest difficulty encountered in the examination of the relationship between love deprivation and delinquency is defining love. In addition to being "many a splendored thing," it is also a many a faceted thing. It cannot be encompassed by noting only one aspect, such as physical abuse, or by using "broken home" as a proxy for love deprivation, as did Andrew (1977:243) because "love is still somewhat difficult to measure." I take my definition from Montagu, who is perhaps science's foremost expositor of the role of love in human conduct. He defines it thus: "Love is a relationship between persons which contributes to the welfare and development of each" (1970:464). He purposely defines love broadly because no one indicant of the concept can adequately define it. Each of the indicants of the concept enumerated in the last paragraph are indicative of the lack of regard for the welfare and development of the child. Collectively, they represent a cold and hostile home environment, the lack of care and supervision, and the modeling of antisocial behavior patterns, all of which are hardly conducive to a child developing positive self-esteem.

The intimate connection between love and self-esteem has been emphasized by William Glasser, who makes them the theoretical underpinning of his reality therapy. He asserts that human beings have two basic psychological needs that must be fulfilled: the need to love and be loved, and the need to feel worthwhile. Glasser goes on to describe how these two needs are interrelated: "Although these two needs are separate, a person who loves and is loved will usually feel that he [or she] is a worthwhile person, and one who is worthwhile is usually someone who is loved and can give love in return" (1975:11). In another of his works, Glasser estimates that about eighty-five percent of those in regular and violent conflict with the law have not had these needs met (1976:187).

There is evidence that Glasser is correct in his observation that low self-esteem breeds violence, and that the taproot of self-esteem is love. Two recent studies of love and self-esteem did indeed find the two variables to be closely linked. Buri, Kirchner, and Walsh (1987) found that only "parental nurturance" among a set of variables in a regression model was able to independently account for significant variance (33%) among a sample of college students. Using a community sample, Walsh and Balazs (1990) report a standardized beta of .63 between the amount of love their respondents reported receiving from others and self-esteem in a six-variable regression model.

There have been some recent attempts to show that youngsters seek out deviant ways to bolster damaged self-esteem (Berman and Siegal, 1976; Buikhuisen, 1987). Yablonsky (1990:449) writes that violent youths are "because of their low self-esteem, acting out self-destructive behavior; they have limited concern about whether they live or die." Dembo et al. (1987) found high relationships between parental abuse, antisocial behavior, and self-derogation among a sample of detained juvenile delinquents. Violent and aggressive responses to the experience of a lacklove childhood have been observed in children as young as two and three years old. George and Main concluded their study of abused and aggressive toddlers by noting: "Compared with their matched controls, we found abused children aggressive, inhibited in approach, and avoidant in response to friendly overtures" (1979:316).

### Is Criminality Inherited?

Studies attempting to link the lack of loving parental care to later violence have been criticized on the grounds that innate "natural abilities [and] physiological predispositions" may mediate both abuse/neglect and violent behavior (Widom, 1989:251). In other words, infants and children may be the cause of their own victimization because they possess temperaments that are not conducive to loving responses from parents (Wilson and Herrnstein, 1985:253). This raises the issue of whether some people are born more predisposed to crime and delinquency—

mediated by temperaments that are not conducive to receiving love—than others.

Several studies have been conducted over the years that appear to indicate that criminality is partially an inherited trait. For instance, McClearn and DeFries (1973) report the concordance rate for criminality among monozygotic twins, averaged over seven studies, was 72 percent. The averaged concordance rate for diaygotic twins was reported as 23 percent. Walters and White (1989:467) point out that when stricter definitions of criminality (i.e., "real" crime as opposed to the usual self-reported "misbehaviors') are used, the concordance for monozygotic twins is 41 percent and for dyzygotic twins it is 25.8 percent. Since it is assumed that all twin pairs share common family environments (an assumption that is not always tenable), the difference between these concordance rates for mono- and dyzygotic twins is taken as a measure of the influence of genetic factors on criminality.

Another method of studying the effects of genes on a given trait is the adoption method. A study by Mednick, Gabrielli, and Hutchings (1984) among a large number of Danish adoptees found that 24.5 percent of adopted boys whose biological and adoptive fathers were both criminal were themselves criminals. If the adoptive father was criminal but the biological father was not, 14.7 percent of the boys were criminal. The former figure illustrates genetic × environment interaction, and the latter figure illustrates environmental influences only, as does the 13.5 percent of criminal boys with neither biological or adoptive criminal fathers. If the biological father was criminal but not the adoptive father, 20 percent of adoptees were criminal. The authors take this latter figure as representing genetic influences.

The percentage difference between the children who became criminal whose adopted but not biological father was criminal (14.7%), and whose biological but not adopted father was criminal (20%), is only 5.3 percent. Although this is suggestive of some sort of genetic influence, it is much smaller than the percentage of boys who became criminal who had neither a biological or adoptive criminal father (13.5%). This makes any genetic contribution seem relatively unimpressive, as does the 80 percent of the adoptees who did not become criminal whose biological fathers were criminal but whose adoptive fathers were not.

More impressive than the analysis of the entire cohort was the authors' analysis of chronic offenders among the adoptees. Among the 3,718 male adoptees, 37 had biological fathers with three or more criminal convictions.

This mere 1 percent of adopted boys accounted for no less than 30 percent of the male adoptee convictions. The relationship between biological father's recidivism and adoptee recidivism is therefore very strong. The strength of the relationship within this small subsample reduces the strength of the relationship among the entire cohort (since we are eliminating 30 percent of the convictions by abstracting this segment from the whole). This suggests that genetic influences beneath some unknown threshold may be nonexistent, while such influences beyond that threshold may exert a major influence.

There is indeed a relationship between parental criminality and offspring criminality that cannot be attributable to chance. But this is not necessarily a function of simple genetic inheritance. Children of criminals inherit a milieu as well as a set of genes from their parents, and being raised in the same family environment does not mean that all children, even twins, are treated alike. There is evidence that some children are "selected out" for positive or negative treatment within the same family (Yablonsky and Haskell, 1988:120). This is an important point because it has been consistently shown that non-shared (within-family) environment is much more important to trait outcomes than shared environment (see Plomin and Daniels, 1987, for a review). Such findings, by definition, diminish the importance of traditional sociological explanations of crime such as SES and cultural values because such variables contribute only to shared (between-family) environmental variance.

In two consecutive issues of the *American Journal of Psychiatry* Lewis, Shanok, and Balla (1979a 1979b) compared medical histories through age 16 of delinquent children with criminal parents (N = 20), delinquent children with non-criminal parents (N = 85), and non-delinquent children (N = 109). The three groups differed significantly from one another on number of hospital visits, particularly for "accidents" and injuries. Differences in medical histories were most striking before the age of four, a particularly crucial stage of central nervous system (CNS) growth. Based on these data, Lewis and her colleagues discount the idea of genetic transmission of deviant behavior, suggesting instead that parental criminality influences the delinquency of their offspring through abuse and neglect: "This physical trauma, especially to the CNS at an early age, impedes a child's ability to perceive accurately, make sound judgments, and control impulses" (1979a:292). These CNS impediments are reflected in a child's IQ scores, as well as later delinquency.

In a subsequent study of 84 incarcerated delinquents matched with a similar number of non-incarcerated delinquents, Lewis et al. (1979b) found more serious medical histories among the incarcerated delinquents, especially in terms of head injuries sustained before the age of two. A separate analysis of violent and non-violent delinquents found that violent delinquents were significantly more abused and neglected, and that the history of abuse for the violent delinquents began significantly earlier than for the non-violent delinquents. The authors suggest that the combination of early central nervous system trauma, parental psychopathology, and social deprivation is primarily responsible for the serious violent delinquency so prevalent in our society.

A similar study by Mednick and his colleagues (1982) of the relationship between abuse and neglect and violent delinquency among a cohort of children born between 1959 and 1961 in Copenhagen found similar results. Perusing the records of children who later became violent delinquents at infancy and then at one year of age, they found a systematic and significant change in the medical and neurological status of these children over the one-year period. This indicated to them that children who later became violent had suffered serious damage to the CNS during this crucial stage of development. These studies strongly suggest that social, psychiatric, and neurological factors combine synergistically in the abused child to produce a potentially violent individual.

Sarnoff Mednick has produced many first-rate studies based on the excellent Danish cohort data available to him. He is also in the forefront among scholars exploring the role of the autonomic nervous system in syndromes such as psychopathy and schizophrenia. Given his access to such data, one wonders why he has not combined his interest in the genetics of criminality with his interest in the role of abuse and neglect in producing criminality. For instance, the children of criminal biological fathers who were adopted and who later became criminal in the Mednick, Gabriellii and Hutchings study (1984) may have suffered the CNS damage noted in the Mednick et al. study (1982) prior to being adopted. If this were the case, it might turn out that genetics have even less influence, if any at all, on offspring criminality that is not mediated by the effects of abuse and neglect. It might be particularly interesting to learn of the infancy experiences of that 1 percent of the 1984 study that accounted for 30 percent of the convictions.

From the above studies we see that identifiable biological differences between violent and non-violent individuals are probably far more attributable to negative childhood experiences than to genetics. A major problem with studies purporting to demonstrate the heritability of criminality is the interpretation placed on them by biologically naive readers. Part of the problem is that such studies rarely attempt to identify the mechanisms by which certain genotypes produce criminal behavior. As previously indicated, genes are molecular, self-replicating proteins that code for physiological, hormonal, and metabolic processes. They do not code for behavior, least of all for behavior that is socially defined as good or bad. They do code for certain predispositions, such as temperament, conditionability, and intelligence, variations of which may put certain individuals at risk for criminal labeling. But there is no neat linear cryptography by which genes code for certain types of brains, which in turn code for certain kinds of behavior. Genes work in intimate relationship with the environment and do not produce a phenotype in isolation from it.

From the neurophysiological research reviewed in Chapter three, we gained insight into the mechanisms by which negative infant experiences translate into the kind of neurological deficits that are related to later delinquency. We know that the kind of stimulation an infant receives during the sensitive period of neuronal growth strongly predisposes the synaptic connections associated with that stimulation to be dominant. If an infant's experiences are positive and loving, the neural pathways to its pleasure centers will be well-trodden. These firmly entrenched neural circuits will strongly predispose the individual, in later life, to perceive many of his or her experiences with others as positive and loving. In the terminology of psychiatrist Eric Berne's (1964) transactional analysis therapy, the individual will interact with life from an "I'm O.K., you're O.K." position. The loved individual will know that he or she is "O.K." because the taproot of self-esteem or personal "OKness" is love.

On the other hand, if an infant's experiences are of a cold, abusive, and neglectful kind, its neural circuitry will be "wired" to its displeasure centers. His or her storehouse of personal memories will reflect the early negativity of experience. Such individuals will tend to interpret subsequent experiences negatively, pessimistically, and possibly react to them with violence. They will probably confront the world from an "I'm not O.K., you're not O.K." life position. Their self-esteem will have been seriously compromised, and, since so many early experiences with significant others were negative, they will generalize that negativity to the outside world. He or she will have difficulty establishing positive peer relationships in childhood (Flaherty and Richman, 1986) and romantic and sexual relationships in adulthood (Kernberg, 1974).

Neurologist Richard Restak sums up the importance of early and loving tactile stimulation for human development when he writes:

> Touch, it turns out, is as necessary to normal infant development as food and oxygen. Mother opens her arms to the infant, snuggles him, and a host of psychobiological processes are brought into harmony. Disrupt this process because the mother cannot or will not caress, touch or otherwise make skin-to-skin contact with the infant and psychobiological processes go askew... physiological imbalances, behavioral peculiarities, hostilities, suppressed anger and rage. (1986:141.)

## Love Deprivation and Intellectual Imbalance

It was suggested in Chapter four that love deprivation could lead to intellectual imbalance in the direction of P > V. Support for this suggestion is offered in Table 6.1. Subjects are divided into three categories based on love deprivation scores: (1) those with scores one standard deviation below the mean; (2) between plus and minus one standard deviation; and (3) one standard deviation above the mean. Using these love deprivation categories we can compare P > V and violence means. It is seen that boys who are one standard deviation or more above the love deprivation mean have P > V and violence means more than twice as large as boys in the between plus or minus one standard deviation category, and more than three times the means of the boys in the minus one standard deviation category. Love deprivation does appear to have a substantively significant effect on P > V discrepancy, possibly through its effect on ANS functioning. Whatever the effect of love deprivation on ANS functioning, it most certainly has a striking effect on violence. A two-way ANOVA revealed the interactive effect of the two variables on violence, with love deprivation ($F = 41.01$, $p < .00001$) being more powerful than P > V ($F = 3.16$, $p < .05$) when both variables are examined simultaneously.

The violence means presented above represent category averages of the seriousness and frequency of violent delinquency. They do not tell us how many boys in each category had committed a violent crime, nor do they tell us how many boys were violent recidivists. Recidivism, of course, is a particularly important concern. Since the ANOVA results revealed significant interaction, it would be fruitful to assess the combined effects of love deprivation and intellectual imbalance on violent recidivism.

TABLE   6.1


P > V and Violence Means by Love Deprivation

| Love Deprivation Category | N | P > V mean | Violence mean |
|---|---|---|---|
| 1 s.d. below mean | 98 (a) | 3.56c | 39.42c |
| Between _ 1. s.d. | 333 (b) | 6.46c | 53.58c |
| 1 s.d. above mean | 82 (c) | 14.40ab | 123.80ab |
| F ratio | | 17.20 | 45.37 |
| sig. | | .0000 | .0000 |
| eta | | .25 | .39 |

Note: a b c = means differing at < .05, Scheffe test.

In order to determine this, I first divided the sample into three approximately equal categories (low, medium, high) on love deprivation. I then computed a composite variable composed of: (1) boys who were high on love deprivation and who were P > V intellectually imbalanced, (N = 77) and (2) boys who were low or medium on love deprivation and who were either V > P or V = P (N = 436). I then cross-tabulated these dichotomous categories with (a) the commission of at least one violent offense and (b) with two or more violent offenses. The results are presented in Table 6.2.

The dichotomized categories are highly related to violent delinquency. In part A of the table we see that the majority of boys in both categories committed at least one violent crime, with the high love deprivation/ P > V boys being significantly more likely to have done so. The conditional odds of committing a violent crime among the low love deprivation/non-P > V boys are 1.17:1 in favor. The conditional odds for high love deprivation/P > V boys are 4.92:1 in favor, and the ratio of the two conditional odds is 4.2:1. In other words, the odds of committing at least one violent crime among high love deprivation/ P > V boys are 4.2 times greater than among low love deprivation/ non-P > V boys.

In part B of the table we see that just over one-third of the total sample were violent recidivists. However, only 28.4 percent of the low love

TABLE 6.2

Juveniles who have Committed at Least One Violent Crime (A)
and Who Have Committed Two or More Violent Crimes (B) by
Love Deprivation and P > V Imbalance

| (A) | | | | | (B) | | | | |
|---|---|---|---|---|---|---|---|---|---|
| Committed Violent Crime | High Love Deprivation and P > V Imbalanced | | | | Committed two or more Violent Crimes | High Love Deprivation and P > V Imbalanced | | | |
| | No | Yes | Total | | | No | Yes | Total | |
| No | 201 46.1% | 13 16.9% | 214 41.7% | | No | 312 71.6% | 19 24.7% | 331 64.5% | |
| Yes | 235 53.9% | 64 83.1% | 299 58.3% | | Yes | 124 28.4% | 58 75.3% | 182 35.4% | |
| Total | 436 | 77 | 513 | | Total | 436 | 77 | 513 | |

$X^2$ = 21.8, df = 1, p = .0000

$X^2$ = 68.1, df = 1, p = .00000

Q = .62, odds ratio = 4.2:1

Q = .77, odds ratio = 7.7:1

deprivation/non-P > V boys were violent recidivists (conditional odds = 2.52:1 against violent recidivism), while 75.3 percent of the high love deprivation/P > V boys were recidivists (conditional odds = 3.05 in favor of recidivism). The ratio of these conditional odds is 7.7:1. These odds are impressive, and they strongly assert the predictive power of love deprivation and intellectual imbalance acting in concert.

## Different Environments, Different Explanations

Most tests of criminological theory regress a set of favored predictor variables on the criterion variable across all subjects in the sample. There is obviously nothing wrong with this strategy if one is seeking to tease out the best explanatory variable(s) across a wide range of subjects. Another approach has been suggested by Trasler (1978). He suggests that it is not tenable to suppose that all predictor variables have similar explanatory power across subjects in delinquent samples, and that we develop specific theories based on ANS reactivity and child-rearing practices across various SES levels. Likewise, Buikhuisen and his colleagues (1984:311) stress that while social deprivation theories are adequate to explain crime among the lower social classes, "They cannot be generalized for instance to criminals who have grown up under favorable conditions." Among the 82 "privileged" offenders they studied, only individual differences such as high extraversion, high impulsiveness, and low anxiety (all of which are associated by the P > V profile) contributed to violent offenses.

In Chapter Two we saw that heritability studies of IQ suggest that genes contribute less to phenotypical IQ among socioeconomically disadvantaged groups than they do among more advantaged groups. Genes contribute less within disadvantaged groups because genetic expression is suppressed by the disabilities suffered within such groups. If some socioeconomic environments suppress the optimal expression of IQ and others allow for the full expression of IQ potential, it is also likely that P > V and love deprivation may have different effects on violent behavior across environmental ranges. All behavior is the result of kinds of people meeting kinds of environments. Some environments overwhelm individual differences and innate propensities; other environments are less intrusive and allow greater leeway for "kinds of people" explanations for behavior. The more socioeconomically disadvantaged the environment, the more we may expect that love deprivation will be related to both P > V and violence. In such an environment we may also expect that P > V will have limited impact on violence independent of love deprivation.

It may be that in socioeconomically advantaged environments love deprivation does not reach the threshold level (whatever that level may be across individuals) necessary for it to be a serious causal candidate for violent behavior. In advantaged environments, P > V discrepancy, like IQ itself, may be much more a function of genetic inheritance than a reaction to environmental conditions. The studies of McFie (1973) lead him to the conclusion that differences between the cognitive abilities represented by VIQ and PIQ are at least partially genetic in origin. If such is indeed the case in advantaged environments, the mechanisms previously discussed as being associated with P > V may be sufficient to account for violent propensities quite independent of love deprivation. As Nachshon and Denno (1987:209) have pointed out, we should expect relatively more psychologically and neurologically deviant subjects among delinquents from higher SES environments, where resistance to crime is high, than among delinquents from lower SES environments, where resistance to crime is low.

Disadvantage/advantage, of course, are relative concepts. Wilson (1987) has called attention to the need to explore the determinants of "senseless" violence in what he calls "truly disadvantaged" environments. Wilson's conception of the truly disadvantaged individual includes people who are socially isolated urbanites, low SES, and victims of discrimination. Thomas Bernard (1990) has proposed a theory, based on social cognitive and physiological variables, for explaining the "senseless" violence so often observed among the truly disadvantaged. He argues that an urban environment, discrimination, and low SES leads to an inability to cope and to frequent intense arousal. Frequent arousal leads to angry aggression, which leads to social isolation of the aroused group, and subsequently to an exacerbation of an already aggressive environment.

To test the differential effects of love deprivation and P > V across different environments, including the "truly disadvantaged," I divided the white juveniles into three environmental groups roughly considered to be (1) homogeneous/disadvantaged (H/D), (2) heterogeneous (HT), and (3) homogeneous/advantaged (H/A) on the basis of SES. To arrive at these groupings I took the approximate bottom and top 10 percent of the SES scale for the H/D and H/A groups, respectively.[3] The remaining white juveniles were placed in the HT category. Black juveniles are analyzed separately because of the race-specific disabilities assumed to impact this group.

The measure of relative advantage/disadvantage are the sizes of the SES means, and the measures of relative homogeneity are the sizes of the coefficients of variation. Table 6.3 presents these values, as well as their respective VIQ and PIQ means and associated C.V.'s.

TABLE 6.3

SES, VIQ, and PIQ Means and C.V.'s Within Each Group

| Group | N | SES Means | C.V. | VIQ Means | C.V. | PIQ Means | C.V. |
|---|---|---|---|---|---|---|---|
| Homo./Disadvantaged | 58 | 11.12 | 9.89 | 84.69 | 15.70 | 95.67 | 15.37 |
| Heterogeneous | 280 | 27.07 | 30.54 | 92.19 | 15.32 | 99.06 | 16.81 |
| Homo./Advantaged | 50 | 48.48 | 5.57 | 93.90 | 10.97 | 104.48 | 9.03 |
| Blacks Only | 83 | 24.17 | 38.76 | 83.25 | 12.08 | 85.31 | 14.83 |

A comparison of the SES means shows that the H/A group has a mean more than four times greater than the H/D group, and that the HT SES mean is more than twice as large as the H/D group. A comparison of the coefficients of variation reveals that there is 3.09 times more SES variation in the HT category than in the H/D category, and 5.31 times more than in the H/A category. The categorization renders the groups sufficiently different from one another in terms of environmental advantage/disadvantage and homogeneity/heterogeneity to allow us to explore the differential effects of love deprivation and P > V across them.

Table 6.4 shows that the H/D boys have a violence mean almost twice as large as the HT and H/A boys. Although blacks have a higher violence mean than whites in the sample as a whole, the H/D white violence mean exceeds that of the blacks. We also see that the H/D boys have the largest love deprivation and P > V means of all groups.

More important than violence means per se are the patterns revealed in the correlation matrices for each group. In the H/D group, both love deprivation and P > V are significantly related to violence, but love deprivation is much more powerful. Although both predictor variables are significant predictors of violence in the HT group, both are only weakly related to violence, with love deprivation being the stronger of the two. We observe a reversal among the H/A boys in terms of the variable exerting most influence on violence. Within this group, P > V is by far the most powerful predictor of violent delinquency, with the love deprivation/violence correlation being smaller than it is in any of the other categories. Among the black juveniles, love deprivation has the stronger correlation with violence.

Turning to the relationship between the predictor variables, we see that the effects of love deprivation on intellectual imbalance are strongest within the disadvantaged environments. Love deprivation accounts for 30.6 percent of the variance in P > V among the H/D boys, and 38.8 percent among the blacks. Among the H/A boys, love deprivation only accounts for 7.4 percent of the variance in P > V, and among the HT boys it accounts for only 1.7 percent. Thus, environmental factors do not affect the development of a P > V intellectual profile in the same way across class and racial groupings.

These results are consistent with the environmental advantaged/disadvantaged hypothesis in terms of the heritability of IQ posited by Scarr-Salapatek (1973) and Fischbein (1980) discussed in Chapter Two. That is, among disadvantaged groups a larger proportion of P > V variability is accounted for by environmental conditions than is the case

TABLE 6.4

Correlation Matrices (r), Means, and Coefficients of Variation
for Each of the Three White SES Conditions and for Blacks

| Variables | Violence | P>V | Lovedep. | X̄ | C.V. |
|---|---|---|---|---|---|
| **Panel 1. Homogeneous/Disadvantaged Whites (N = 58)** | | | | | |
| Violent Delinquency | 1.000 | .352b | .528a | 100.27 | 64.07 |
| P > V Discrepancy | | 1.000 | .553a | 11.14 | 162.67 |
| Love Deprivation | | | 1.000 | 30.36 | 39.85 |
| **Panel 2. Heterogeneous Whites (N = 280)** | | | | | |
| Violent Delinquency | 1.000 | .141b | .292a | 54.31 | 136.04 |
| P > V Discrepancy | | 1.000 | .131c | 6.99 | 183.03 |
| Love Deprivation | | | 1.000 | 25.27 | 51.30 |
| **Panel 3. Homogeneous/Advantaged Whites (N = 50)** | | | | | |
| Violent Delinquency | 1.000 | .705a | .262c | 56.02 | 105.83 |
| P > V Discrepancy | | 1.000 | .272c | 10.48 | 115.64 |
| Love Deprivation | | | 1.000 | 17.78 | 48.85 |
| **Panel 4. Blacks Only (N = 83)** | | | | | |
| Violent Delinquency | 1.000 | .371a | .570a | 80.93 | 85.37 |
| P > V Discrepancy | | 1.000 | .623a | 2.15 | 474.42 |
| Love Deprivation | | | 1.000 | 20.14 | 79.94 |

a = p < .001,  b = p < .01,  c = p < .05

in advantaged groups. Conversely, P > V scores within advantaged groups are less correlated with environmental conditions than they are in the disadvantaged groups. Within disadvantaged groups, miseries multiply and restrict optimum gene expression. Within advantaged groups, genetic potential is allowed fuller expression due to the relative lack of environmental restrictions.

The results are also consistent with Venables' (1987) study of delinquency and tonic heart rate (a measure of ANS activity) among British delinquents. He found a significant negative correlation of −.36 (p < .025) between tonic heart rate and delinquency among high SES delinquents, but a non-significant (r = −.10) correlation between the two variables among low SES delinquents. Venables (1987:119–120) comes to the same conclusion as do I: "[B]iological variables should show more clearly in high social-class subjects," and that "delinquency in low-social-class situations may owe more to social than to biological factors."

In that the environmental conditions I have measured do not impact on P > V very much at all in the H/A group, we are left only with genetics (insofar as genetics are implicated in the P > V profile) to account for the variance in this group. Of course, part of the variance in the H/A group might be attributable to unmeasured environmental variables. However, in light of the fact that the variables that *have* been measured impact so strongly on the disadvantaged groups, and in light of the fact that the H/A is so much higher in SES than the H/D and black groups, it is reasonable to assume that any unmeasured variables would have minimal impact on IQ variation in this group. Furthermore, any unmeasured environmental variable that serves to suppress genetic expression is more likely to occur in disadvantaged groups and would thus function to further accentuate the differences between the advantaged and disadvantaged groups.

We now turn to the multiple regression models in Table 6.5. As we move from left to right (from the most disadvantaged to the most advantaged group), we note that P > V becomes increasingly more powerful in accounting for variance in violent delinquency. Similarly, we see that love deprivation becomes decreasingly less powerful as we move in the same direction. Among the black juveniles, only love deprivation significantly impacts on violence, with the model accounting for 31.9 percent of the variance in violent delinquency. Among the H/D boys, P > V has no significant independent effect on violence after love deprivation has explained all the variance it can. This model accounts for 25.8 percent of the variance in violent delinquency. Among the H/A boys we observe the opposite pattern, with this model accounting for 49.5 percent of the variance in violent delinquency. Only among the HT boys do both variables have significant independent effects, but both variables together only account for 8.9 percent of the variance in violent delinquency.

Because P > V is not significant at < .10 in the H/D group and love deprivation is likewise not significant in the H/A group, we can elimi-

## TABLE 6.5

Standardized Betas for the Effects of P>V Discrepancy
and Love Deprivation for H/D, HT, H/A and Black
Groups on Violent Delinquency

| Variable | Blacks | White Groups | | |
| --- | --- | --- | --- | --- |
| | | H/D | HT | H/A |
| P>V discrepancy | .015ns | .086ns | .104c | .696a |
| Love deprivation | .570a | .481a | .278a | .078ns |
| Adj. R squared | .319 | .258 | .089 | .495 |
| F ratio | 20.24 | 10.91 | 14.66 | 25.07 |

a = p < . 001, b = p < .01, c = p < .05

nate them from their respective models and simply square the zero-order
correlations between violence and love deprivation and P > V in the
H/D and H/A groups, respectively. Thus, love deprivation explains
26.6 percent of the variance in violence among the H/D group, and P > V
explains 50.1 percent of the variance in violence among the H/A group.
Among the black sample, a similar situation obtains, and we can thus say
love deprivation alone accounts for 32.5 percent of the variance in
violence among blacks.

We may conclude that love deprivation and P > V impact differentially
on violent delinquency within different environments. Within disadvantaged SES groups (H/D and black), environmental experiences weigh
more heavily than cognitive functioning in terms of explaining variance
in violent delinquency. Within the advantaged group, cognitive func-
oning totally overwhelms the effects of love deprivation. These findings
support those who contend that different explanations are required for
higher status delinquency, and that these explanations must be sought

within the person more than within his environment (Trasler, 1978; Buikhuisen et al., 1984; Venables, 1987).

### Conclusion

Love deprivation as conceptualized here does seem to exert a powerful impact on violent crime, especially among delinquents from "truly disadvantaged" environments. But we must look beyond simple demographics such as urbanism and low SES to look at what goes on (apparently more frequently) in such environments. Not all youths suffer the specific disabilities emphasized here within these environments, and many, those who are loved, go on to be productive members of society. Nettler (1978:324) points out that how we are today is a result of three classes of causes: "These determinants lie in our neurophysiological constitutions, in *how* we are reared, and in *what* we are taught" (emphasis in original). Nettler's statement can stand as a succinct definition of what the biosocial perspective of human behavior is all about.

The destructiveness of a loveless environment spills over into adult violence of the worst kind. Summing up Merilyn Moore's profile of serial killers, a profile which, incidentally, closely conforms to my conceptualization of love deprivation, Dillingham (1988:24) writes: "The serial killer is likely someone who grew up in a single parent home, was abused as a child, often sexually, and had family members who were addicted to drugs or alcohol." Colin Wilson (1984) adds parental promiscuity and offspring illegitimacy to this list of disabilities as he sums up the life histories of a number of notorious violent criminals such as Carl Panzram, Albert DeSalvo, Jack Abbott, and Charles Manson. After reviewing the histories of these and other criminals, Wilson (1984:623) is led to conclude: "And so insecure social bonds prevent a capacity for love and affection from being channeled into stable relationships, and the resentment lies dormant, like a volcano, waiting to be detonated into violence by stress."

### ENDNOTES

1. We should not confuse the terms "love" as used by these writers with the common denotation of love. They were not writing about romantic love, which is merely a subconcept contained in the more inclusive concept. For these men, love was viewed as a broad form of human relatedness that one grows in, not "falls in" (Walsh, 1986).

2. Wilson and Herrnstein (1985:237) criticize Schaefer (1959) for his use of the dimension "love versus hate" as an aspect of maternal behavior, stating that "we suspect that few parents lack any love for their children." However, I would agree with Schaefer that it is of little use for cold, rejecting, or abusing parents to protest that they "really do" love their children. Love must be *demonstrated* to be perceived as such; verbal claims to the contrary that are not behaviorally expressed are empty. The effects of love deprivation are just as real whether or not parents "really do" love their children in the abstract.

3. Broken home and illegitimacy was added to the former measure of love deprivation for this analysis for two reasons: (1) it is consistent with Walsh and Petees' (1987) original measure, and (2) it is recommended that there be about 20 cases for each predictor variable included in a multiple regression model to arrive at reliable estimates (Hays, 1988:655). Entering these two variables separately would have required at least 80 cases in each model for reliable estimates. We have two predictor variables (love deprivation and $P > V$) and model N's of 58 and 50.

# Chapter Seven

# FEMALE VIOLENCE

*Sexism and Biological Determinism*

Exploring sex differences in violent behavior from a perspective that includes biological thinking is another one of criminology's taboo areas (Henson, 1980). To insist on doing so, especially if the writer is male, is to risk charges of sexism. This should not surprise, since writing about race and crime sometimes involves the risk of being labeled racist, and writing about IQ and crime carries with it the risk of being tagged with all sorts of pejorative labels. I have already said that I reject such labels when they are applied to those engaged in serious science as unwarranted, silly, and serving to limit freedom of inquiry. Some of the most distinguished women in behavioral science—Alice Rossi, Carol Jacklin, Anke Ehrhardt, June Reinisch, Eleanor Maccoby, Sandra Scarr, and Julianne Imperto-McGinley—are actively engaged in the study of the biology of human sex differences. I would challenge anyone to come up with a list of equally distinguished female behavioral scientists from among those who might want to pin the sexist label on the women on my list.

Critics of behavioral biology set up the ideological agenda by asserting that any posited biologically based sex difference necessarily implies (1) something called "biological determinism," and (2) that there is a natural inferiority/superiority between the sexes, and that these assertions of inferiority/superiority are used to perpetuate a male-dominated sexist society (Andersen, 1988).

Determinism is commonly understood in science as nothing more sinister than the assumption that all events have causes. To attack determinism in this sense is to attack any theory of causation, and thus to impugn the whole business of science. If by "biological determinism" critics mean that behavioral biologists make such hard statements as: "In the presence of biological factor X, behavior Y *will* occur," the critics are wrong and they know it. Behavioral biologists, like all other scientists, work in a probabilistic, not a deterministic, world. The practice of purposely confusing "probabilistic" and a fatalistic "determinism" is a crafty strategy designed to push a social philosophy rather than to attack a particular epistemology.

As for the second concern, it is true that to talk about differences is to imply a hierarchy of attributes about which we can make judgments of superiority/inferiority if we are so inclined. Men and women are different across a wide range of natural (biological) attributes; whole books have been devoted to enumerating them (Montagu, 1974; Hoyenga and Hoyenga, 1979; Khan and Cataio 1984). Men are superior to women in some ways; women are superior to men in others. To recognize this does not imply that either sex is inferior or superior any more than it implies that I am inferior or superior to you because I have some traits that are superior to yours, and you have some that are superior to mine. Inferiority/superiority judgments are trait-specific and do not apply to judgments about the whole person, and certainly not to an entire sex.

If we take the critics of behavioral biology at their word (that differences imply superiority/inferiority), then as far as criminal activity is concerned, women would definitely have to be considered, by a very wide margin, the morally superior sex. There is no doubt at all that across time, national boundaries, and types of crime (excluding prostitution), females commit far fewer crimes than males. From international crime data, Wilson and Herrnstein (1985:104) conclude that "Males are five to fifty times [depending on the country] more likely to be arrested as are females." If we consider only violent crimes, the gap between the sexes is even wider. In 1987, males constituted 89 percent of all arrests for violent crimes and 76 percent of all arrests for property crimes in the United States (Reid, 1990:90).

## The Male "Chivalry" Hypothesis

Are these huge discrepancies in male/female crime an accurate reflection of actual sex differences in behavior or of something else? In a variation of the differential detection hypothesis relating to IQ, some criminologists (Pollak, 1950; Reckless and Kay, 1967; Simon, 1975) view the relationship between sex and violent crime as largely spurious. The higher rates of male arrests and convictions, they reason, are largely a function of differential reporting and the differential application of formal arrests rather than actual different rates of violence committed by males and females. Ignoring massive evidence from the biological sciences regarding a profound sexual dimorphism, they cling to the worn doctrine of a sexless equipotentiality for violence. To explain the differential arrest rates, they turn to old standby explanations located outside of the individuals whose behavior is to be explained. The assertion is that there is a bias in favor of women which disposes victims not to report crimes committed against them by women, and a similar bias in the "chivalrous" criminal justice system which is revealed in the unwillingness of police officers to arrest women and in the unwillingness of the courts to convict.

To determine if such pro-female bias actually exists, Hindelang (1979) compared Uniform Crime Report (UCR) data and National Victimization Survey (NVS) data for the years 1972 through 1976. He found that the official and self-reported rates of victimization accorded extremely well with one another, especially for violent crimes. The percentage of females arrested for rape was 1 percent for both the UCR and NVS data, and for simple assault the percentages were again identical at 14 percent. For robbery (UCR = 7%, NVS = 4%) and aggravated assault (UCR = 13%, NVS = 8%), official reporting was greater than survey reporting. Hindelang (1979:154) concluded his report by stating: "The results presented here give increased confidence that, for the United States as a whole, arrest data for the kinds of crimes considered are reasonably accurate indicators of the basic demographic characteristics of offenders, certainly with respect to race and sex." It seems that the attempt to deny reality with respect to sex-based levels of violence has proven to be as vacuous as the IQ/differential detection hypothesis when subjected to the test of empirical data.

## Why are Females Less Violent?

Freda Adler (1975:16) acknowledges puzzlement over the fact that researchers continue to find a large disparity between the sexes in the commission of violent as females become more liberated. Many other sociologists echo her puzzlement. Their puzzlement arises because the ratio of female-to-male crimes of an economic nature has been decreasing over the past two or three decades as female opportunities to commit such crimes have increased (Wilson and Herrnstein, 1985:109). As long as sociologists view the commission of any type of crime, including violent crimes, as simply a function of differential opportunities and ignore basic biological differences between the sexes, they will remain puzzled. The biological fact is that males are more "prepared" to do violence than females whether we look at infants, adolescents, or adults, and regardless of the culture in which it takes place (Nettler, 1978:84). As Weis (1982:163) pointed out in his self-report study of gender and violence: "The girls are *least involved* in the 'typically masculine' offenses included in the *Aggression* factor . . . the girls are virtually non-violent" (emphasis in original).

Simple observation tells us that males are more violent and aggressive, and that females are more nurturant. This observation is not confined to Western societies; it is universal (Maccoby and Jacklin, 1974; Wells, 1980). Andersen (1988:55) disputes this by stating that this assertion is "a fact that simply does not stand up to the cross-cultural evidence." She quotes as her sole source of evidence Margaret Mead's ethnographic studies of the Arapesh, Tchambuli, and Mundugumor peoples of New Guinea contained in her book, *Sex and Temperament in Three Primitive Societies* (1935). In this book, Mead reported that the Arapesh were a gentle people who held that what we would consider the feminine temperament to be ideal for both sexes, and the Mundugumor considered the masculine temperament to be proper for both sexes. Strangest of all reported by Mead were the Tchambuli. The Tchambuli valued sex-based differences in temperament, but the ideal temperament for males was reported to be "feminine," and for females the ideal was "masculine."

Mead's research is treated as gospel in many sociology textbook discussions of gender roles to perpetuate the notion that culture, not biology, determines masculinity and femininity: "Mead's research is therefore strong support for the conclusion that gender is a variable creation of society" (Macionis, 1989:317). The criticism of Mead's research in the anthropological literature has been virtually ignored in the feminist and sociological literature, despite the fact it has been coming in since the 1930's (Brown, 1991:20–23).

It turns out that Mead's three tribes were not all that different from other societies in terms of sex-based behavioral expectations after all. Fortune's (1939) study of the Arapesh pointed out that they did not expect the two sexes to have the same temperament, that warfare was a well-developed art among these "gentle" people, and that the warriors among them were exclusively male. The Mundugumor women were considerably more masculine in their behavior than Western women, but far less so than their menfolk. Scott (1958) showed that although the Tchambuli males may have been effeminate with respect to some Western male behaviors, the defense of the tribe was their responsibility, and they thoroughly enjoyed the "manly" pursuit of headhunting. More recent fieldwork by Deborah Gewertz (1981) among the Tchambuli showed that males were clearly dominant in that society.

In light of mountains of cross-cultural and historical evidence pointing to the opposite conclusion, it is quite remarkable that Mead's study, based on subjective observations of three very small and quite exotic cultures, should have been so readily accepted. The continued citation of Mead's work to "prove" the extreme malleability of masculinity/femininity is either an example of the intrusion of ideology into science or a sad comment on the nature of interdisciplinary communication. Culture can and does mold masculine and feminine characteristics in many diverse ways, and some women are more aggressive and violent than some men. But we cannot change the fact that males everywhere are simply more prepared to do violence than are females.

Why are males more "prepared" to do violence, and why are aggressive crimes "typically masculine?" As already observed, for the radical environmentalist the answer lies in differential socialization of the sexes. For them, apart from the obvious physical differences and separate reproductive roles of the sexes, the natural human gender condition is androgynous. Any gender differences other than those mentioned are considered to be trivial and entirely the consequence of social conditioning (May, 1980).

We are reminded again that Alice Rossi has pointed out the poverty of such a view of sex role behavior in her ASA Presidential Address, in which she warned that it carries "a high risk of eventual irrelevance" in light of the growing evidence of sexual dimorphism from the biological sciences and neurosciences (1984:4). Lee Ellis, another biologically oriented sociologist, has written the most comprehensive review of the evidence of neuroandrogenetic origins of sex roles that I have seen. Every social scientist should read Ellis's article and pay heed to his conclusion: "Social scientists in the future should avoid attributing sex differences in human behavior to training and social expectations until they have first given careful attention to neurohormonal factors" (1986:537).

Mccoby and Jacklin (1974) do not ignore the evidence from the more basic sciences. They outline their reasons for believing that violence and aggression are based on biological sex differences:

(1)  Males are more aggressive than females in all human societies for which evidence is available. (2)   The sex differences are found too early in life, at a time when there is no evidence that differential socialization pressures have

been brought to bear by adults to "shape" aggression differentially in the two sexes.... (3) Similar sex differences are found in man and subhuman primates. (4) Aggression is related to levels of sex hormones that can be changed by experimental administration of these hormones. (1974:242–243.)

The cross-cultural evidence has already been briefly argued. One would have to be particularly talented in sophistry, and be prepared to rest one's case on the weakest of data, to attempt to refute Maccoby and Jacklin's first point. The same can be said of their third point.

Their second point is also well-supported by the literature, although one could argue that it is never too early for the social sex-typing process to begin (Newman, 1979:134). Males and females certainly receive sex-segregated messages beginning very early in life, but surely these messages largely conform to the biology of the person receiving them. Ellis (1986:51) argues that social training could serve to *blunt* sexual differences rather than cause them, and I have argued the same point elsewhere in terms of sexual behavior (Walsh, 1991:232–233). Regardless of the arguments adduced in support of either position, the data on which they stand are descriptive rather than explanatory. That is, males are *observed* to be more aggressive than females at all ages. The why's behind these observations requires an examination of biological differences between males and females, albeit differences that are reinforced by a gender-typing socialization. This brings me to the last of Maccoby and Jacklin's four points, the role of the adrenal-gonadal hormones.

### Hormones and Violence

The links between testosterone and aggression and violence are more complicated than popular accounts imply. These complications lead some theorists to discount their influence altogether. For instance, Andersen (1988:56) disparages the influence of hormones on behavior by correctly noting that postmenopausal women have lower levels of the female hormones estradiol and progesterone than males of the same age. She goes on to say: "Because there is no empirical evidence that older men are more feminine that older women, we must doubt the conclusion that hormonal differences explain differences in the behavior of the sexes." Since Andersen appears to believe that higher levels of female hormones "should" lead to feminization of older males but don't, it would seem that she holds the deterministic "push-pull-click-click" idea of hormonal influences on behavior that she accuses others of holding.

Andersen's "conclusion," while based on a true premise, is a poor syllogism. She either ignores or is unaware that hormonal influence on sex-typed behavior is not simply a function of absolute levels of sex hormones but is rather a function of their ratios and how and where they act on the brain. These steroid hormones function in the brain as regulators of the genes that control the production of the various neurotransmitters (Udry, 1990). Male and female brains have certain structural differences and are differentially sensitive to the various steriod hormones (Khan and Cataio, 1984).[1] As Olweus et al. (1988:268) have pointed out: "There is little doubt that circulating levels of testosterone during the fetal stage have profound organizational effects on the brain of human and nonhuman primate males. These effects include an increased readiness to engage in aggressive behavior."

It is generally assumed that the "standard" human brain is female unless influenced between the sixth and eight week of gestation by male hormones secreted by the testes of an XY fetus (Khan and Cataio, 1984:13). This secretion of male hormones in utero is commonly known as the "androgen bath." The effects of androgenization first sensitizes the male brain to the effects of androgens, and later it activates the male brain to engage in male-typical behavior.[2] It is thought that progesterone protects genetic females from the effects of androgen during this period, assuring that XX humans develop along feminine sexually dimorphic lines (Ehrhardt and Meyer-Bahlburg, 1981).

The so-called sex hormones interact differently with male and female brains in areas sensitized in utero to be receptive to them. Both the estrogens and androgens act on the limbic system, the brain's emotional center, in areas known to be structurally different in males and females. Testosterone is transformed in the brain into sex-specific variations— estradiol in females, dihydrotestosterone in males. Estradiol promotes nurturing behavior in females by lowering the threshold for firing the nerve fibers in the media preoptic hypothalamic area (Konner, 1982:318). Testosterone, on the other hand, lowers the firing threshold of the amygdala, the area of the brain most associated with violence and aggression (Konner, 1982:117). The male preoptic area responds to testosterone but not to estradiol, and the female preoptic area does not respond to testosterone (McEwen, 1981:1307).

Administering testosterone to animals of either sex increases fighting, while administering estradiol reduces it. It has been shown that castrated males (removing the gonadal source of testosterone production) become less aggressive, and that administering estrogen (neutralizing the effects of testosterone) is fairly successful in treating aggressive sex criminals (Khan and Cataio, 1984:105). There is an abundant literature indicating that estradiol increases nurturing behavior—the antithesis of violence—and that testosterone diminishes nurturing behavior, even among females (Terkell and Rosenblatt, 1972; Zarrow, Denenberg, and Sachs, 1972; Konner, 1982). Females taking progestogen-dominant contraception pills report strong feelings of nurturance and affiliation and feel irritable and hostile when progesterone levels are low (Asso, 1983:64). If we want to understand violent behavior in terms of male/female differences we must come to grips with the accumulating evidence that "sex differences in masculine and feminine behaviors appear to be dependent upon differences in neural organization laid down during early development" (Ader, 1983:260).

## Premenstrual Tension Syndrome and Female Violence

Desmond Ellis and Penelope Austin conclude their study of female aggression in a correctional center by writing: "In the case of the woman who kills her husband, lover, child . . . this study suggests that it is important to ask: What was her menstrual condition at the time of the event?" (1971:395). The emotional ups and downs experienced by women at various points of their menstrual cycle has received a lot of research attention over the years. For instance, Cooke (1945) found that 84 percent of all reported violent crimes committed by women were committed during what is known as the paramenstruum period (four days prior to onset and four days into the menstrual period). Over a number of similar studies, it is estimated that 62 percent of violent crimes committed by women are committed during this period (Taylor, 1984). If the females' monthly hormonal cycle had nothing to do with acts of violence, we would expect such acts to be evenly distributed throughout the cycle rather than highly concentrated at this one eight-day period.

These studies have been criticized on methodological and interpretive grounds. A study designed to accommodate such criticisms was conducted by d'Orban and Dalton (1980). Using a refined methodology, they did find a smaller percentage of violent crimes committed by women during the paramenstruum. However, the percentage (44%) was still significantly in excess of the expected rate of 29 percent ($\chi^2 = 5.8$, p < .02). They were also able to dismiss the various social learning alternative explanations posited by various critics. Nevertheless, they do not propose that hormonal changes "cause" violence among women unalloyed by experience.

They argue that the paramenstruum acts as a triggering factor probably only for "a group of women who are also prone to unstable and aggressive behaviour at other times" (1980:358).

Although the great majority of women manage to deal with the mild mood swings associated with the monthly cycle, a small number experience deep mood changes that they have difficulty dealing with. Such women are said to suffer from premenstrual tension syndrome (PMS). Although there are a number of theories about the causes of PMS, the most usual is the progesterone deficiency theory. Hormonal assays of progesterone do appear to consistently indicate that women with PMS have lower levels than non-PMS women, and the administration of progesterone alleviates the symptoms of PMS for most women (Trunnell, Turner, and Keye, 1988).

During the paramenstruum period progesterone levels drop almost to zero, estradiol levels drop to 50 percent of mid-cycle baseline measures, and testosterone remains relatively high at 82 percent of baseline (Utain, 1980:32). Norepinephrine levels are also probably higher during this period (Asso, 1983:142). Recalling the putative "feeling" effects of these substances, we might speculate with Wilson (1981:36) that the male-like violence sometimes expressed by women who suffer extreme PMS is a function of these women being chemically more "male-like" at this time. Possible support for this view is the review of the literature on the physiological fluctuations accompanying the menstrual cycle by Barfield (1976:71–73). Some of these studies report premenstrual increases in metabolic rate and visual-spatial sensitivity, and decreases in sensitivity to touch, sound, and smell. The characteristics that increase are those in which males normally excel, and those that decrease are areas in which females normally excel.

The regulation of the menstrual cycle involves complex interactions between neurotransmitters, pituitary gonadotropins, and the ovarian steriods. Since all women experience some degree of mood change over the cycle, it has been suggested that those who suffer extreme symptomology be considered to be suffering from "premenstrual dysphoric disorder" rather than the more common PMS (Haskett, 1987). Haskett cautions that the state of our knowledge about the pathophysiology of this disorder is poorly known. We can therefore do little more than speculate about the mechanisms relating this disorder to female violence at present.

### Environmental Influences on Hormonal Secretion

Let us not fall into the radical reductionist trap of implying that testosterone "causes" violence and aggression unalloyed by social experience. In a review of 18 studies using various kinds of samples and various definitions of aggression, Rubin (1987) found only one study in which testosterone level was related to aggression as "strongly positive." Five studies showed a "weakly positive" relationship, six showed a "moderately positive," and six showed no relationship. It would seem that testosterone only activates aggression when the amount of circulating testosterone is radically altered. According to Rubin, Reinisch, and Haskett (1981:1320): "There is a demonstrated activation effect of androgens on certain aggressive behaviors in men, but only when the amount of circulating androgen is altered to a great extent." Usually, but not always, this alteration of circulating androgen levels is brought about by environmental experiences.[3]

Rose, Holaday, and Bernstein (1971) have dramatically demonstrated the responsiveness of testosterone levels to environmental experience. They took a number of male rhesus monkeys and placed them individually into colonies consisting of thirteen or more female monkeys. In every instance, the lone male assumed dominance and settled into a blissful existence which included frequent copulation with all females. After several weeks of simian heaven, testosterone assays were taken of the male monkeys. It was found that, compared to baseline levels, each male's level of circulating testosterone showed an approximate fourfold increase.

The researchers then removed each of their experimental monkeys from the all-female colonies and placed them individually into different colonies of all-male monkeys. Dominance hierarchies in these all-male colonies were already established. The intruder monkeys were immediately set upon by the other monkeys and utterly subjugated. After thirty minutes of this treatment, each monkey was removed from its respective colony and their testosterone levels were again assayed. It was found that in every case, the testosterone that was so blissfully banked from their experience in the female colonies had declined precipitously after their experience in the male colonies.

The relationship between testosterone levels and dominance is not limited to non-human subjects. Ehrenkranz, Bliss, and Sheard (1974) found that socially dominant and aggressive prison inmates had significantly higher testosterone levels than did a control group of prisoners identified as non-aggressive and non-dominant. Schalling (1987) found among a group of Swedish delinquents that high testosterone levels were associated with various measures of aggression (physical, verbal, and preference for physical sports), as well as as extraversion. Correlations were particularly strong among youths who had obtained pubertal maturity, a period during which males experience a tenfold to twenty-fold increase in testosterone (Udry, 1990:3). The correlations for overall aggression, preference for physical sports, extraversion, and monotony avoidance were .56, .61, .48, and .50, respectively.

Researchers exploring the link between aggression and testosterone are careful to emphasize that the direction of causation is not clear. Experience may have a greater effect on testosterone production (and on the production of other hormones) than endogenous hormonal production has on behavior. It is probable that high testosterone levels function as an additional risk factor for individuals predisposed by social factors to be violent. Certainly, youths inhabiting Wilson's (1987) "truly disadvantaged" environments have many occasions to react violently. Successful violence may then lead to even higher levels of testosterone and to a greater risk of further violence. The synergistic nature of biological/environmental interaction is perhaps nowhere more evident than in the ups and downs of the gonadal steroid hormones.

We may conclude, as did one expert in the field of the chemistry of violence, that "overall there are fairly consistent data indicating that vertebrate male aggression is organized by the early influence of androgens [on the developing brain] and is triggered post pubertally by androgens" (Thiessen, 1976:75).

### Sex Differences in Visual-Spatial Ability

In Chapter three it was said that interpersonal violence can be viewed as a visual-spatial ability, and that violence can be suppressed by individuals possessing good verbal skills. Across a wide variety of studies and types of tests utilized, males have been shown to be superior to females in visual-spatial abilities, and females have been shown to be superior in males in verbal abilities (Wells, 1980; Durden-Smith and deSimone, 1983; Johnson and Meade, 1987; Maccoby, 1988). Reliable sex differences in visual-spatial ability shows up as early as seven years of age, increases at puberty (indicating gonadal hormonal influence), and continues throughout the life span (Linn and Petersen, 1986).[4] Likewise, females show a marked superiority to males in verbal abilities throughout the life span, and verbal disabilities such as stuttering and dyslexia are 4 to 10 times more likely to appear in males than in females (Sutaria, 1985; Skinner and Shelton, 1985; Witleson, 1986).

The dominant (usually left) hemisphere organization of the female brain is superior to that of the male, while the usually non-dominant right hemisphere organization of the male brain is superior to that of the female (Flor-Henry, 1978). The female brain is less specialized or "lateralized" than the male brain, a feature that has many positive implications for females.[5] Man's evolutionary history as a hunter and fighter endowed him with greater muscular and bone strength than that of women, a metabolism and vascular system more geared to an active life-style, and a brain attuned to the visual-spatial aspects of his environment (Geary, 1989). Females were more diverse in the tasks they had to perform in the hunting and gathering societies that have characterized the life of the species for 99.9 percent of its history. Females were thus subjected to a different and less specialized selection process that was perhaps responsible for their lesser degree of brain laterality (Mellen, 1982). Woman's role as nurturer, caregiver, comforter, and peacekeeper exerted pressure for the selection of social skills such as language and greater emotional sensitivity.

Various theorists have commented on how the lesser laterality of the female brain influences the female experience of the emotional life in ways considered more psychologically healthy than it is experienced by males. Psychoneuroendocrinologist Paul Pearsall believes that the more left-brain male tends to be more "self-oriented," while the more integrated female brain tends to be more "other" and "us-oriented." He goes on to write that the "whole brain" orientation is "more in tune with the principles of healthy living in our world and for our world" (1987:33).

Pearsall's biological insight is augmented from the sociological point of view by Jane Miller. Miller (1984:1) sees male development of self as entailing a process of separating, of becoming "one's own man," and the female process as more "encompassing." She also sees the female process as "closer to the elementary necessities from which our dominant culture has become unnecessarily removed" (1984:5). So, whether we arrive from a biological or a sociological position, we arrive at the same conclusion: females in general are more affiliative, nurturing, empathetic, and altruistic, and are therefore less prone to violence.

There are some indications that the magnitude of sex-related differences in cognitive abilities may be becoming less pronounced (Feingold, 1988). Although there is little doubt that biological differences direct the focus of male and female activities in different directions (baseball versus needlework, math versus French, and so forth), culture does exaggerate these differences. To the extent that each sex is encouraged socially to partake in the favored activities of the other, we should expect some divergence of the cognitive abilities associated with such activities. Critical reviews of Feingold's work (Geary, 1989; Halpern, 1989), while agreeing that there should be some closing of the gap separating male and female cognitive abilities with greater similarity of experience, also agree that significant difference between the sexes will remain. Significant differences in violent criminal behavior between the sexes will also remain with us.

### Hormones and Brain Hemisphericity

It was indicated in Chapter four that exaggerated right-hemisphere functioning is associated with psychopathy and the P > V profile (Flor-Henry, 1978). There is a possible sex hormone explanation for why exaggerated right-hemisphere functioning only appears to translate into violent behavior among males. It has been found in many monoamine oxidase (MAO) assays that males have, on average, about 20 percent less MAO than females at all ages (Zuckerman, Buchsbaum, and Murphy, 1980). MAO is an enzyme that removes neurotransmitters by oxidation after they have performed their excitatory task, thereby exerting a dampening and regulatory effect on behavior governed by some of the major neurotransmitters such as norepinephrine, dopamine, and serotonin.

Lower levels of MAO among males may well account for a great deal of the difference between the sexes in schizophrenia, psychopathy, crime rates, and in sensation-seeking behavior in general. A study by Coursey, Buchsbaum, and Murphy (1979) among 375 college students of both sexes showed that low MAO subjects had more psychiatric contacts and used more drugs and alcohol than high MAO subjects. Low MAO males reported more attempted suicides and had more criminal convictions than high MAO males. The negative relationship between MAO concentrates (low) and all kinds of sensation-seeking behavior (high) is one of the most well-established findings in psychophysiology (Zuckerman, Buchsbaum, and Murphy, 1980). Even in male-only studies, the sensation-seeking psychopath has been shown to have lower MAO than non-psychopaths (Lidberg et al., 1985), and low MAO activity has been shown to significantly differentiate violent and non-violent criminals (Davis et al., 1983).

How does this translate into an increased propensity among males to engage in violent criminal behavior? All behavior is at bottom a function of neurotransmitter activity responding to environmental cues. Among males, the experiencing of stressful events has the effect of increasing norepinephrine (the "action hormone") secretion and increasing right hemisphere (the "action hemisphere") brain activity. The opposite effect is usually seen in females, for whom stressful events tend to lead to a decrease in norepinephrine secretion and a decrease in right hemisphere activity. For females, stressful events tend to be experienced in the left hemisphere, leaving them more prone to depression as they verbally mull over the event (Durden-Smith and deSimone, 1983:155). Low MAO among males would have the effect of allowing for the prolonged activity of the increased norepinephrine secreted during periods of stress, and hence an increased probability of violence.

Testosterone itself has the effect of increasing the intensity of stress resulting in greater secretion of norepinephrine (Bardwick, 1976), and certainly the behavioral and personality characteristics of high testosterone males are very similar to those of low MAO males (Schalling, Edman, and Asberg, 1983). Further, it appears that there is an inverse relationship between androgen levels and MAO activity (Bardwick, 1976; Asso, 1983). MAO concentrations increase with age, and testosterone levels decrease with age (Mawson and Mawson, 1977). Increasing age is also accompanied by a very large decrease in the male propensity to engage in violent and other antisocial behaviors, as well as a withdrawal from sensation-seeking behavior in general. National arrest data show that per capita arrest rates for males fall precipitously after about age 30, with 15- to 19 year-olds being arrested about 16 times more often than fifty- to fifty-four-year-olds (Wilson and Herrnstein, 1985:128–129). Declining testosterone levels perhaps allow for increased MAO activity (or vice versa) and correspondingly better-behaved individuals.

In concert with this line of thinking is a study conducted by Rushton and his colleagues (1986) on the heritability of aggression and altruism among 573 adult twin pairs. They found that the heritability coefficients for both characteristics to be about .5. More importantly for our purposes, they found strong age and sex differences on both variables, with females and older people being significantly more altruistic, and males and younger people being significantly more aggressive. In terms of our previous discussion on the hormonal basis for aggression, nurturance, empathy, and altruism, the conclusion offered by Rushton et al. (1986:1197) is enlightening: "[L]arger amounts of a gonadal hormone such as testosterone predisposes toward aggressiveness, which in turn decreases empathy. This would explain the negative relationship between aggression and altruism, as well as the age and sex differences, for testosterone production is known to decrease with age and to differentiate the sexes in the predicted direction."

In common with the Rowe and Osgood (1984) study of genetics and differential association discussed in Chapter 4, this study also found negligible non-genetic variance in either aggression or altruism to be associated with common shared environment. Most of the non-genetic variance was attributed to each twin's specific environment (1986:1196).

In females, regardless of any exaggerated right-hemisphere dysfunction, the differential activity of norepinephrine should help to preclude a violent reaction to stress. Recall that women are more likely to exhibit violent reactions to stress during the paramenstruum period if they suffer from extreme PMS. Perhaps stress induces the male pattern of norepinephrine (levels of which appear to be higher during paramenstruum) and all that it implies during this period. Supportive of this view is a British study that found that women over 30 are responsible for nearly half of all crimes committed by women, but males over 30 are responsible for less than one-fourth of male crimes (Taylor, 1984:89). Although women at all ages commit far less crimes than men at all ages, these figures perhaps reflect the changes in the balance of the sex hormones in men and women with advancing age as the gonadal hormones tend toward equilibrium.

The conjectured process of ANS adjustment in response to parental rejection discussed in Chapter 4 might provide us with clues about how early childhood stresses tie in with the noted left-hemisphere dysfunction and exaggerated right-hemisphere functioning. With regard to brain laterality and environmental experience, there is a fair amount of evidence that early experience (handling and stroking) positively influences hemispheric integration, at least in animals (Denenberg, 1984). Parental rejection, by definition, means less tactile stimulation, interaction, and communication between parents and child, leading to deficits in left hemisphere development that are reflected in the child's poor verbal abilities. Conversely, efforts to avoid punishment may favor the development of the visual-spatial skills of the right hemisphere. As was hypothesized in Chapter 4, if children are to avoid as much punishment as possible, they have to become sensitive to environmental cues that punishment is imminent. They may develop exceptional visual-spatial skills and the ability to associate these cues with verbal cues. The constant association of verbal and visual cues as threatening may explain the abused child's tendency to respond to some forms of verbal stimuli in a violent way as he or she grows older.

If this speculation has any merit, it would apply more to boys than girls because of the greater hemispheric specialization of males. Females are better protected from exaggerated right hemisphere functioning by less strict brain lateralization, perhaps due to the larger female splenium of the corpus callosum.[6] Since, in addition to possessing significantly smaller spleniums, males are also generally less secure in the left hemisphere than females, it may be that a similar lack of communication experience will affect males more adversely. Boys do seem to suffer the trials of an abusive environment less well than girls. Perhaps this is because they are more "modifiable,"[7] or because girls have more positive ways of dealing with stress, such as a more open display of emotion.[8]

### The Family Background of Female Delinquents

Since female criminality and delinquency is comparatively rare, it would seem to follow that females who become delinquent are more atypical of their sex than delinquent boys are atypical of their sex. The reasoning is that since females generally tend to be more conforming in their behavior than males, the delinquency threshold is much higher for females than for males. That is, it takes a greater level of criminogenic conditions to propel females over the line dividing deviance from non-deviance.

Although there is a relative dearth of studies of specifically female delinquency, what studies there are tend to support the contention that female delinquents come from more dysfunctional families than their male counterparts (Reige, 1982; Rosenbaum, 1989). The Reige (1972) study found that female delinquents are more sensitive to and more engaged in intrafamily conflicts than were their non-delinquent siblings. Another study found that: "There was more mother-adolescent conflict/hostility and a trend for more parental conflict/hostility in families of female delinquents than in the families of male delinquents" (Henggeler, Edwards, and Borduin, 1987:206). Summing up her study of 240 girls committed to the California Youth Authority, Rosenbaum (1989:38) states:

"Not only did these girls suffer from their parents' broken marriages and multiple relationships, alcoholism, and mental illness, but they typically lacked the nurturing youth require." In a study of male and female sociopaths, Cloninger, Reich, and Guze (1975:20) state that there existed "many kinds of more frequent disruptive home experiences in female sociopaths compared to male sociopaths." It has also been found that females are less sensitive than males to criminogenic factors in the environment that are located outside the family (Wolkind and Rutter, 1973; Cadoret, 1982).

Our data support the proposition that female delinquents come from more dysfunctional homes than delinquent boys. Females were 4.34 times more likely to come from broken homes than were boys ($X^2$ = 19.5). The greater tendency of female delinquents to come from broken homes has previously been noted (Datesman and Scarpitti, 1975). Females were also 3.24 times more likely than boys to be born out of wedlock ($X^2$ = 21.1), and their SES mean is significantly lower (t = 2.35, p < .02). Female delinquents in the present sample had a love deprivation mean significantly greater than males (means 31.6 and 20.9, respectively, t = −6.52). These findings are consistent with the findings of Kovar (cited in Kratcoski and Kratcoski, 1979:149) who "demonstrated that delinquent girls she worked with tended to have come from homes in which there was little love for the girl, to have been abandoned or misused by their families, and to have in their family history patterns of neglect and deprivation."

Despite the greater disabilities suffered by the girls in the sample, only 16 (21.6%) committed a violent offense, whereas 58.3 percent of the boys had. These 16 girls had a violence mean of 82.1 but were less violent than the boys who had committed at least one violent offense ($\overline{X}$ = 104.05). Only 9 (12.2%) of the girls committed two or more violent offenses compared to 35.4 percent of the boys. The violent and non-violent girls had practically identical love deprivation means. The lack of association between love deprivation and violence among females was also found by Widom (1989:265), who comments: "Although abused and neglected subjects overall had substantially higher rates of arrests for violent offenders [sic], thus supporting the cycle of violence hypothesis, this was due primarily to the males in the abused and neglected group. This difference was not evident among the females."

It is interesting to note how the 74 girls compare with boys regarding the number who are intellectually imbalanced and how this balance relates to delinquency. Of the 74 girls, 45 (60.8%) were P = V, and 29 (39.2%) were P > V imbalanced. None of the girls showed the V > P imbalanced profile, further emphasizing the atypicality of female delinquents. The goodness-of-fit test comparing these girls with the expected frequency in each profile according to Kaufman's (1976) normative sample of girls was highly significant ($X^2 = 26.2$). Since the P > V profile is also overrepresented among female delinquents, with the V > P profile being completely absent, we have further evidence that P > V is a marker of antisocial behavior, and V > P is a marker of conforming behavior. Male and female delinquents did not differ significantly on FIQ, VIQ, PIQ or verbal/performance discrepancy scores.

Delinquent boys had a violence mean more than three times greater than that of the delinquent girls (62.1 versus 19.6, t = 7.78, p < 0001). Within the female subsample, the violence means for the P = V and P > V were practically identical (t = 1.09). While our data support the assertion that V > P is a marker of good behavior, and that P > V is a marker of delinquent behavior among girls as well as boys, it appears that intellectual imbalance does not significantly affect the seriousness of violent delinquency among girls who are already delinquent.

Comparing girls who committed a violent offense with the non-violent girls, it was found that P > V discrepancy scores were significantly different for the violent ($\overline{X} = 13.94$) and non-violent girls ($\overline{X} = 7.26$), t = 2.31, p < .01. Unlike the boys, among whom elevated PIQ most strongly contributed to P > V, among the girls low VIQ rather than elevated PIQ is responsible for the discrepancy. This is exactly what one would expect from Flor-Henry's (1978) brain hemisphericity theory of violence. Violent boys have high scores on tests that tap abilities lateralized to the hemisphere where they are most dominant relative to scores lateralized to the hemisphere where they are least dominant. Violent girls have low scores on tests that tap abilities lateralized to the hemisphere where they are most secure relative to scores lateralized to the right hemisphere. The violent girls have a mean VIQ of 79.29, and the non-violent girls have a mean of 94.81 (t = 4.13, p < .001). PIQ means (violent = 96.41, non-violent = 101.61) were not significantly different. The only other notable differentiation between the two groups is that all the violent girls had histories of drug abuse. However, 61.4 percent of the non-violent girls also had such histories.

Table 7.1 assesses the effect of sex on violent delinquency controlling for the effects of other variables in the model.

TABLE 7.1

Subject's Sex and Other Variables Regressed on Violent Delinquency

| Variables | b | s.e. | $\beta$ | t | sig. |
|---|---|---|---|---|---|
| Love Deprivation | 1.70 | .19 | .337 | 8.76 | .0000 |
| Sex (male/female) | -52.96 | 7.87 | -.255 | -6.73 | .0000 |
| Large Family/middle born | 41.39 | 6.40 | .281 | 6.47 | .0000 |
| Substance Abuse | 13.17 | 3.43 | .140 | 3.83 | .0001 |
| Race (white/black) | 25.78 | 7.42 | .132 | 3.48 | .0005 |
| Only Child | 37.04 | 11.52 | .122 | 3.22 | .0014 |
| Small family/middle born | 24.37 | 8.20 | .119 | 2.97 | .0031 |
| P > V Discrepancy | .52 | .20 | .100 | 2.59 | .0099 |
| Large family/first born | 34.88 | 13.20 | .100 | 2.64 | .0084 |
| Small family/last born | 18.09 | 8.07 | .089 | 2.24 | .0255 |
| (Constant) | -27.19 | 8.00 | | -3.40 | .0007 |

Adj. R Squared = .291,    F = 21.45,    P = .00000

NOTE:   The Constant = large family/last born.    Small family/middle
born and SES did not enter the equation.

The sex difference in violent delinquency increases when the effects of all other variables are included in the model. Before the inclusion of the other predictors the male/female difference was 42.5, with the predictors included the difference becomes 52.96. This underscores the fact that females in the sample suffered greater levels of the criminogenic disabilities included in the model.

## Conclusion

The evidence is unequivocal: males are far more violent than females. This is a general statement of difference, for there are some females who are more violent than the "average" male. With changes in the social system we will see a convergence of male and female rates, but a significant gap will remain. The effects of culture on sex-based violence was made obvious in Wolfgang's (1958) study of homicide in Philadelphia. Wolfgang (1958:55) found that although black males had a homicide rate four times that of black females, black females had a homicide rate three times that of white males. This study highlights the biology of within-group sex differences (in both black and white communities males had a higher homicide rate) and the sociology of between-group differences (black females were more homicidal than white males).

Biological differences between the sexes have been emphasized to explain the difference in violent delinquency. But it should also be emphasized that the sexes are a lot more alike than they are different. There is enormous overlap between the sexes in any distribution of attributes such as empathy, altruism, visual-spatial ability, and even sometimes in patterns of hormonal secretion. Sex differences must be viewed in terms of group or mean differences only, and not necessarily applicable to any given individual. Even the sex difference that is perhaps most pronounced (i.e., upper-body strength), some females engaged in extensive weight training are able to exceed untrained male means on various tests of upper-body strength. Sex differences along many other dimensions should also be minimized, but not eliminated, as patterns of experience become less sex-segregated.

However, our evolutionary history has produced males and females that differ behaviorally along sexually dimorphic lines. Nowhere is this more obvious than in the greater readiness of males to engage in aggressive and violent behavior, and the greater readiness of females to engage in nurturing behavior. Culture certainly directs the extent to which these behaviors are engaged in and their methods of expression, but differentiated male and female brains and hormonal secretion patterns assure that the two sexes are differentially sensitized to environmental cues eliciting such behavior. Culture does not go to work on a biological tabula rasa, but the sex-differentiated biological baggage we bring with us into this world does not necessarily mean that we are unequivocally "what we secrete."

## ENDNOTES

1. The modifier "sex" in "sex hormones" loses its descriptive power after the reproductive phase of the human life span is over. These steroid hormones actually represent different stages of biosynthesis rather than being strictly distinct substances. Using cholesterol as their major precursor, the testes and the ovaries, as well as the adrenal cortex, convert it into the steroid hormones. Both the testes and the ovaries secrete male and female hormones, sex differentiation being a function of the secretion patterns, and the amount and availability of these hormones at various stages of sexual development (Khan and Cataio, 1984:15).

2. The term "androgenization" may be something of a misnomer. The complicated

nature of neuroandrogenic processes is emphasized by findings that indicated that it is the "female" hormone estradiol that masculinizes XY brain tissue. Testosterone is converted to estradiol in the brain via the enzyme aromatase. Thus, while estradiol has a masculinizing effect on the brain, at least during the period of neuronal sex differentiation, it has feminizing effects outside the brain (Waber, 1977; Ellis, 1986).

3. The biophysiological activity of sex hormones depends on their free availability. Only those hormones (about 10%) not bound to sex hormone binding globulin (SHBG) are available for activity. By the end of puberty, males have only about half their former level of SHBG, resulting in more free gonadal hormones. Thus, although men have about 15 times the concentration of total testosterone that women have, they have about 30 times more free (process-activating) testosterone (Khan and Cataio, 1984; Udry, 1990).

4. The evidence for hormonal influences on cognitive abilities comes mainly from studies of individuals with sex chromosome abnormalities. Turner's syndrome (XO chromosomes) females have low androgen levels and are deficient in visual-spatial skills. One study (Sherman, 1975) found XO females, who are extremely nurturing, to have a mean VIQ of 106 and a mean PIQ of 86. XYY males (relatively high androgen levels) show a superiority in PIQ ($\overline{X}$ = 88) over VIQ ($\overline{X}$ = 79), although both scores are significantly below population norms.

5. Although males and females differ in visual-spatial ability, these differences do not show up on the PIQ subtest of the WISC–R as presently constructed. When initially constructing his scales, Weschler found that there was a great deal of interaction across the sexes with regard to verbal and performance IQ, with females showing marked VIQ superiority and males showing marked PIQ superiority. In the process of standardizing the tests, Wechsler pruned the items most responsible for the sex-based differences (Wells, 1980:115). By doing so he eliminated the interaction and provided us with a sex-neutral measure of general IQ. He did so, however, at the cost of leaving us without a commonly administered scale that would discriminate more strongly between verbal and visual-spatial abilities. Needless to say, such a scale would improve the P > V measure.

Wechsler's "test pruning" to eliminate sex differences moves some to ask why the same could not be done to eliminate race and SES differences. Gordon and Rudert (1979) address this issue by pointing out that the great bulk of the items in the original WISC scale showed no sex differences, and that those that did produced a definable interaction effect. This interaction effect is not found, as we have already pointed out, in race and SES comparisons. Gordon and Rudert go on to say that if we were to prune the items that discriminated between and among racial and SES groupings, "all of the items would have to go" (1979:179).

6. The splenium, the posterior portion of the corpus callosum, has been found to be significantly larger in females than in males (de Lacoste-Utamsing and Holloway, 1982). While cautious in their interpretation of this finding, the implication is that the more fibers contained in the splenium, the greater is the capacity for inter-hemispheric information transfer and thus less brain

laterality. Any brain injury that may be the result of abuse is less likely to be permanently disruptive of brain processes because any information associated with the specific injured area can be transferred to the other hemisphere. It is consistently found that female stroke victims, for instance, recover more readily from its ravages than do male victims (Witelson, 1976).

7. There is an abundant literature indicating that males are more "modifiable" then females, i.e., greater variability around the male mean on a given attribute than there is around the female mean. Males lack the "stability" provided by a second X chromosome and are therefore more susceptible to the effects of the appearance of genetic recessive characteristics that may be either advantageous or disadvantageous (Wilson, 1981).

8. Some interesting observations relating to the greater propensity of women to openly express their emotions have been made by Fry and Langeth (1985). It appears that crying offers not only psychological relief but also has positive somatic consequences. An analysis of tears reveals that they contain by-products of stress-related chemicals. By crying we rid ourselves of these damaging chemicals and more quickly restore our bodies to chemical balance. Crying also tends to decrease testosterone levels in both males and females when levels of this hormone are high. The implication of this is that crying may have the consequence not only of helping to prevent stress-related diseases such as ulcers, hypertension, and other cardiovascular problems but also of reducing aggressive responses to stress.

## Chapter Eight

# STRUCTURAL AND STATUS INFLUENCES ON VIOLENT DELINQUENCY

*Birth Order, Family Size, and Violent Delinquency*

There is a plethora of studies in psychology attesting to the influence of birth order (the sequential birth position of a child among his or or siblings) on personality, achievement, and intelligence. Firstborns, on average, have consistently been shown to have higher IQ's than later-born siblings (Scarr and Weinberg, 1978). Perhaps as a consequence of greater IQ, firstborns are highly overrepresented among scholars and professors, U.S. Presidents, astronauts, *Who's Who* members, and many other markers of achievement and eminence (Mednick, Higgins, and Kirschenbaum, 1975). In terms of personality, firstborns tend to be more affectionate, responsible, and conforming, while middle-borns tend to be more outgoing and show a greater need to affiliate (McNeil and Rubin, 1977).

Despite the excitement that birth-order research generates among personality theorists, it is a much neglected variable in sociological criminology. Yablonki and Haskell (1988:143) express their surprise at this neglect, and assure us that "the ordinal position that a child occupies in a family has a great affect on the eventual personality and the possibility of being delinquent." Across a wide range of studies and settings, it seems that being middle-born (born in any sequential position other than first or last) puts a child at greatest statistical risk for delinquency, and that being firstborn renders a child least likely to become delinquent.

The Cambridge-Somerhill study found that middle-born children were particularly prone to becoming delinquent; of the 121 middle-born children, 47 percent had a juvenile record. Eldest children were the next most delinquency-prone, with 34 percent acquiring a record. By way of contrast, 27 percent of the firstborn children acquired a record (McCord and McCord, 1958:118). The effects of birth order are not as straightforward as this simple enumeration of percentages would imply. The effects vary with such factors as sex, birth spacing, same sex/opposite sex, SES, and family size (Kreppner, 1988). Family size appears to be the most important variable mediating the effects of birth order (Murrell, 1974).

For instance, Murrell's study of 72 youthful offenders found that firstborns (especially those from small families) score highest on the Gough socialization scale and had higher self-esteem than middle- or last-born children. In this study, last-borns rather than middle-borns were the least socially adaptive, but last-borns were also significantly more likely to come from broken homes than were boys in the other two ordinal positions. In Rahav's (1980) much larger study of Israeli children it was found that middle-born children were more likely to become delinquent than first and last-borns, but this was particularly so in large families. Regardless of family size, Rahav found that middle-born boys were more likely to become delinquent than first or last-borns, but the relationship was more pronounced as family size became larger.

In Werner and Smith's (1982) study of a birth cohort of Hawaiian children it was also found that being firstborn and having three or fewer siblings (along with high IQ and having an affectual bond with mother) was predictive of non-delinquency. Guided by findings reported above, I divided the male sample into categories based on birth order and family size. Consistent with Werner and Smith (1982) and Murrell (1974), a family of four or fewer children was considered small, and a family with five or more children was considered large. Only-children were considered separately. The groupings are given in Table 8.1.

From Table 8.1 we can see that there is considerable interaction between family size and birth order. Firstborn children from small families were the least violent of all groupings. Firstborn children from large families were the most violent, but they differed significantly only from first-borns from small families. Family size does appear to have a significant effect on violent delinquency for firstborns. The small number of first-borns from large families, however, does not make the finding compelling. Firstborns from small families also had the lowest mean P > V score.

As expected from the results of previous research, middle-born children from large families were statistically significantly more violent than the small/first, large/last, and small/last-born boys. This same group of boys also showed the highest P > V scores of all other groups. These findings support those of Rahav (1980): middle-born boys are more seriously involved in delinquency, and the relationship is more pronounced for large families. No significant differences among the groups were found on love deprivation. No significant mean violence differ-

TABLE   8.1

Violence, P > V and SES Means by Family Size/Birth-Order Group

| Family Size/ Birth-Order | | N | Violence | P > V | SES |
|---|---|---|---|---|---|
| Small/first | (a) | 106 | 35.04fg | 1.47cf | 27.87e |
| Large/Last | (b) | 53 | 40.73f | 6.73 | 23.55c |
| Small/last | (c) | 70 | 52.36f | 8.68a | 31.53be |
| Small/second | (d) | 57 | 55.39 | 8.52 | 26.78d |
| Only Child | (e) | 24 | 71.25 | 3.83 | 15.59acdf |
| Large/Second | (f) | 186 | 86.76abc | 10.10a | 25.91 |
| Large/First | (g) | 18 | 89.72a | 5.22 | 26.12 |
| Total | | | 62.37 | 7.12 | 26.51 |
| F ratio | | | 8.61 | 5.55 | 6.42 |
| Eta | | | .30 | .25 | .28 |

abc = means that differ significantly at < .05, Scheffe test

ences were found among the female delinquents based on these birth order/family size groupings. Wilkinson, Stitt, and Erickson (1982) also found that middle-borns had the highest rate of delinquency, last-borns the next highest, and firstborns the lowest in their study of three-child families. The relatively high mean violence score for only-children may best be interpreted in light of their low SES score (these boys tended to be the children of single mothers).

Dividing the boys into gross categorizations consisting of middle-born (N = 239) and "other" (N = 274), and disregarding family size, it was found that the middle-born boys were significantly more violent (means = 79.28 and 47.12, respectively, t = 5.27, p < .0001). Middle-born boys were also significantly higher on P > V (means = 9.73 and 4.95, t = 4.12, p < .001). No significant differences were found on VIQ, PIQ, love deprivation, or SES.

Examining family size and disregarding birth order, boys from large families (N = 253) were found to be significantly more violent than boys from small families (N = 258). The respective means were 77.28 and 47.65 (t = 4.48, p < .001). Boys from large families also differed significantly on P > V (means = 9.05 and 5.23, t = 3.25, p < .001). They did not differ on love deprivation, VIQ, PIQ, or SES.

There is an insufficient number of females in the present study to perform the same set of analyses with them as I did with the boys. A series of t-tests were performed using the female sample dichotomized into groups consisting of middle-borns (N = 27) and "others" (N = 47). The middle-born girls had a significantly lower FIQ mean (85.03) than the rest of the female sample (101.13). Apart from this substantial FIQ difference, there were no other statistically significant findings.

Behavioral differences among children of different birth orders are easier to find than to explain. Why are firstborns least likely to become delinquent and, when they do, to be less seriously involved in it? Conversely, why are middle-born children more likely to become delinquent and, when they do, to be more seriously involved in it? Birth order per se explains nothing. Biologically, it is known that the intrauterine environment varies with the number of previous pregnancies and with mother's age, that infant health tends to vary inversely with mother's age, and that fetal stress is less likely during the first than during subsequent pregnancies (Kagan, Reznick, and Snidman, 1987). However, these differences are not great and may only be of any importance at all when differences in the age of the mother at the birth of her children are extreme.

Differences in the family environment experienced by children of different birth orders provide better explanations. For some period in their lives, firstborns are free of sibling competition for their parent's attention and have only adult role models. When other children arrive on the scene, the first child is often expected to perform quasi-parental roles, roles that often generate feelings of responsibility, superiority, self-worth, and identification with parents (Kammeyer, 1968). Experimental evidence supports the notion that firstborns are more parental and adult oriented and more dependent on parents and adults for approval and affection (Mednick, Higgins, and Kirschenbaum, 1975:419). It is apparently this sense of self-worth, responsibility, and adult orientation that serves as a prophylactic against delinquency for many firstborns (Warren, 1969).

Kreppner (1988:157) has indicated that the birth of the first child has a tremendous impact on a couple's life and status not matched by the birth of subsequent children. Given the emotional importance of the birth of the first child, it is no surprise that parents tend to lavish more attention on it than they do on subsequent children. Kreppner's (1988:160) review of this phenomenon concluded:

> Jacob and Moss' (1976) investigation unveiled that mothers spent significantly less time in social, affectionate, and caretaking interactions with their second borns compared to the time spent with the first child. This replicated earlier results by Robarth (1971) and Thoman et al. (1972) indicating that primiparous mothers provided more stimulation to their newborn infants than multiparous mothers.

Based on a number of research reports, Yablonsky and Haskell (1988:144) remark that "middle-born children seem to have the greatest need for attention and affection and are the very ones who are less apt to get it." The relative lack of affection and attention received within the family constellation generates a search for affection and attention among the peer group. Other studies have found that second-born boys tend to display more aggression and, by way of contrast with firstborns, more peer than adult orientation, variables known to be associated with delinquency (Sutton-Smith and Rosenberg, 1970). Middle-born children can be expected to be less apt to abide by the values and standards of their parents and to be more apt to abide by those provided by their peers, which are less likely to be acceptable in terms of middle-class standards of behavior.

Last-born children occupy an intermediate position in terms of becoming delinquent and, if they do, being less seriously involved in it. It has been speculated that the social learning experiences of later- and last-borns mirror those of firstborns in many respects (Kammeyer, 1969:209–210). Although parents have less time and energy to devote to later-borns than they did to firstborns, this is compensated somewhat by the greater solicitude of the older children toward the youngest child. Firstborn children are less apt to view last-borns as competitors for parental affection and will tend to assume more of a positive caretaking role with them. Additionally, parents will have become more experienced in their parental roles and will have perhaps become more emotionally and financially secure by the time their last children are born.

It appears, then, that middle-born children are literally "caught in the middle." They have the same need for love and attention as all children, but are less likely to get as much as they need from parents as firstborns and less likely than last-borns to get it from their older sibling. Being caught in this situation, the literature indicates that they tend to have lower feelings of self-worth and that they tend to turn away from adult values and become more peer oriented. Thus, an exploration of the birth-order literature points once again to the importance of love during childhood to the development of a healthy prosocial personality.

### Broken Homes and Delinquency

Few purported causes of delinquency have been studied more than broken homes. Despite all this research activity, there is little consensus in the literature as to its influence on delinquency rates. Some recent studies find small or no apparent effect of family structure on delinquency (Rosen and Neilson, 1982; Johnson, 1986), while others find some support for its affect (Gove and Crutchfield, 1982; Rankin, 1983). There is no doubt, however, that a disproportionate number of jail and prison inmates (about 48%) grew up primarily in broken homes compared with about 25 percent of the general population (U.S. Department of Justice, 1988:48). As more and more homes depart from the traditional two-parent nuclear family (less than 10% in 1960 to approximately 25% in the early 1980s [Bureau of Census, 1984]), the issue takes on more importance.

It would seem that the primary reason for the noted inconsistency of findings is the inconsistency of methodologies and definitions. We see more juveniles from broken homes than from intact homes in juvenile institutions (Rosen and Neilson, 1982), but this can be partially attributed to the greater tendency of the authorities to retain jurisdiction over juveniles from broken homes and to release juveniles from intact homes to the care of their parents. This tendency only holds true for trivial or routine offenses, however (Wilson and Herrnstein, 1985:247). The problems of self-report data in relation to serious offenses noted in Chapter 5 could lead to a serious underestimation of the impact of family structure on such offenses.

We cannot assume that a broken home has a transactional effect; i.e., that this one stress increases the likelihood of the occurrence of others stresses productive of delinquency, although Sack, Mason, and Higgins (1985) found a rate of child abuse in single-parent homes to be almost twice as high as that found in two-parent homes. Recent studies have shown that family functioning (family "quality") is far more important than family structure in explaining delinquency (Cernkovich and Giordano, 1987; Van Vooris et al., 1988). Broken homes may have little or no effect on juveniles who are otherwise insulated, but could severely affect those juveniles already predisposed to delinquency. In this case, "broken homes would affect the incidence or the severity more than the prevalence of crime" (Wilson and Herrnstein, 1985:248).

Wells and Rankin (1986:81) have remarked that the usual broken/intact conceptualization of family structure is "so conceptually amorphous that they are only crudely meaningful, masking more variation than they reveal." How a home was broken may be more important that the simple fact that it is broken. A home broken by divorce reveals a certain amount of familial discord prior to the fracture, but possibly less than one broken by desertion. On the other hand, a home broken by death reveals nothing about prior family dynamics. West and Farrington (1973) found that boys from homes broken by divorce or desertion were more likely than boys from intact homes to become delinquent, but boys from homes broken by death were not. Among the already delinquent, we may also observe that boys from homes broken by divorce or desertion to be significantly more violent than boys from homes broken by death or from intact homes.

In light of the above, I decided to explore violent delinquency in four different family structures: intact homes and homes broken by death, divorce, and desertion. In Table 8.2, it is observed that boys from homes broken by desertion (in every case it was the father who deserted the home) are significantly more violent than boys from all three other family conditions, and that none of the other family conditions differed significantly among themselves. A simple "broken/intact" dichotomy revealed no significant difference on violent delinquency, thus supporting Wells and Rankin's (1986) assertion that such a conceptualization of family structure may mask more than it reveals.

How can we account for this large difference in violent delinquency between boys from homes broken by desertion and the rest? We see that the boys from homes broken by desertion also have the highest $P > V$ and love deprivation means and the lowest SES mean. However, when I adjusted for these effects, plus the effects of race, the boys from homes broken by desertion still had a significantly higher mean than all other categories (87.3 versus 66.74 for intact homes, 53.85 for divorced homes, and 31.84 for boys from homes broken by death).[1] Desertion, therefore, exerts an effect on violent delinquency independent of other measured variables. It can only be speculated that the family dynamics prior to desertion were particularly poor. It is reasonable to assume that there are important characterological differences between fathers who simply desert their families and those who go through the process of divorce. A

TABLE 8.2

Violence, P > V, Love Deprivation, and SES Means
by  Type of Family Structure

| Family Structure | | N | Violence | P > V | Love Dep. | SES |
|---|---|---|---|---|---|---|
| Divorced | (a) | 269 | 55.99c | 6.44bc | 21.57 | 26.86 |
| Death | (b) | 30 | 45.83c | 13.56ad | 21.87 | 21.20d |
| Desertion | (c) | 35 | 110.29abd | 19.94ad | 26.86d | 17.74ad |
| Intact | (d) | 179 | 64.59c | 4.75bc | 18.56c | 28.39c |
| Total | | 513 | | | | |
| | F ratio | | 6.92 | 16.29 | 6.42 | 11.05 |
| | eta | | .20 | .30 | .28 | .26 |

divorced father may continue to financially support his family and to visit his children. A father who deserts his family shows self-centeredness and a lack of responsibility, characteristics which probably had adverse effects on family dynamics prior to his departure.

### Illegitimacy and Delinquency

Illegitimate birth could reasonably be considered the first social status that could influence a child's future. Such births have risen dramatically over the last 25 years in the United States. The illegitimacy rate per thousand live births for females aged 15 to 19 in 1960 was 15.3; in 1982 it was 28.9 and climbing (Hanson, Myers, and Ginsburg, 1987:241). Approximately 800,000 illegitimate children are born to teenage mothers in the United States each year (Wallis, 1987:11).

Although illegitimate birth does not carry the social stigma that it once did, it still presents many practical difficulties that are inimical to good parenting and child socialization. Mothers of illegitimate children often lack the wide network of social support enjoyed by mothers of legitimate children (Crnic et al., 1984). Social support is a valuable resource for emotional well-being (Flaherty and Richman, 1986). It nestles us in a network of mutual obligation and assures us that we are appreciated, respected, and loved. Social support also has the potential for mediating everyday stresses associated with maternity and serves as "a preventative function for parent-child difficulties, such as child abuse" (Crnic et al., 1984:225). It has been frequently shown that abusing parents, regardless of their children's birth status, tend to be socially isolated and that mothers of illegitimate children are less responsive and less attached to their children (Crockenberg, 1981; Ricks, 1985).

Growing up in a numerically truncated and possibly abusive home can retard a child's cognitive skills (Srouf, 1979). Shinn's (1978:316) review of 54 studies relevant to this issue led her to conclude, "low levels of parent-child interaction are important causes of poor [intellectual] performance among children in single-parent families." Although the studies reviewed by Shinn (1978) were of families that were either intact or broken by divorce or death, there is no reason to assume that father absence would not have similar effects on the intellectual performance of illegitimate children. In fact, any deficit in performance attributable to father absence would be exacerbated in such a home because there was never a father present from the start. Growing up in a home atmosphere deficient in verbal stimulation, more likely in a single-parent home, can lead to poor development of the left hemisphere of the brain, as manifested by low VIQ. However, an illegitimate child who subsequently becomes part of a two-parent family may not be significantly different in intellectual performance from legitimate children from intact homes.

Illegitimacy appears to impact negatively on many areas of an individual's life and may be especially relevant in the exploration of delinquency. For instance, it has been pointed out by Leyton (1986:316) that the incidence of illegitimate birth among serial killers (e.g., David Berkowitz, Ted Bundy, Charles Manson, Henry Lucas) is far greater than would be expected by chance. Nonetheless, studies exploring the influence of birth status on delinquency are rare; I was only able to locate one such study (West and Farrington 1973). Although their sample contained only 25 illegitimate boys, West and Farrington (1973:197) concluded that "the boys born illegitimate were singularly delinquent-prone."

Regardless of birth status, a child may become part of a single-parent household because of divorce or some other event that fractured the household, and an illegitimate child can become a part of a two-parent household due to the mother's subsequent marriage. There are no theoretical guidelines available which would allow us to formulate a hypothesis regarding the relative advantages or disadvantages accruing to an illegitimate child who remains fatherless throughout his minority in comparison to one who later becomes part of a two-parent household. Certainly, it appears reasonable that children who do later become part of a two-parent household would enjoy certain objective advantages. One such advantage could be an extended support network which could both reduce the kinds of stress on the mother alluded to above and at the same time increase the environmental stimulation required for better cognitive development. The presence of a father in the household should also contribute substantially to the family income and to all the benefits that accompany a larger income.

There are 85 boys in the sample who were born out of wedlock. Rather than performing analyses on birth status alone, it was decided to explore the effects of birth status and family structure jointly. The male sample was divided into four categories determined by their joint distribution on these two variables: legitimate/intact home, legitimate/broken home, illegitimate/single-parent, and illegitimate/two-parent.

In Table 8.3 we have the means for violent delinquency, love deprivation, P > V discrepancy, VIQ, and PIQ for each of the four-family structure/ birth status categories. We see that the illegitimate boys from one-parent homes are significantly more violent than legitimate boys from both broken and intact homes, but they do not differ significantly from illegitimate boys whose mothers subsequently married. Illegitimate boys whose mothers subsequently married are also more violent than boys in both legitimate birth categories.

Illegitimate boys from one-parent homes also had a significantly higher love deprivation mean than all other groups. We may be seeing here the reflection of the effects of struggling to raise a child without the financial and emotional support of a spouse and an extended family. This finding supports previously cited studies indicating a higher level of abuse and neglect in single-parent homes (Sack, Mason, and Higgins, 1985). It might be speculated that the potential for abuse and neglect is increased when one has had to cope from the beginning of the child's life without the aid of a spouse.

In terms of intellectual functioning, it is noted that illegitimate boys from one-parent families have a much higher mean P > V discrepancy score than all other three categories, none of which differed significantly among themselves. This 19.28 discrepancy is far in excess of the 12 points necessary for significance at the .05 level. It is also noted that the illegitimate boys from broken homes have both the lowest verbal IQ and the highest performance IQ means. This finding supports the proposition that growing up in a numerically truncated home, one that lacks broad-based social support and intellectual stimulation, results in retarded

TABLE 8.3

Violence, Love Deprivation, and Cognitive Measure
Means by Family Structure/Birth-Status Categories

| N | Family Structure/ Birth Status | | Violence | Love Deprivation | P > V |
|---|---|---|---|---|---|
| 170 | Intact/Legitimate | (a) | 55.45bd | 19.88cd | 3.63d |
| 35 | Intact/Illegitimate | (b) | 88.86ac | 21.69d | 4.18d |
| 258 | Broken/Legitimate | (c) | 53.74bd | 26.00d | 7.29d |
| 50 | Broken/Illegitimate | (d) | 109.16abc | 33.42abc | 19.28abc |
| F ratio | | | 11.41 | 16.87 | 19.39 |
| sig. | | | .0000 | .0000 | .0000 |
| eta | | | .251 | .301 | .320 |

| | | | VIQ | PIQ | |
|---|---|---|---|---|---|
| | | | 90.35d | 94.45cd | |
| | | | 86.17 | 89.31cd | |
| | | | 92.78d | 100.00ab | |
| | | | 83.03ac | 102.24ab | |
| | F ratio | | 8.74 | 8.85 | |
| | sig. | | .0000 | .0000 | |
| | eta | | .22 | .22 | |

verbal skills (Shinn, 1978). The high PIQ mean of these boys relative to those in the two intact home groups, as well as their significantly higher love deprivation scores, lends support to those who believe that growing up in such deprived homes is conducive to developing a hyporeactive ANS (Wadsworth, 1976) and/or relatively good visual-spatial skills (DeLozier, 1982).

## *Alcohol and Drug Abuse*

Substance abuse has a tremendous impact on crime. About one-third of all arrests are for alcohol-related crimes; about 75 percent of robberies and 80 percent of homicides involve a drinking offender and/or victim (Masters and Robertson, 1990:274). During a three-month period in 1989, between 50 and 85 percent of male arrestees and between 44 and 87 percent of female arrestees in thirteen of the nation's largest cities tested positive for one or more drugs other than alcohol (Wish and O'Neil, 1989). A large-scale survey of inmates in American prisons found that 37 percent admitted using cocaine and 30 percent admitted using heroin in contrast to surveys of the general population in which 12 percent and 1 percent of respondents admitted to using cocaine and heroin, respectively (U.S. Department of Justice, 1988:50).

Drugs (including alcohol) affect brain functioning in one of four ways: (1) they stimulate or speed up the release of neurotransmitters, (2) they inhibit or slow down their release, (3) they prevent the reuptake of transmitters after they have been released, or (4) they break down transmitters more quickly. Depending on the type of drug taken, the individual's feelings and/or behavior are speeded up or slowed down, intensified or reduced, stimulated or mellowed.

In one sense, then, the motivation to ingest exogenous chemicals is to exchange one mood state for another considered more desirable. People drink alcohol or take drugs to alter their moods for a variety of reasons — some acceptable, others not so acceptable. Some do so just to be sociable and to liven up parties, some to sedate themselves, and some to anesthetize the pains of life. The habitual use of chemical comforters by some segments of our society indicates that there is a rather large proportion of people who find little meaning in life. As Nettler (1978:342) has remarked: "People whose lives are 'good in themselves' do not need the deadening chemicals. However, persons who receive as much pain as pleasure when they look at reality each morning need what comfort they can get."

In a statement with which control theorists and reality therapists would concur, the President's Task Force on Drunkenness concluded that the chronic drinker is a person who "has never attained more than a minimum of integration in society. . . . [H]e [or she] is isolated, uprooted, unattached, disorganized, demoralized, and homeless (1967:11–13). A similar statement regarding drug addicts was made by Chein et al. (1964:273): "In almost all addict families, there was a disturbed relationship between the parents, as evidenced by separation, divorce, open hostility, or lack of warmth." The common theme here is that substance abusers, lacking attachment and emotional warmth, think of their pharmacopoeia of chemical happiness not in terms of what it does "to" them but rather in terms of what it does "for" them. Lacking the endogenous chemicals released in response to the warmth of others that make them naturally "high" on life, they turn to exogenous chemicals sources.

It is not enough to identify people who are at risk for substance abuse, nor is it enough to indicate that such people are also at risk for committing crimes. A National Institute of Justice study concluded: "It is our judgment that alcohol use is an important factor in the occurrence of some crime. If we begin to understand *how* alcohol use exerts its causal influence, the relative importance of alcohol use to the occurrence of criminal behavior can be estimated" (Collins, 1983:1). Let us survey some research relevant to this question.

Alcohol is a depressant drug that affects behavior by inhibiting the functioning brain. As more and more alcohol is ingested, we are taking a trip back into evolutionary history as our behavior becomes less and less inhibited. The rational neocortex is affected first as it surrenders control of the organism to the more primitive limbic system. Raw basic emotions are then allowed free rein without benefit of first being channeled by rational considerations. The drinker may become excessively jolly, amorous, sad, or aggressive, depending on both the situation in which the drinking takes place and the emotion to which the drinker is most neurologically disposed. The rate at which this surrender to raw emotionality occurs depends on a number of variables such as the alcohol content of the drink and the amount and speed with which it is drunk, the weight of the drinker, the amount of food in the stomach, the time of the day, and the state of the drinker's metabolic system.

Ethanol alcohol is broken down in the body via enzymatic action into a molecule called acetaldehyde (AcH). AcH is a toxic chemical that produces unpleasant reactions, such as nausea and headaches, and may be considered a built-in negative reinforcer against overindulgence in alcohol. Schuckit and Rayses (1979) have shown that children of alcoholics produce significantly higher levels of AcH concentration than a control group. Since AcH is a "punishing" chemical, one might suppose that higher concentrations of if would militate against excessive drinking. In fact, disulfiram (Antabuse) is sometimes used in the treatment of alcoholics because it functions to maintain high levels of AcH by retarding further metabolic reactions.

According to one model of alcoholism, AcH is rapidly converted into a morphine-like substance called tetrahydropapaveroline (THP), or some other highly addictive opiate-like alkaloid, in individuals prone to the disease (Schuckit and Rayses, 1979; Rosenfeld, 1981, Applewhite, 1981). There is no conclusive proof for this line of thinking, but if true it may explain why the vast majority of those who drink do not become alcoholics, while those who quickly metabolize AcH into THP are at risk. This is not to assert that those who commit violent crimes under the influence of alcohol are necessarily alcoholics, or that alcoholics necessarily commit violent crimes.

A number of studies have related alcoholism and problem drinking to low MAO activity (Gottfries, 1980), a trait that appears to be under strong genetic control (Oreland, 1983). Failkov (1985:248) cites studies that have shown that the lifelong expectancy rate for alcoholism among males ranges between 3 and 5 percent, but only between 0.1 and 1.0 percent for women. This is intriguing because, as we saw in Chapter Seven, males have an average of 20 percent less MAO than women (Zuckerman, Buchsbuam, and Murphy, 1980). It was also shown in Chapter Seven that low MAO is associated with many kinds of pathological and sensation-seeking behavior, which are themselves strongly associated with being male.

We know that the early effects of alcohol are to increase activity, thus giving the impression that alcohol is a stimulant. In fact, it has been shown that low levels of alcohol (pre-intoxication) cause an increase in norepinephrine secretion (Hoffman and Tabakoff, 1985). It is only after a certain threshold is reached, which is different for different individuals, that alcohol reduces neural activity and becomes a depressant. At the chemical level, it may be that the increased norepinephrine accompanying drinking and further enhanced by stress, coupled with low MAO activity, is the link between alcohol and violence. We know that other drugs classified as stimulants, such as cocaine and the amphetamines, increase neural activity and inhibit MAO.

### Drug Abuse

Turning our attention to drugs other than alcohol, it is obvious that there are far too many different kinds of drugs for me to present a survey of their physiological effects here. I will concentrate on just two: heroin and cocaine. These two drugs have been selected because heroin and cocaine abusers constitute the majority of arrestees in most jurisdictions in the United States (Wexler et al., 1988).

Heroin is a derivative of morphine, a powerful painkiller. The brain secretes its own morphine-like substances called endorphins (for "endogenous morphine-like substances"). The endorphins are a class of neurotransmitters known as peptides and are concentrated in the limbic system. When under emotional stress, the endorphins help to keep us on an even keel by providing us with a perfectly legal "tonic." When an infant is separated from its mother, its endorphin level falls and the level of the stress hormone cortisol rises, triggering anxiety and distress crying. In experiments with animals, it has been found that, among a wide variety of drugs tried, only endorphins mollify infants separated by their mothers in the same way that actual reunion will (Liebowitz, 1983:106). Liebowitz (1983:134), who calls the endorphins "attachment juice," states that when we are isolated and unattached our endorphin activity temporarily shuts down.

The presence of these natural-occurring analgesics provides clues to the addictive process. It has been suggested that some people become addicted to opiates because they have insufficient emotional attachments to others, and hence less natural endorphin secretion (Applewhite, 1981:132). Lacking normal amounts of nature's "tonic" precipitates a search for artificial substitutes to correct the deficit. It has also been suggested that the frequent injection of heroin affects the brain's natural capacity to release endorphins in much the same way that too much thyroid extract will eventually cause the body to cease its own production of the thyroid-stimulating hormone (Restak, 1979:344–355).

If the line of thinking presented by Liebowitz, Applewhite, and Restak has any merit, the narcotics addict is caught in a catch-22 spiral. That is, addicts may turn to heroin as a temporarily satisfying substitute for the emotional attachments missing in their lives. The frequent use of heroin may cause a shutdown of the endorphin system, and a closed or malfunctioning endorphin system would have the effect of making addicts chemically incapable of forming attachments to other people. Such a progression would make the addict even more dependent on the drug as his/her only source of attachment pleasure.

Heroin has no direct influence on violence; i.e., taking heroin does not increase the individual's potential and readiness to engage in violence. In fact, taking heroin wafts the individual into a euphoric state of sweet indifference, a state that makes violence highly improbable. It has been reported that in countries where narcotics are supplied to registered addicts, these addicts have lower rates of criminal activity than the general population (Hartman, 1978:404). It is the street hustle to obtain the drug and the turf wars that are responsible for the association between heroin and violence.

Cocaine, and closely allied drugs such as methamphetamine, are stimulants. These stimulant drugs, along with the depressant drug, alcohol, have the most immediate association with violent crime. As one writer dramatically (and perhaps exaggeratedly) put it:

> Cocaine gives an icy-cold high that freezes your heart and makes you believe that you are all-powerful, invincible, and righteously correct in all of your appetites and impulses. It is the most self-deceiving of drugs, and the most insidious, quietly turning every user into a Mr. Hyde. If grass is the drug of peace, cocaine is the drug of war. (Bogdanovich, 1985:143.)

Stimulant drugs mimic the activity of the sympathetic branch of the ANS to increase arousal and a sense of well-being. They are the drugs of choice for individuals who seek excitement and adventure, the driven, the easily bored, and the chronically underaroused (Grabowski, 1984). It has been characterized as "the most powerful reinforcer known" (Holden, 1989:1378). Cocaine works by releasing and then blocking the reuptake of the neurotransmitter dopamine at the synaptic terminals, thus keeping the individual in an extended state of arousal. This blockage of reuptake may be exacerbated by low MAO levels among chronic cocaine and methamphetamine users (Woolvertaon and Kleven, 1988). The presence of low MAO levels among chronic cocaine abusers fits in pharmacologically with the sensation-seeking, non-conventional profiles of such people noted previously.

It is interesting to note the effects of strong stimulant drugs on some kinds of socially deprived monkeys. We are all aware of the pathological behaviors displayed by maternally deprived monkeys from the seminal work of Harry Harlow and his colleagues (1958, 1962). Certain of these monkeys were found not to differ behaviorally from maternally raised monkeys, although such monkeys were distinctly a minority. However, when given amphetamines these maternally deprived monkeys, although usually behaviorally "normal," were much quicker to show long-term alterations in behavioral and neurochemical systems than were maternally raised monkeys (Kraemer et al., 1983). This intriguing finding suggests that maternal deprivation somehow "primes" the system to be extra responsive to stimulant drugs, and, since low MAO individuals are particularly susceptible to stimulant drugs (Liebowitz, 1983), that somehow early deprivation experiences may have an impact on MAO levels. Lidberg and his colleagues (1985) do suggest that early childhood experiences may affect MAO levels, but do not specify what they might be.

We should not go too far in ascribing biological, psychological, or social pathologies to people who use drugs once in awhile on an experimental basis any more than we should ascribe them to the casual user of alcohol. Most people who experiment with drugs during adolescence do not become addicted, nor are they likely victims of future poor physical or psychological health (Marlett et al., 1988). Of more concern is those individuals whose use of drugs becomes *abuse* of drugs. The characteristics of such individuals are very much the characteristics descriptive of delinquents and criminals, suggesting that substance abuse and antisocial behavior share a common set of causes.

Summing up a number of studies that have attempted to discover if certain personality profiles are more prone to drug abuse than others, Goode (1988:62) finds that sensation seeking is high on the list of characteristics that separate users from non-users. Other characteristics include rebelliousness, peer orientation, hedonism, non-conformity, and acceptance of deviant behavior. These are characteristics that also describe the delinquent and criminal. Goode (1988:63) goes on to say that the stronger these characteristics define a given individual, the more seriously he or she is involved with drugs (and, of course, crime and delinquency).[2]

The personality characteristic most frequently implicated in drug abuse is low self-esteem (Franklin, 1985). We have already seen that the taproot of low self-esteem is the inability to get one's love needs fulfilled. In addition to low self-esteem, Franklin (1985) lists many of the disabilities discussed in this book (parental abuse, neglect, and substance abuse, poverty, poor school performance, and so on). All individuals who suffer these disabilities obviously do not become substance abusers, although they are at risk for becoming so if they are also biologically at risk.

I was able to determine the substance abuse histories of 388 of the male delinquents. Only 21.6 percent of those for whom a substance abuse history was available had no known history of such abuse. Unfortunately, I was not able to determine what the drugs of choice were. These subjects were divided into four groups: (1) alcohol abusers only, (2) drug abusers only, (3) those who had no history of abusing either alcohol or drugs, and (4) those who abused both. As see in Table 8.4, the evidence linking substance abuse and frequency and severity of violent delinquency is ambiguous. Delinquents who use *both* alcohol and drugs were significantly more violent than those who used either substance alone. They were not, however, more violent than delinquents who had no recorded history of any kind of substance abuse. Delinquents with no recorded history of substance abuse had a significantly higher violence mean than those who abused alcohol only. Comparing the groups in terms of ever or never having been convicted of a violent offense, 63.7 percent of those who abused both alcohol and drugs, 60.7 percent of those who abused neither,

37.8 who abused only alcohol, and 21.7 percent who abused only drugs committed at least one violent offense.

TABLE 8.4

Tests of Significance of Violent Delinquency, VIQ, PIQ, and SES Means for Alcohol, Drug, and both Alcohol and Drug Abusers

| Group | | N | Violence | VIQ | PIQ | SES |
|-------|---|---|----------|-----|-----|-----|
| Alcohol only | (a) | 37 | 19.30cd | 90.03 | 97.24 | 32.19c |
| Drugs only | (b) | 46 | 24.13d | 94.89c | 105.37c | 24.16 |
| Neither | (c) | 84 | 57.43a | 87.02bd | 94.56bd | 23.50a |
| Both | (d) | 221 | 73.08ab | 93.97c | 101.67c | 27.76 |
| | F | | 11.26 | 6.00 | 5.94 | 4.39 |
| | eta | | .28 | .21 | .21 | .19 |

abcd = means that differ at < .05 using the Scheffe test

There was no significant difference among the four groups on love deprivation or P > V. Differences on VIQ, PIQ, and SES among the groups are not substantial. The most noteworthy finding is that non-abusing delinquents had the lowest means on all three variables. Also worthy of note is that 78.4 percent of the boys in the sample had reported histories of substance abuse, with 57 percent having a history of abusing both. It appears that abusing one substance places one at risk for abusing another; 82.8 percent of the boys who abused alcohol also abused other forms of drugs.

### Adolescence as a Causal Factor

There are certain other causal factors of a biosocial nature that are applicable to juvenile delinquency that should be addressed. Most juvenile delinquents do not become adult criminals (Boucher, 1985), a fact that points toward unique aspects of this youthful period of life that may increase the probability of antisocial behavior. Among the factors not previously discussed as possible causes of antisocial behavior are the psychosocial problems associated with adolescence, that sometimes confusing period between childhood and adulthood. This strange and some-times frightening stage of life we call adolescence begins at puberty, a period of profound biological change that occurs most generally between the ages of 11 and 18, with onset and termination being about two years earlier in girls. Puberty is the period in which the body begins to produce the sex hormones in larger quantities, leading to the greater visible sex differentiation of males and females.

Prior to puberty, males and females have approximately the same level of testosterone. During puberty girls' testosterone levels double and boys' increase between 10 and 20 times. Testosterone is a major activator of aggressive behavior, and its elevation during adolescence corresponds with major increases of antisocial behavior of all kinds (Udry, 1988). But sex differences in testosterone cannot be considered apart from sex differences in sex hormone-binding globulin (SHBG), to which most of the gonadal hormones in the body are reversibly bound. Levels of SHBG are about equal in both sexes prior to puberty, but thereafter females have about twice the male level. This means that postpubescent males, even if testosterone levels were equal between the sexes, would have twice the level of *free*, i.e., unbound, testosterone available for behavioral activation. In actuality, then, postpubescent males have a concentration of free testosterone about 40 times greater than postpubescent females (Khan and Cataio, 1984:10). It is against this backdrop of greatly enhanced biological predisposition toward the breaching of social controls that the social and psychological problems of adolescence should be viewed (Udry, 1988:710).

Psychologically, adolescence has been considered everything from a normal developmental period accompanied by a few mild disturbances experienced by about half of all teenagers (Offer, 1975), to a stage of life that is very emotionally disturbing for just about all teenagers (Thornburg, 1971). From a review of the literature, Udry (1990:2) lists the following changes that typically occur among high-school-age adolescents: "They complete puberty, lower academic achievement values, increase values of independence, increase tolerance for violation of adult standards, decrease religiosity, decline in church attendance, increase reported alcohol and drug use, and increase sexual activity." Except for the completion of puberty, these changes are not likely to be welcomed by parents and other authority figures, and they certainly represent a gap between biological and social maturity that must be bridged.

In psychologist Erik Erikson's (1963) *Eight Ages of Man* model of human psychosocial development, he identifies eight stages in the human life cycle in which individuals are confronted with new challenges and interactions with themselves and with their environment. Each of these stages involve crises that can lead to opposite (positive or negative) personality outcomes, depending on how the crises are confronted and resolved. Adolescence is identified as a stage in which the two polar outcomes are *identity vs. role confusion.* In reality, of course, these outcomes are never either/or dichotomies. Most teenagers emerge from this stage situated somewhere on a shifting continuum.

During this stage young people start asking philosophical questions about themselves: "Who am I?" "What is my place, and where am I going?" "What does this or that person think of me?" They also start to form opinions and theories and asking questions about many aspects of their environment that they formerly took for granted. Their surging hormones, abundant energies, and new questioning orientation make them impatient, action orientated, and imbued with an aura of omnipotence. If, thanks to loving parents, they were successful in navigating previous developmental states (trust vs. mistrust, autonomy vs. doubt, initiative vs. guilt, and industry vs. inferiority), they will emerge with a positive identity and very little role confusion.

If mistrust, doubt, guilt, and inferiority were previous outcomes, role confusion is the likely outcome of this stage. To seek out an identity they will turn away from neglectful parents and toward others in the same sorry boat as themselves. Needless to say, such a strategy is not a good one. The identity likely to be achieved in such groups is very likely to be negative—"delinquent," "doper," "punk"—but even a negative identity is better than no identity at all as long as it is accepted by the groups to which we belong.

Even youths from well-adjusted homes often conform more with their peers' expectations than with their parents' during adolescence. This is a normal part of growing up and part of finding one's own way in life. The trick is to find the right set of peers. Well-loved youths will generally be prosocial and will seek the company of others like themselves, but: "Rejected and neglected children who do not find love and affection, as well as support and supervision, at home, often resort to groups outside the family; frequently these groups are of a deviant nature" (Trajanowicz and Morash, 1983:90). About two-thirds of the children who run away from home do so in response to parental abuse (Hyde and Hyde, 1985:2). Rejected children, being unsure of themselves, will often overidentify with the heroes of cliques and crowds or with the heroes the media provide for them to hold themselves together.

With the well-publicized breakdown or diminished authority of the family, religious, and educational institutions in the United States, behavior, attitudes, and values have come more and more under the influence of other forces. I believe that a good case could be made for the proposition that we have abrogated much of the responsibility for socializing our young to peer groups and to television, both of which represent immature and often antisocial visions of reality. Groups have a morality and direction of their own that is often radically different from the sum of their individual parts. Already unsure of identity and direction, juveniles in peer groups easily defer to the collective judgment. With internalized standards submerged in the group and with responsibility diffused among them, we sometimes see horrible manifestations of antisocial "group think" such as the brutal "wilding" of the so-called Central Park jogger in 1989.

Television, the other half of the socialization equation, provides our youth with models and standards of behavior. More than anything else, television models and sells greed, hedonism, impatience, and impulsivity ("Go out and buy this or that and you'll feel great and the boys/girls will love you. Do it now!"). Our kids grow up seeing all kinds of complex problems solved in one hour (often by violent means) with six commercial breaks designed to sell us the "good life." Is it any wonder that our kids become narcissistic, lower their thresholds for violence, become desensitized to the suffering of others, and have difficulty delaying gratification? If kids are watching television an average of 6.8 hours a day (Roberts and Bachen, 1981), their highly impressionable minds have to be influenced by it.

The themes of many television and movie shows often appear as though they were produced by some malignant juvenocracy specifically to challenge traditional notions of decency and good character. Teachers are portrayed as helpless, bumbling idiots who are easily manipulated, intimidated, and outsmarted by crude (but "awesome") teenagers. Youths who study and behave respectably are characterized as "nerds" or "geeks" and are ostracized by the in crowd. Parents are "squares" and hypocrites (which, unfortunately, is all too often the case) who indulge their own sexual and chemical appetites while condemning those of their children. The family warmth of Ozzie and Harriet (although smarmy and unrealistic) has been replaced as a family role model by the equally unrealistic, and totally dysfunctional, Bundy and Simpson families. In the metallic crotch-raw cacophony that passes for teenage music today, females are viewed as little more than sexual playthings whose favors, if not granted, may simply be taken. A particularly revolting example is a rap number by the Geto Boys in which some moron slits a woman's throat, watches her die, and then has sex with her corpse. Obnoxious self-indulgence of all kinds is promoted, while sensitivity, responsibility, altruism, and other indications of decency and character are pooh-poohed.

It seems plain that adolescence is a period in which enhanced biological abilities and a permissive environment conspire to produce America's terrible delinquency problem. Every generation believes that its youth is "going to hell," Plato even thought so 4,000 years ago. Obviously, the hormonal surges of adolescence occur regardless of time and place, but no generation before has experienced the frightful combination of drugs, alcohol, single-parent homes, negative role models, and the availability of guns that today's American youth experience. As Edwards and Nuckols (1991:25) dramatically put it: "Statistically speaking, the United States is the most dangerous country on the planet for adolescents." They may be quite right. In a television interview just after the Gulf War, Louis Sullivan, secretary of the Department of Health and Human Services, commented that there are more young people killed on our urban streets ever 100 hours than killed in the 100 hours of the land phase of that war. This is a sorry situation, and we are in desperate need of a solution.

### Conclusion

This chapter emphasizes structural effects on violent delinquency and cognitive development. Middle-borns, children from homes broken by desertion, and illegitimate children were found to be more violence-prone than children from other groups. But structure per se has little effect on either violent delinquency or cognitive development. The important variable appears to be the amount of care and affection available to children. Perhaps the most interesting findings of this chapter were found for the juveniles who were illegitimate and whose mothers remained unmarried. Not only were these boys significantly more violent than the others, they were found simultaneously to have the lowest mean VIQ and the highest PIQ. These boys were also found to have the highest love deprivation mean. Although findings based on such a small number can hardly be said to be either definitive or compelling, taken in conjunction with supporting literature, they do point suggestively to the importance of affectionate variables for healthy psychological and behavioral development.

The findings relating to substance abuse produced no surprises: boys who abused both alcohol and drugs were the most violent of all four groups. However, boys who abused neither substance were significantly more violent than boys who abused alcohol only. The boys with no recorded history of substance abuse were also found to have the lowest IQ means and the lowest SES mean. Other than the factors mentioned, there was no particular variable profile obtained that could further differentiate among the groups. Since 90 percent of the boys for which information was available abused alcohol, drugs, or both, it appears that substance abuse is very much a concomitant of delinquency. Rather than invoking substance abuse as a "cause" of delinquency, however, it is more likely that some third variable is largely responsible for both behaviors. The literature review points to what I have chosen to call love deprivation as a strong candidate.

Although I have chosen to emphasize biosocial variables, it is plain that no adequate explanation of linkages between substance abuse and crime and delinquency can ignore sociocultural factors. There are many fine works exploring these factors. Robert Cloninger, one of the top researchers in the genetics of alcoholism, supports this view when he writes: "The demonstration of the critical importance of sociocultural influences in most alcoholics suggests that major changes in social attitudes about drinking styles can change dramatically the prevalence of alcohol abuse, regardless of genetic predisposition" (in Peele, 1990:58). Supposedly, the same can be said for other kinds of chemical abuse.

The trying period of adolescence could not be left out of any discussion of juvenile delinquency. During this period an increasing biological propensity to violate norms interacts with an environment, which, in today's society, seems to work synergistically to help produce the kinds of antisocial behavior that are so prevalent. The biosocial model's usefulness is potentially at its best when we are attempting to account for behavior during the confusions attending adolescence.

## ENDNOTES

1. Means were adjusted for the effects of other independent variables by entering the family structure variable as $k - 1$ dummy variables into a regression equation and computing as follows:

$$\overline{Y}' = a + b_1 d + b_2(\overline{X}_2) + b_3(\overline{X}_3) \ldots b_k(\overline{X}_k)$$

where $a$ = Y intercept, $b$ = unstandardized beta,
$\overline{X}$ = mean of non-dummy independent variables (Walsh, 1990:294)

# Chapter Nine

# CONCLUSIONS AND IMPLICATIONS

## Summarizing the Present Research

Throughout this book violent delinquency has been defined and explained in terms of its relationship to love deprivation and intellectual imbalance. The literature reviewed and the original empirical findings presented lead me to conclude that these variables impact more strongly on the frequency and seriousness of violent delinquency than do other factors such as SES and race. I do not intend this chapter to be a comprehensive summary of all the research findings reported here, but certain points deserve some repetition.

Repeated violent delinquency is the kind of delinquency that most concerns us all. We saw that boys high on love deprivation and who were also P > V imbalanced were over seven times more likely to have committed two or more violent crimes than boys not in this category. This is an extremely substantively significant within-sample difference; I am unaware of any other two-variable composite that has such a powerful influence on violent delinquency.

Although lacking a control group of non-delinquents with whom to make comparisons, we are fortunate in having population norms with which to make such comparisons. It was seen that P > V imbalanced boys were overrepresented by a factor of 2.2 in the delinquent sample in relation to the proportion of P > imbalanced boys in the general population. It was also shown that P > V boys were more than 5 times more likely to be represented in a delinquent sample than were V > P boys. Intellectual imbalance was shown to be a rather useful predictor of good (V > P) or delinquent (P > V) behavior when VIQ and PIQ scores differ significantly, i.e., by 12 or more points.

A link common to both the P > V profile and violence is love deprivation. Love deprivation, conceptualized as an overlapping set of emotional and physical disabilities indicative of a lack of proper care and regard for the well-being of children on the part of their caregivers, is a terrible cross to bear. All crosses, of course, are not of equal weight.

174

Some people carry them and emerge strong and healthy, others are emotionally crushed under their oppressive weight. There are also those who are deprived hardly at all who become violent, some for constitutional reasons, some because they get involved with substance abuse, some for purely situational reasons, and some for any combination of reasons. We saw, for instance, that P > V had no independent impact on violent delinquency after love deprivation had explained all the variance it could among youths living in extremely disadvantaged environments. Among youths from relatively advantaged environments, on the other hand, love deprivation had no unique effect on violent delinquency after P > V explained all the variance that it could.

One thing is clear, the disabilities subsumed under the general rubric of love deprivation has a pervasive impact on child development. Depending on the intensity of the deprivation suffered and on the individual's sensitivity to it, it will leave its mark etched in the brain's neurophysiology. We have seen that although genetic differences are perhaps most responsible for differences in synaptogenesis and neurotransmitter metabolism, repeated experiences with strong emotional content can produce similar synaptic structures and similar psychopharmacologies. What some call emotional programming is actually habituated neurotransmitter secretions along well-trodden synaptic pathways. Liebowitz explains how these established neurological patterns intrude on behavior in later life:

> If someone grows up in a cruel, neglectful, uncaring or cold family atmosphere [read "love deprived"] the chances are that as an adult he or she is going to have a store of painful memories. What this means is that there will be a series or well-established links between memory and displeasure centers. As adults these people will be more prone to depression, sadness, or pessimism. Anytime an unhappy childhood memory is evoked, the displeasure circuits will be activated. Also, new interactions that touch on any of these old memories will often cause excessive emotional reactions in people who may not even be consciously aware of the connection between present and past. (Liebowitz, 1983:45.)

Although the "hard" neurological evidence relating to the role of early experience has been necessarily limited to the study of animals (they are often sacrificed so that their brains can be closely examined), there is no reason to doubt that similar experiences do not have similar neurological and behavioral consequences for humans. These similar effects can be assessed using less intrusive methods such as EEG and

PET scan readings and bioassays of substances such as MAO. The fact that humans are cultural as well as biological animals does not change the fact that we share with other primates a desperate need for love and attachment. Because we are cultural animals, meaning that our behaviors are more open to learned patterns than are those of the lower primates, we are even more likely to be affected by our early experiences than lower animals are. Our plastic brains internalize experience, we remember it, we respond to further experiences influenced by it, we stew over it—and we get even.

A small "earliest memory" literature shows the extent of such early experience introjection. In contrasting the earliest reported memories of criminals with those of a control group, Hankoff (1987) found that the earliest memories of offenders revolved much more often around unpleasant, violent, hostile, and loveless family experiences than did those of the control group. According to Hankoff (1987), such results are consistently found in this body of literature. As Liebowitz (1983) suggests, it is not difficult to see how these disturbing memories impose themselves on the interpretation of present experiences and causing "excessive emotional reactions." Such reactions are the stuff of violence.

### What can be Done?

Everyone agrees that criminal violence is a serious social problem, and everyone agrees that steps should be taken to reduce it. However, slipping back and forth between the imperative and indicative moods is fraught with difficulty. Conservative lovers of individual responsibility like to emphasize moral training in "traditional values," religion, and punitive measures "with teeth in them," as solutions to violence. Liberals like to emphasize reductions in income inequality, educational and job training programs, and a "deeper understanding" of the individual criminal. I am not about to embark on a critical evaluation of any of these nominated solutions, all of which have some degree of merit. Nor do I propose to attack the problem of violence by concentrating on the violent offender himself or herself, but rather by focusing on the family. The dysfunctional family is the cradle of violence. It is here that we have to attempt to apply the scotch to the kind of parental behavior that appears to breed violence in their offspring by attempting to reduce stressors and enhancing coping resources.

The kinds of disabilities I have subsumed under the rubric of love deprivation have their roots in a variety of biological, psychological, and social causes. Because the causes are diverse and interactive, any treatment strategy designed to ameliorate the problem must be similarly diverse. In short, a biosocial perspective on the problem is needed. Most ameliorative strategies to date have concentrated on trying to change the thinking and behavioral patterns of parents already known to be abusing their children. While there is merit in such strategies and they should be continued, psychological counseling/therapy of identified child abusers has had limited success. One evaluation of 11 federally funded programs found that there was a known reoffending rate of 30 percent *during* treatment (Cohn, 1979), and Herrenkohl et al. (1979) found that more than two-thirds of treatment families reabused their children within a short time after treatment. It is probably futile to think that counseling offenders will have much more than temporary and limited impact on an established pattern of behavior, especially when these offenders remain mired in a social-psychological environment that remains conducive to child abuse and neglect.

Neither the problem of child maltreatment in all its forms or its solution is simple, and it is highly unlikely that it can ever be eradicated. It occurs in families in all SES groups, although it is more pervasive and serious among lower SES families (Brown, 1984). It is clear that we must go beyond the current strategy of punishing and/or counseling its perpetrators. Whether we punish or treat (and this applies equally to abusers and the abused child who becomes delinquent), we are responding reactively rather than proactively. What is needed is some form of prevention strategy in addition to the current efforts to bridle the horse after it has bolted the stable and run amok.

The strategy I propose is one that Gendreau and Ross (1987) call the "early/family intervention" strategy. According to them, such a strategy must pay attention to the literature of genetics, developmental psychology, pediatrics, family sociology, and various other disciplines. They see the early/family intervention strategy as having the possibility of enjoying a firm consensus among professionals and laypersons alike for three main reasons:

> First, a broad social-philosophical constituency supports early intervention. "Just society" philosophers (e.g., Rawls) argue cogently that justice, in contemporary sociopolitical terms, must insist that universal liberties are accessible to all. . . . The U. S. Surgeon General's task force has given highest priority to preventative activities in the most comprehensive sense.

Second, the rapprochement between psychobiological and sociological theories has been a most welcome development.

Third, the viability of early prevention has been confirmed in an exceptionally rich process literature documenting the functioning of families at risk with the law. (Gendreau and Ross, 1987:358–359.)

One strategy is to try to increase the emotional attachment between mother and child.

### Increasing Mother-Infant Attachment

In 1979 the Canadian Standing Senate Committee on Health, Welfare and Science set itself the task of determining what factors occurring in a child's first three years of life led to later violent behavior. The committee summoned expert witnesses from the full spectrum of the behavioral and medical sciences to help them with this task. The prenatal, perinatal, and early childhood periods were focused on. Many of the disabilities discussed in Chapter Three—lack of prenatal care, low birth weight, malnutrition, maternal substance abuse, lack of tactile stimulation, and so forth—were emphasized by these scientists as leading to child maltreatment, learning disabilities, and later violent behavior.

A report on the findings of this committee (Harvey, 1980) emphasized the value of early mother-child attachment and breast-feeding. Acknowledging that "It seems strange to have a discussion of hospital practices alongside a discussion of the origin of psychopathic and violent behavior," Harvey (1980:5) goes on to write:

> Yet, in the perinatal period our hospitals don't do nearly enough to promote the bonding or maternal attachment of mother and child. If the capacity to establish strong interpersonal relationships is the cornerstone of personality, the lack of such capacity is a distinguishing characteristic of the psychopath. Hospitals, preoccupied with smooth routine, do little during the important first few hours and days to promote the mother-child contact essential to the growth and development of the child's personality. The early isolation of the infant in the nursery and the lack of bonding is often the beginning of a trail that leads to neglect and abuse.

Central to the committee's conclusions as reported by Harvey (1980) is the development of mother-infant bonding or attachment. Attachment is central to criminology's control theory, but as the term is used in developmental neurophysiology it implies a deep biological symbiosis between mother and infant that confers physical and emotional benefits on both. Reite (1987:598) points out that the great weight of the developmental neurophysiology literature supports the notion that lack of attachment produces "physiological effects that interfere with subsequent physiological maturation and/or normal physiological/behavioral interactions." It is far too simplistic to propose that an infant's early interactive experiences with its mother entirely, or even primarily, account for its subsequent personality and behavior; there are just too many intervening events to make the proposition viable. It is more realistic to propose that these early experiences lay down a physiological substrate which makes it more or less probable that subsequent experiences will be perceived and responded to in a more positive (prosocial) way.

From the evidence presented in Chapter Three regarding the neurological and other developmental effects of tactile and other forms of stimulation on newborn infants, surely it would be beneficial if hospital staff were to educate new mothers to such simple procedures. The evidence relating to the neurological development and attachment benefits of such practices far outweigh any disruption of a hospital's "smooth routine." We also need to educate parents about the vital role of loving stimulation in the development of the child's brain, and we need to support this learning by making it possible for mothers to be in close contact with their infants as much as possible during the most active stage of neuronal growth, i.e., at least for the first four to nine months (Fischer, 1987). There is also a large literature pointing to the importance of keeping mother and child in constant skin contact for the first hour after birth and extended contact throughout the early postpartum days for bonding purposes (Klaus and Kennell, 1982).[1] Some studies suggest that extended perinatal contact significantly reduces the risk of future child maltreatment (O'Connor et al., 1980; Olds, 1984).

There is a convergence of the observational/clinical data and the neurophysiological evidence regarding the importance of these early developmental periods. It was discussed earlier how the brain develops to some extent according to the experiences of the human organism. We saw how many aspects of neuronal development are genetically coded so that the organism responds normally to the vital and ubiquitous information contained in its environment that shape the sensory and motor systems. Greenough, Black, and Wallace (1987) call this aspect of brain development *experience-expectant*. They call the more plastic aspects of neuronal development, those aspects of the organism's environment that are unique to it, *experience-dependent*. It is these experience-dependent aspects that determine which of the excess synaptic connections in the infant's brain will survive according to their use or disuse. Because basic synaptogenesis during early sensitive periods is probably qualitatively different from later experiential effects and because synaptic pruning is most active in the first few months of life, it seems that the clinical people have been right all along in their assertion that the early months of life are vital for the human task of learning how to love.

We can help to assure the continuity of mother-infant contact after the hospital period by making paid maternal leave a right guaranteed to all mothers. This is hardly a novel, radical, or utopian suggestion. No less than 117 other nations give such a guarantee, in many cases with full pay for as long as nine months and with assurances that any employment they held at the time of pregnancy would be waiting for them at the end of their leave (Walsh, 1988b). We gave such guarantees to young men when the military draft was a part of American life. If we can make such guarantees to draftees while we taught them how to kill, why not to mothers while they teach their infants to love?

It is not simply desirable that the United States take this step, it is morally and legally obligated to do so. This nation is a signatory to the *United Nations Convention on the Elimination of all Forms of Discrimination against Women.* Along with other signators, the United States agreed to "introduce maternity leave with pay or comparable social benefits without loss of former employment, seniority or social allowances" (Townson, 1984:1). The United Nations manifesto was introduced based on the evidence presented by neuroscientists attesting to the significance of mother/infant interaction for neurological development. A review article by Hopper and Zigler (1988) points out many medical and social science bases for the implementation of such a policy.

Although most of the evidence cited by Hopper and Zigler (1988) issued from American research, we alone apparently choose to ignore it. According to the 1989 Labor Department's survey of fringe benefits, only two-fifths of America's female workers in medium to large companies were eligible for maternal leave. The average leave time workers could take was 20 weeks, and, more significantly, it was unpaid (UPA, 1990). In other words, the poorest working mothers, those most in need of paid leave, are the least likely to take advantage of it.

An important component of the bonding process appears to be the practice of breast-feeding. Breast-feeding provides the extended skin-to-skin contact that is so important to the developing infant and helps to cement the attachment bond that acts as a buffer against maltreatment.

Ashley Montagu comments on the benefits conferred on mother and child by breast-feeding: "Physiologically, the nursing of her babe at her breast produces in the mother an intensification of her motherliness, the pleasurable care of her child. Psychologically, this intensification serves to further consolidate the symbiotic bond between herself and her child. In this bonding between mother and child, the first few minutes after birth are crucial" (1978:63).

This is not the place for an extensive survey of the extremely large literature on attachment and bonding and the influence of breast-feeding on the process. Some researchers have suggested that the hormone oxytocin, which is released during the act of breast-feeding, is "the hormone of love" (Klopfer, 1971; Nelson, 1971). Experimental administration of oxytocin has been shown to initiate maternal behavior in non-human mammals. Other researchers have shown that lactating human mothers show a greater sensitivity to their infants than non-lactating mothers, and that this sensitivity shows up on various physiological measures (Wiesenfeld et al., 1985). None of this means that bottle-feeding mothers cannot be excellent mothers, or that breast-feeding mothers are necessarily superior mothers. Nor does it mean by any stretch of the imagination that bottle-fed babies will inevitably be developmentally retarded or suffer disastrous consequences later in life, or that breast-fed infants will all become pillars of the community. But breast-feeding does appear to be a practice that benefits both mother and child, and it is a shame that this "head start" in life seems to depend so much on whether or not a mother can financially afford to practice it for an extended period.

Nevertheless, the feeding of the infant at the mother's breast is a phylogenetic trait of all mammals, and phylogenetic traits are traits because they somehow contribute to the inclusive fitness of the species. Humans are not exceptions to this rule. Quite apart from any posited attachment benefits associated with breast-feeding, breast milk is the most nutritious food a human being will ever ingest. In addition to its well-known immunological qualities, human milk is rich in cystine, an amino acid that is thought to be essential to the infant's developing brain, especially for myelination (Restak, 1979).

In a recent article decrying the decline of breast-feeding in third-world countries, Winikoff and Laukaran (1989) conclude that: "Mothers do want to breast-feed, but in order to do so successfully, they need informed health advisors and a supportive environment. Without attention to these factors, 'modernization' may well mean the loss of a superior health technology—to the detriment of both mothers and children." Such a conclusion also applies to the developed world where the convenience of bottle-feeding has cut deeply into the practice of breast-feeding, particularly among the poor. Based on 1988 census data, it has been reported that white college-educated mothers were the most likely (about 72%) to breastfeed their infants, followed by mothers with less than a high school education (about 28%), and that black mothers (about 22%) were least likely to breast-feed (LeFrancois, 1990:167). Given the nutritional, emotional, and tactile advantages accompanying breast-feeding, it is not unreasonable to suppose that a fair proportion of the non-genetic variance in measured intellectual functioning that differentiates the races and the various SES groups may be attributable to variance in infant feeding methods.

One of the strategies suggested by Winikoff and Laukaren (1989) to increase breast-feeding among lower income mothers is to provide health advisors and a supportive environment. Attempts to do this in the United States have had encouraging results. Lyons-Ruth, Connell, and Grunebaum (1990) conducted a study in which infants considered at risk for a number of social and psychological disabilities (low SES, maternal depression and inadequate caretaking) received home visit services from professional and paraprofessional workers. These infants were compared with a matched at-risk group who did not receive the service and with infants in the community considered not at risk on a number of developmental variables. The treatment at-risk families were provided with services for 18 months. The services rendered were in the form of counseling and advice to the mother on many areas of practical life (how to get basic needs such as legal, health, financial and educational needs met), parenting skills, and how to decrease social isolation by encouraging participation in parenting groups and providing an accepting relationship.

Lyons-Ruth and her associates (1990) concluded that the home services provided had a significant positive impact on both mothers and infants. Treated infants outperformed non-treated infants by an average of 10 points on the Bayley Mental Development Index, mother-infant attachments were shown to be much more secure, and treated mothers were less depressed and socially isolated. The researchers point out that earlier follow-up studies (Lazar and Darlington, 1982) showed that treatment effects remain fairly stable, and that the continued effects of treatment were, in large part, attributable to the strengthening of the attachment relationship between mother and child.

Despite the applicability of these studies to the human development process, the traditional criminologist may feel uncomfortable and may agree with Harvey (1980) that it does indeed seem strange to be discussing perinatal infant care within the context of a work on violent delinquency. There is, after all, a tremendous distance between the crib and a jail cell, and numerous other life events intervene and impact on behavioral outcomes. I would agree that it is obviously naive to posit that all of life's ills have their origin in the failure of early nurturing. This point notwithstanding, I am in broad agreement with Selma Fraiberg, who has spent a lifetime studying child development, when she writes:

> The condition of non-attachment leaves a void in the area of personality where conscience should be. Where there are no human attachments there can be no conscience. As a consequence, the hollow men and women contribute very largely to the criminal population. It is this group, too, that produces a particular kind of criminal, whose crimes, whether they be petty or atrocious, are always characterized by indifference. The potential for violence and destructive acts is far greater among these bondless men and women; the absence of human bonds leaves a free "unbound" aggression to pursue its erratic course (1977:62).

### Prenatal and Post Hospital Intervention

What happens perinatally builds on what has happened prenatally. Many factors affect the health and viability of the fetus, and most of these factors are associated with SES. It is estimated that at any one time more than 35 million Americans are not covered by private or public health insurance plans (David and Rowland, 1986). Without access to adequate prenatal medical care, the probability of some sort of fetal disability that may later impact on behavior increases. This lack of prenatal care is reflected in the United States' dismal infant and maternal death rates compared with those of other industrialized nations (Walsh, 1988b). Children born to poor parents in this country are twice as likely to die within the first year of life than are children born into more privileged families (Gortmaker, 1979).

According to the Physician's Task Force on Hunger in America (Farley, 1990:464), up to 20 million Americans, primarily the poor, suffered malnutrition at some time during the early 1980s. Maternal (and hence fetal) malnutrition has a retarding effect on the infant's motor and intellectual capacities, especially if malnutrition continues for an extended period after birth (LeFrancois, 1990:141). LeFrancois lists many other prenatal risks that are associated with SES such as maternal stress, unwed motherhood, and the ingestion of toxic chemicals such as alcohol, drugs, and tobacco. All this points to the need for massive educational efforts on the part of our schools. A fourth "R"—responsibility—should be an integral part of the school curriculum.

Reducing these prenatal risk factors and assessing the outcome of doing so were the goals of the federally funded Prenatal/Early Infancy Project (Olds, 1984). This project provided a comprehensive array of medical, educational and counseling services, and nurse visitation services to young, unwed, lower SES women both prenatally and postnatally. Compared with a matched control group of women, women who received services gave birth to fewer premature and low birth-weight babies, smoked and drank less, were more likely to return to school, viewed their infants more positively, and played with them more often. Six percent of the serviced mothers were reported to have abused or neglected their infants compared to 20 percent of the unserviced mothers. The incidence of child maltreatment among the unserviced mothers rose over time, but no such trend was observed among the serviced mothers. This sophisticated longitudinal study showed that appropriate early intervention can significantly reduce the stresses and disabilities so prevalent among at-risk mothers. Reducing such stresses reduces the probability of abuse and neglect, improves the intellectual functioning of the children, and reduces the risk of future delinquency.

Although it is beyond question that the kinds of intervention studies reported produce positive outcomes, little or nothing is done on a society-wide scale to implement the kinds of strategies studied. We are far behind Canada and Western European nations in actually applying what we know to be useful and beneficial. These countries provide all their citizens with equal medical care (often at no cost), they provide paid maternal leave, and many pay family allowances for each dependent child. These services are available to all, not only to those who have demonstrated a special need (Coleman and Cressey, 1987:180). The United States has rates of violent crime (murder, rape, robbery, and so forth) approximately five times higher than any of these countries (National Institute of Justice, 1987); one cannot help but wonder how much of this difference is attributable to the less generous provisions we make for our citizens, especially our less fortunate citizens.

According to Fagan's (1990) analysis of violent delinquency, the stable but persistently high rates of juvenile violence is destined to continue, especially given the hardening of poverty in the 1980s. Blacks, the most violent of our citizens, are particularly hurt by the hardening of poverty. Many see such programs as Affirmative Action producing a black society bifurcated by class as the cream of the black culture is skimmed, leaving the rest locked into something of a permanent jobless underclass (Whitman et al., 1987; Norton, 1987). A combination of the legacy of slavery and white racism (Norton, 1987), combined with an excessive reliance on the legal and welfare systems to ameliorate black disabilities (Loury, 1987), has helped to create America's lumpenproletariat. Even Martin Luther King described the black family over twenty years ago as "fragile, deprived and often psychopathic" (cited in Norton, 1987:53).

The black family, as well as poor families of every race, would benefit most from a comprehensive approach to the problem of juvenile violence. The following table indicates what I see as the major programs that we should implement as a society. Specific programs for families identified as abusing/neglecting that take a strictly psychosocial approach, such as anger, self-esteem, and substance abuse counseling, are not included here. Such programs are adequately identified and discussed elsewhere (Wolfe, 1987). There will certainly be those who will consider such a broad approach as drastic and unrealistic. But we must do something both drastic and meaningful if we are to apply the scotch to youthful violence, a problem that Curtis (1985) has called a "slow riot." And I would remind such people that such programs are already in place in many other industrialized nations, and that some are in place piecemeal in various parts of the United States.

### Conclusion

In writing this chapter I was ever mindful that while it is relatively easy to identify wrongs, it is inordinately difficult to write meaningful prescriptions for ameliorating them. For instance, Gelles and Cornell (1990) devote 138 pages of their excellent book on family violence to the scope of the problem, but only one page to prevention. This one page offers some excellent prescriptions, most of which I would heartily agree with, but the *how to* of their implementation was not addressed. They are not addressed because neither the authors nor anyone else has the slightest idea about how they would be implemented. How does one, for instance, "eliminate the norms that legitimize and glorify violence" (1990:139)? The authors suggest the elimination of corporal punishment

TABLE 9.1

Major Programs Which Should Be Implemented in Society

| Strategy | Assumed Benefits |
|---|---|
| 1. Provisions for adequate prenatal health care available to all without needs test. | No stigma of needs test. Reduction of premature and low birth weight infants. Adequate maternal nutrition. |
| 2. Parenting education and sex education as required courses in high schools. | Inculcation of knowledge about responsible sexual and parenting behavior. Reduced illegitimate births and increased parenting skills. |
| 3. Paid maternal leave of nine-months' duration with guarantee of previous employment at termination of leave. | Mothers who must or who wish to have the opportunity to maintain contact with infant during most active phase of neuronal development. Increase breast-feed, continuation of the attachment process. |
| 4. Family allowances paid for each dependent child. | Helps with cost of raising families eases financial burden of parents. |
| 5. Free medical care (including dental and optical) for children at least to age 18. | Assure healthy, well-nourished children regardless of family income. |
| 6. Home visitor concept for families identified as being in need. Visitors would include nurses, counselors, or other experts as determined by supervising social worker. | Educational and counseling services relating to parenthood, help and support relating to all aspects of family life (financial, health, employment, family discord, social support). |

## HOSPITAL PRACTICES

| | |
|---|---|
| 1. Less use of analgesic drugs. Encourage mother/infant skin contact for one hour or more immediately after birth, and as much contact as possible during hospital stay. | Mother is fully cognizant during the birthing process. Bonding and attachment is increased. No abrupt change in infant's environment, less stress. |
| 2. Encourage breast-feeding via education and modeling. | Cements bonding and attachment. Intensifies maternal behavior. Most nutritious for infant, aids in neuronal development. |
| 3. Educate mothers in the importance of tactile and other forms of stimulation. Show mothers how to perform full-body nude massages of infant. | Aids motor and intellectual development of infant. Intensifies attachment. |
| 4. Include fathers in the birthing and educational processes. | May facilitate father/infant bonding. Father shares in early parenting process. |

in the home and in the school, gun control, the elimination of media violence, and the abolition of the death penalty. These issues have moral, legal, and ideological aspects of tremendous emotional importance attached to them far removed from their possible link to criminal violence. Only massive government intrusion into areas, some of which are considered sacred by many Americans and which would therefore be stoutly resisted, could accomplish such goals.

Gelles and Cornell's other prescriptions, changing the sexist nature of society, integrating families into a network of kin and community, and reducing poverty, inequality, and unemployment, are laudable goals but far, far easier said than done. How does a society return to the halcyon state of "community," how does a society go about providing meaningful work for everybody? The distasteful truth is that it cannot. The prescriptions are also eerily reminiscent of the Marxist agenda, and we all know what human outrages Marxist attempts to mold social perfection led to. Recent history has surely informed us that we cannot force people to do what some ideological philosophy, however well-meaning, considers to be "in the best interest of all."

The biosocial program outlined here offers no grand approach aimed at changing the fabric of society. But the comprehensive nature of the biosocial perspective, the attempt to understand the genetic, biological, developmental and social factors involved in delinquent behavior, may lead to benign and effective intervention strategies. The program is formulated on relatively hard science as opposed to philosophy, and its intervention strategies are modeled on successful strategies (paid maternal leave, family allowances, and the home visitor concept) already in place in nations with sociopolitical systems most like our own, not on fatuous utopian strategies that have been shown to be abject failures, as well as major insults to the human condition. The biosocial approach steps on few ideological toes because it is based primarily on hospital practices and education. Even the ideas of maternal leave and a comprehensive medical care system are losing their ideological content, and what ideological content that does remain does not incite the passions the same way that some of the suggestions of Gelles and Cornell (1990) do.

On the other hand, the biosocial approach to violent and troubled families is more ambitious than approaches that concentrate on that small portion of abusive and neglectful families who are officially identified as such. The biosocial approach "catches" every mother and every family, regardless of whether or not it is at risk for child abuse and neglect, because it is a society-wide approach. It concentrates on improving three important factors associated with violence: (a) it facilitates mother/infant attachment, (2) the processes involved in attachment facilitate intellectual development, and (3) it eases the financial burdens of raising children and offers additional supports for families needing such support.

In summary, the biosocial approach to juvenile violence concentrates on the earliest years of a person's family life. There are many other extrafamilial factors that are conducive to violence with which the individual must contend and about which this approach says nothing. The best that we can hope for is that the strategies outlined here will provide most youths with the necessary emotional and intellectual capacities to resist reacting violently within the often exciting, and sometimes mad, world of the teenage peer culture.

## ENDNOTES

1. The term "bonding" in a human context should not be confused with the term popularized by the ethologists. There is no "critical" period (hours or days) in which specific events *must* occur if the development of attachment is to proceed normally (Lamb and Hwang, 1982). Rossi (1987) indicates that such a fixed and temporary-specific period for infant/mother bonding among the human species would make no evolutionary sense.

# Appendix

# MEASUREMENT OF THE VARIABLES USED
# IN THIS STUDY

VIOLENT DELINQUENCY. The measure of violent delinquency is the Andrew Violence Scale (Andrew, 1978). Andrew (1982) reports reliability coefficients for the scale ranging between .62 and .85. Crimes used in this study are only those in which the offender confronted the victim and used or threatened to use force. They include homicide, rape, aggravated assault, robbery, and various other kinds of assaultive behavior. Crimes are given a score based on seriousness of the crime. Each juvenile's violence score combines the number of violent crimes committed and the seriousness rating of those crimes.

LOVE DEPRIVATION. Love deprivation is measured by Walsh and Petee's (1987) love deprivation scale. This scale is based on the ratings of juvenile probation officers and child social workers who were asked to rate a number of items according to how they viewed them as indicators of the concept of love deprivation. Each item was rated on a scale ranging from zero (a poor indicator) to 10 (a very good indicator). Only indicators with a mean score of 6 or more were retained. The scale has an interrater reliability of .731. These items and their rounded mean scores are given below.

| ITEM | $\overline{X}$ |
|---|---|
| Physical Abuse of Child | 9 |
| Psychological Abuse of Child | 9 |
| Parental Substance Abuse | 9 |
| Child States Feels Unloved | 8 |
| Parental Sexual Promiscuity | 7 |
| Child Illegitimate | 6 |
| Child from Broken Home | 6 |

The theoretical importance of each of these items is commented upon throughout the text and has been enumerated by many researchers whose works have been reviewed here. The reliance on official data for the measure of love deprivation might be criticized. However, I agree with McCord (1979) that the coding of treatment records that have been collected over a long period of time by trained observers is a reliable method of tapping the concept. The index is based on multiple indicators of the concept derived from theory and from the combined judgments of a number of professionals in daily contact with the problem.

INTELLECTUAL IMBALANCE. Intellectual imbalance is measured by the standard method of subtracting an individual's PIQ score from his or her VIQ score.

SES. SES is a composite of annual income and occupational status of the head of household as suggested by Van Dussen and Zill (1975).

All other variables used in the study are self-explanatory or explained in the text.

# BIBLIOGRAPHY

Ader, R. (1983). "Developmental psychoneuroimmunology." *Developmental Psychobiology, 16:*251–267.

Adler, F. (1975). *Sisters in Crime: The Rise of the New Female Criminal.* New York: McGraw-Hill.

Anastasi, A. (1976). *Psychological Testing.* New York: Macmillan.

Andersen, M. (1988). *Thinking About Women: Sociological Perspectives on Sex and Gender.* New York: Macmillan.

Andrew, J. (1974). "Delinquency, the Wechsler P > V sign, and the I-level system." *Journal of Clinical Psychology, 30:*331–335.

Andrew, J. (1977). "Delinquency: Intellectual imbalance?" *Criminal Justice and Behavior, 4:*99–104.

Andrew, J. (1978). "Violence among delinquents by family intactness and size." *Social Biology, 25:*243–250.

Andrew, J. (1980). "Verbal IQ and the I-level classification system for delinquents." *Criminal Justice and Behavior, 7:*193–202.

Applewhite, P. (1981). *Molecular Gods: How Molecules Determine Our Behavior.* Englewood Cliffs, NJ: Prentice-Hall.

Asso, D. (1983). *The Real Menstrual Cycle.* New York: John Wiley.

Associated Press. (1990). "Maternity leave benefits increase." *Idaho Stateman,* April 13, p. 2.

Austin, R. (1975). "Construct validity of I-level classification." *Criminal Justice and Behavior, 2:*113–129.

Austin, R. (1981). "I-level and rehabilitation of delinquents." In Kratcoski, P. (ed.), *Correctional Counseling and Treatment.* Monterey, CA: Duxbury Press.

Baltes, P. and Nesselroade, J. (1984). "Paradigm lost and paradigm regained: Critique of Dannefer's portrayal of life-span developmental psychology." *American Sociological Review, 49:*841–846.

Banton, M. and Harwood, J. (1975). *The Race Concept.* New York: Preager.

Baratz, S. and Baratz, J. (1982). "Early childhood intervention: The social science base of institutional racism." In Yetman, N. and Steele, C. (eds.), *Majority & Minority: The Dynamics of Race and Ethnicity in American Life.* Boston: Allyn and Bacon.

Bardwick, J. (1976). "Physiological correlates of the menstrual cycle and oral contraceptive medication." In Sachar, E. (ed.), *Hormones, Behavior, and Psychopathology.* New York: Raven.

Barfield, A. (1976). "Biological influences on sex differences in behavior." In

Teitelbaum, M. (ed.), *Sex Differences: Social and Biological Perspectives.* Garden City, NY: Anchor.

Barnett, R., Zimmer, L., and McCormack, J. (1989). "P > V sign and personality profiles." *Journal of Correctional and Social Psychiatry and Offender Treatment and Therapy, 35:* 18–20.

Baskin, Y. (1986). "The way we act: More than we thought, our biochemistry helps determine our behavior." *Science, 86,* November: 94–101.

Berman, A. and Seigal, A. (1976). "A neurophysiological approach to the etiology, prevention, and treatment of juvenile delinquency." In Davids, A. (ed.), *Child Personality and Psychopathology: Current Topics.* New York: Wiley.

Bernard, T. (1990). "Angry aggression among the 'truly disadvantaged.'" *Criminology, 28:* 73–95.

Berndt, T. (1982). "The features and effects of friendships in early adolescence." *Child Development, 53:* 1447–1460.

Berne, E. (1964). *Games People Play.* New York: Grove Press.

Blau, A. (1943). "Childhood behavior disorders and delinquency." *Mental Hygiene, 27:* 261–266.

Block, N. and Dworkin, G. (1976). "IQ and heritability." In N. Block and G. Dworkin (eds.), *The IQ Controversy.* New York: Pantheon.

Bogdanovich, P. (1985). *The Killing of the Unicorn: Dorothy Stratten 1960–1980.* New York: Bantam.

Bouchard, Jr., T. and McGue, M. (1981). "Familial studies of intelligence: A review." *Science, 212:* 1055–1059.

Bouchard, Jr., T. and Segal, N. (1984). "Environment and IQ." In Woolman, B. (ed.), *Handbook of Intelligence: Theories, Measurements, and Applications.* New York: John Wiley.

Boucher, C. (1985). "A child development perspective on the responsibility of juveniles." In Sullivan, J. and Victor, J. (eds.), *Criminal Justice 85/86.* Guilford, CT: Dushkin.

Braginski, D. and Braginsky, M. (1973). "Psychologists: High priests of the middle class." *Psychology Today, December:* 15–138.

Bridgeman, P. (1955). *Reflections of a Physicist.* New York: Philosophical Library.

Brody, N. (1985). "The validity of tests of intelligence." In Wolman, B. (ed.), *Handbook of Intelligence: Theories, Measurement, and Applications.* New York: Wiley.

Brown, D. (1991). *Human Universals.* New York: McGraw-Hill.

Brown, S. (1984). "Social class, child maltreatment, and delinquent behavior." *Criminology, 22:* 259–278.

Bruner, J. (1972). "The nature and uses of immaturity." *American Psychologist, 27:* 678.

Buikhuisen, W. (1982). "Aggressive behavior and cognitive disorders." *International Journal of Law and Psychiatry, 5:* 205–217.

Buikhuisen, W. (1987). "Cerebral dysfunctions and persistent juvenile delinquency." In Mednick, S., Moffitt, T., and Stack, S. (eds.), *The Causes of Crime: New Biological Approaches.* Cambridge: University of Cambridge Press.

Buikhuisen, W. (1989). "Explaining juvenile delinquency from a biosocial developmental perspective." *International Journal of Offender Therapy and Comparative Criminology, 33:* 185–195.

Buikhuisen, W. and Mednick, S. (1988). *Explaining Criminal Behaviour.* Leiden, The Netherlands: E. J. Brill.

Buikhuisen, W., Bontekoe, E., Plas-Koenhoff, C., and Van Buuren, S. (1984). "Characteristic of criminals: The privileged offender." *International Journal of Law and Psychiatry, 7:*301–313.

Buri, J. Kirchener, P. and Walsh, J. (1987). "Family correlates of self-esteem in young American Adults." The Journal of Social Psychology, 127:583–588.

Buss, D. (ed.). (1990). Biological Foundations of Personality: Evolution, Behavioral Genetics, and Psychophysiology. Special issue of the *Journal of Personality,* vol. 58.

Casler, L. (1973). "Toward a re-evaluation of love." In Curtin, M. (ed.), *Symposium on Love.* New York: Behavioral Publications.

Cadoret, R. (1982). "Genotype-environmental interaction in antisocial behavior." *Psychological Medicine, 12:*235–239.

Cernkovich, S. and Giordano, P. (1987). "Family relationships and delinquency." *Criminology, 25:*295–319.

Chase, N. (1975). *A Child is Being Beaten.* New York: McGraw-Hill.

Chase, T., Fedio, P., Foster, N., Brooks, R., Di Chiro, G. and Mansi, L. (1984). "Wechsler adult intelligence scale performance: Cortical localization by fluoro-deoxyglucose F 18 positron emission tomography." *Archives of Neurology, 41:*244–247.

Clark, C. and Gist, N. (1938). "Intelligence as a factor in occupational choice." *American Sociological Review, 3:*672–672.

Clarke, A. M., and Clarke, A. D. (1976). *Early Experience: Myth and Evidence.* New York: Free Press.

Cloninger, C., Reich, T., and Guze, S. (1975). "The multifactorial model of disease transmission: II. Sex differences in the familial transmission of sociopathy (antisocial personality)." *British Journal of Psychiatry, 127:*11–22.

Cloward, R. and Ohlin, L. (1960). *Delinquency and Opportunity.* New York: Free Press.

Cohen, A. (1955). *Delinquent Boys: The Culture of the Gang.* New York: Free Press.

Cohn, A. (1979). "Essential elements of successful child abuse and neglect treatment." *Child Abuse & Neglect, 3:*491–496.

Coleman, J. and Cressey, D. (1987). *Social Problems.* New York: Harper & Row.

Collins, J. (1983). "Alcohol use and criminal behavior: An executive summary." National Institute of Justice. Washington, DC: U.S. Department of Justice.

Cooke, W. (1945). "The differential psychology of American women." *American Journal of Obstetrics and Gynecology, 49:*457–472.

Corning, W., Steffy, R., and Chaprin, I. (1982). "EEG slow frequency and WISC–R correlates." *Journal of Abnormal Child Psychology, 10:*511–530.

Coser, L. (1971). *Masters of Sociological Thought.* New York: Harcourt Brace Jovanovich.

Coursey, R., Buchsbaum, M., and Murphy, D. (1979). "L. platelet MOA activity and evoked potentials in the identification of subjects biologically at risk for psychiatric disorders." *British Journal of Psychiatry, 134:*372–381.

Crnic, K., Greenberg, M., Robinson, N. & Ragozin, A. (1984). "Maternal stress and social support: Effects on the mother-infant relationship from birth to eighteen months." *American Journal of Orthopsychiatry, 54,* 224–235.

Crockenberg, S. B. (1981). "Infant irritability, mother responsiveness, and social support influences on the security of mother-infant attachment." *Child Development,* 52, 857–865.

Curtis, L. (1985). *American Violence and Public Policy.* New Haven, CT: Yale University Press.

David, K. and Rowland, D. (1986). "Uninsured and unserved: Inequalities of health care in the United States." In Conrad, P. and Kern, R. (eds.), *The Sociology of Health and Illness.* New York: St. Martin.

Davis, B., Yu, P., Boulton, A., Wormith, J. and Addington, D. (1983). "Correlative relationship between biochemical activity and aggressive Behaviour." *Progress in Neuro-Psychopharmacology and Biological Psychiatry,* 7:529–535.

DeFrancis, V. and Lucht, C. (1974). *Child Abuse Legislation in the 1970's.* Denver: American Humane Association.

de Lacoste-Utamsing, C. and Holloway, R. (1982). "Sexual dimorphism in the human corpus callosum." *Science, 216:* 1431–1432.

DeLozier, P. (1982). "Attachment theory and child abuse." In Park, C. and Stevenson-Hinde, J. (eds.), *The Place of Attachment in Human Behavior.* New York: Basic Books.

Dembo, R., La Voie, L., Schmeidler, J., and Washburn, M. (1987). "The nature and correlates of psychological/emotional functioning among a sample of detained youths." *Criminal Justice and Behavior, 14:* 311–334.

Denenberg, V. (1981). "Hemispheric laterality in animals and the effects of early experience." *Behavioral and Brain Sciences, 4:* 1–49.

Deutscher, I. (1967). "The social causes of social problems, from suicide to delinquency." In Mizruchi, E. (ed.), *The Substance of Sociology.* Boston: Appleton-Century-Crofts.

DiCara, L. (1970). "Learning in the autonomic nervous system." *Scientific American, 222:* 30–39.

Dillingham, S. (1988). "Manual on catching ones who kill and kill." *Insight,* February 22, 24.

Dobbing, J. (1973). "The later development of the central nervous system and its vulnerability." In Davis, J. and Dobbing, J. (eds.), *Scientific Foundations of Pediatrics.* London: William Heinemann.

d'Orban, P. and Dalton, K. (1980). "Violent crime and the menstrual cycle." *Psychological Medicine, 10:* 353–359.

Duara, R., Grady, C., Haxby, J., Ingvar, D., Sokoloff, L., Margolin, R., Manning, R., Cutler, N. and Rapoport, S. (1984). "Human brain glucose utilization and cognitive function in relation to age." *Annals of Neurology, 16:* 702–713.

Durden-Smith, J., and deSimone, D. (1983). *Sex and the Brain.* New York: Arbor House.

Eaker, H., Allen, S., and Gray, J. (1983). "A factor analytic study of personality and intellectual variables in incarcerated delinquent males and females." *Journal of Clinical Psychology, 39:* 614–616.

Eckland, B. (1979). "Genetic variance in the SES–IQ correlation." *Sociology of Education, 52:* 191–196.

Edwards, D. and Nuckols, C. (1991). "Identifying kids at high risk." *Adolescent Counselor, 3:*25–40.

Ehrhardt, A. and Meyer-Bahlburg, H. (1981). "Effects of prenatal hormones on gender-related behavior." *Science, 211:*1312–1318.

Ehrenkranz, J., Bliss, E., and Sheard, M. (1974). "Plasma testosterone: Correlation with aggressive behavior and social dominance in man." *Psychosomatic Medicine, 36:*469–475.

Ellis, D. and Austin, P. (1971). "Menstruation and aggressive behavior in a correctional center for women." *Journal of Criminal Law, Criminology, and Police Science." 62:*388–395.

Ellis, L. (1977). "The decline and fall of sociology: 1975–2000." *American Sociologist, 12:*56–66.

Ellis, L. (1986). "Evidence of neuroandrogenic etiology of sex differences from a combined analysis of human, nonhuman primate and nonprimate mammalian studies." *Personality and Individual Differences, 7:*519–552.

Elmer, E. (1977). *Fragile Families, Troubled Children.* Pittsburgh: University of Pittsburgh Press.

Erlenmeyer-Kimling, L. and Jarvik, L. (1963). "Genetics and intelligence: A review." *Science, 142:*1477–1478.

Eysenck, H. (1977). *Crime and Personality.* London: Routledge and Kegan Paul.

Fagan, J. (1990). "Social and legal policy dimensions of violent juvenile crime." *Criminal Justice and Behavior, 17:*93–133.

Failkov, M. (1985). "Biologic and psychosocial determinants in the etiology of alcoholism." In Tarter, R. and Van Theil (eds.), *Alcohol and the Brain: Chronic Effects.* New York: Plenum Medical.

Farley, J. (1990). *Sociology.* Englewood Cliff, NJ: Prentice-Hall.

Farrington, D. (1987). "Implications of biological findings for criminological research." In Mednick, S., Moffitt, T., and Stack, S. (eds.), *The Causes of Crime: New Biological Approaches.* Cambridge: University of Cambridge Press.

Feingold, A. (1988). "Cognitive gender differences are disappearing." *American Psychologist, 43:*95–103.

Fincher, J. (1982). *The Human Brain: Mystery of Matter and Mind.* Washington, DC: U. S. News Books.

Fischbein, S. (1980). "IQ and social class." *Intelligence, 4:*51–63.

Fishbein, D. (1990). "Biological perspectives in criminology." *Criminology, 28:*27–75.

Fischer, K. (1987). "Relations between brain and cognitive development." *Child Development, 58:*623–632.

Flaherty, J. and Richman, J. (1986). "Effects of childhood relationships on the adult's capacity to form social supports." *American Journal of Psychiatry, 143:*851–855.

Flor-Henry, P. (1978). "Gender, hemispheric specialization and psychopathology." *Social Science and Medicine, 12b:*155–162.

Fortune, W. (1939). "Apapesh warfare." *American Anthropologist, 41:*22–41.

Fraiberg, S. (1977). *Every Child's Birthright: In Defense of Mothering.* New York: Basic Books.

Frank, G. (1983). *The Wechsler Enterprise*. New York: Pergamon Press.

Franklin, J. (1985). "Alternative education as substance abuse prevention." *Journal of Alcohol and Drug Education, 30:*12–23.

Freud, A. (1965). *Normality and Pathology in Childhood*. New York: International Universities Press.

Freud, S. (1961). *Civilization and its Discontents*. New York: Norton.

Fry, W. and Langeth, M. (1985). *Crying: The Mystery of Tears*. New York: Winston Press.

Gardener, E. (1972). *Principles of Genetics*. New York: John Wiley.

Garth, D., Tennent, G. and Pidduck, R. (1971). "Criminological characteristics of bright delinquents." *British Journal of Criminology, July:*275–279.

Geary, D. (1989). "A model for representing gender differences in the pattern of cognitive abilities." *American Psychologist, 44:*1155–1156.

Gelles, R. and Cornell, C. (1990). *Intimate Violence in Families*. Beverly Hills, CA: Sage.

Gendreau, P. and Ross, R. (1987). "Revivification of rehabilitation: Evidence from the 1980s." *Justice Quarterly, 4:*349–406.

George, C. and Main, M. (1979). "Social interactions of young abused children: Approach, avoidance, and aggression." *Child Development, 50:*306–318.

Gibbons, D. (1970). *Delinquent Behavior*. Englewood Cliffs, NJ: Prentice-Hall.

Gewertz, D. (1981). "A historical reconsideration of female dominance among the Chambri of Papua New Guinea." *American Ethnologist, 8:*94–106.

Gibbons, D. (1973). *Society, Crime, and Criminal Careers*. Englewood Cliffs, NJ: Prentice-Hall.

Glasser, W. (1975). *Reality Therapy*. New York: Harper & Row.

Glasser, W. (1976). *The Identity Society*. New York: Harper & Row.

Glueck, S. (1956). "Theory and fact in criminology: A criticism of differential association theory." *British Journal of Criminology, 7:*92–109.

Goelet, P., Castellucci, V., Schacher, S., and Kandell, E. (1986). "The long and short of long-term memory." *Nature, 322:*419–422.

Goldman-Rakic, P. (1987). "Development of cortical circuitry and cognitive function." *Child Development, 58:*601–622.

Goode, E. (1988). *Drugs in American Society*. New York: Alfred A. Knopf.

Gordon, R. (1980). "Research on IQ, race, and delinquency: Taboo or not taboo?" In Sagarin, E. (ed.), *Taboos in Criminology*. Beverly Hills, CA: Sage.

Gordon, R. and Rudert, E. (1979). "Bad news about intelligence tests." *Sociology of Education, 52:*174–190.

Gortmaker, S. (1979). "Poverty and infant mortality in the United States." *American Journal of Sociology, 44:*280–297.

Gottfries, C. (1980). "Activity of monoamine oxydase and brain levels of monoamines in alcoholics." In Richter, D. (ed.), *Addiction and Brain Damage*. Baltimore, University Park Press.

Gove, W. and Crutchfield, R. (1982). "The family and juvenile delinquency." *Sociological Quarterly, 23:*301–319.

Grabowski, J. (1984). *Cocaine: Pharmacology, effects and treatment of abuse*. Washington, DC: National Institute of Drug Abuse.

Green, P., Morgan, C., and Barah, D. (1979). "Sociobiology." In S. McNall (ed.), *Theoretical Perspectives in Sociology*. New York: St. Martin's Press.

Greenough, W., Black, J., and Wallace, C. (1987). "Experience and brain development." *Child Development, 58:*539–559.

Gutterman, S. (1979). "I.Q. tests in research on social stratification: The cross-class validity of the tests." *Sociology of Education, 52:*163–173.

Halpern, D. (1989). "The disappearance of cognitive gender differences: What you see depends on where you look." *American Psychologist, 44:*1156–1158.

Hankoff, L. (1987). "The earliest memories of criminals." *International Journal of Offender Therapy and Comparative Criminology, 31:*195–201.

Hanson, S., Myers, D., & Ginsburg, A. (1987). "The Role of responsibility and knowledge in reducing teenage out-of-wedlock childbearing." *Journal of Marriage and the Family, 49,* 241–256.

Hare, R. and Quinn, M. (1971). "Psychopathy and autonomic conditioning." *Journal of Abnormal Psychology, 77:*223–235.

Harlow, H. (1958). "The nature of love." *American Psychologist, 13:*673–685.

Harlow, H. and Harlow, M. (1962). "Social deprivation in monkeys." *Scientific American, 206:*137–144.

Harre, R. (1967). "Philosophy of science, history of." In P. Edwards (ed.), *The Encyclopedia of Philosophy*, vol. 6: pp. 289–296. New York: Macmillan.

Hartl, D. (1981). *A Primer of Population Genetics*. Sunderland, MA: Sinauer Associates.

Hartman, H. (1978). *Basic Psychiatry for Corrections Workers*. Springfield, IL: Charles C Thomas.

Harvey, B. (1980). "Searching for the roots of violence: The first three years of life." *Liaison, 6:*3–8.

Haskell, M. and Yablonsky, I. (1974). *Crime and Delinquency*. Chicago: Rand McNally.

Haskett, R. (1987). "Premenstrual dysphoric disorder: Evaluation and treatment." *Progress in Neuro-Psychopharmacology and Biological Psychiatry, 11:*129–135.

Haynes, J. and Bensch, M. (1981). "The P > V sign on the WISC–R and recidivism in delinquents." *Journal of Consulting and Clinical Psychology, 49:*480–481.

Haynie, R. (1980). "Deprivation of body pleasure: Origin of violent behavior? A survey of the literature." *Child Welfare, 59:*287–297.

Hays, W. (1988). *Statistics*. New York: Holt, Rinehart and Winston.

Heath, A., Berg, K., Eaves, L., Solaas, M., Corey, L., Sundet, J., Magnus, P., and Nance, W. (1985). Education policy and the heritability of educational attainment." *Nature, 314:*734–736.

Henggeler, S., Edwards, J., and Borduin, C. (1987). "The family relations of female juvenile delinquents." *Journal of Abnormal Child Psychology, 15:*199–209.

Henson, S. (1980). "Female as totem, female as taboo: An inquiry into the freedom to make connections." In Sagarin, E. (ed.), *Taboos in Criminology*. Beverly Hills: Sage.

Herrenkohl, R., Herrenkolh, E., Egolf, B., and Seech, M. (1979). "The repetition of child abuse. How frequently does it occur?" *Child Abuse & Neglect, 3:*67–72.

Herrnstein, R. (1971). *IQ in the Meritocracy*. Boston: Little, Brown.

Herrnstein, R. (1980). "In defense of intelligence tests." *Commentary, 69:*40–51.

Herrnstein, R. (1989). "Biology and crime." National Institute of Justice Crime File, NCJ 97216. Washington, DC: U. S. Department of Justice.

Hertzig, M., Birch, H., Richardson, S. and Tizard, J. (1972). "Intellectual levels of school children severely malnourished during the first two years of life." *Pediatrics, 49:*814–824.

Hindelang, M. (1979). "Sex differences in criminal activity." *Social Problems, 27:*143–156.

Hindelang, M., Hirschi, T., and Weis, J. (1981). *Measuring Delinquency.* Beverly Hills, CA: Sage.

Hirschi, T. (1977). "Causes and prevention of juvenile delinquency." *Sociological Inquiry, 47:*322–341.

Hirschi, T. and Hindelang, M. (1977). "Intelligence and delinquency: A revisionist review." *American Sociological Review, 42:*571–587.

Hoffman, P. and Tabakoff, B. (1985). "Ethanol's action on brain chemistry." In Tarter, R. and Van Theil (eds.), *Alcohol and the Brain: Chronic Effects.* New York: Plenum Medical.

Hoffman-Plotkin, D. and Twentyman, C. (1984). "A multimodal assessment of behavioral and cognitive deficits in abused and neglected preschoolers." *Child Development, 55:*794–802.

Holden, C. (1989). "Street-wise crack research." *Science, 246:*1376–1381.

Hopper, P. and Zigler, E. (1988). "The medical and social science basis for a national infant care leave policy." *American Journal of Orthopsychiatry, 58:*324–338.

Hoyenga, K. B. and Hoyenger, K. T. (1979). *The Question of Sex Differences: Psychological, Cultural, and Biological Issues.* Boston: Little, Brown.

Huesmann, L., Eron, L., and Yarmel, P. (1987). "Intellectual functioning and aggression." *Journal of Personality and Social Psychology, 52:*232–240.

Hyde, M. and Hyde, L. (1985). *Missing Children.* New York: Franklin Watts.

Hynd, G. and Willis, W. (1985). "Neurological foundations of intelligence." In Wolman, B. (ed.), *Handbook of Intelligence: Theories, Measurements, and Applications.* New York: John Wiley.

Jacobs, B. and Moss, H. (1976). "Birth order and sex of sibling as determinants of mother-infant interaction." *Child Development, 47:*315–322.

Jefferey, C. (1977). "Criminology—whither or wither?" *Criminology, 15:*283–286.

Jefferey, C. (1979). "Biology and crime: The Neo-Lombrosians." In Jefferey, C. (ed.), *Biology and Crime.* Beverly Hills, CA: Sage.

Jefferey, C. (1990). *Criminology: An Interdisciplinary Approach.* Englewood Cliffs, NJ: Prentice-Hall.

Jencks, C. (1980). "Heredity, environment, and public policy revisited." *American Sociological Review, 45:*723–736.

Jencks, C. (1987). "Genes and crime." New York: *New York Review of Books, 34:*33–41.

Jensen, A. (1969). "How much can we boost IQ and scholastic achievement?" *Harvard Educational Review, 39:*1–123.

Jensen, A. (1974). "Social class, race, and genetics: Implications for education." In G. LeFrancois (ed.), *Little George: A Survey of Child Development.* Belmont, CA: Wadsworth.

Jensen, A. (1977). "Cumulative deficit in IQ of blacks in the rural south." *Developmental Psychology, 13:*184–191.

Johnson, E. and Meade, A. (1987). "Developmental patterns of spatial ability: An early sex difference." *Child Development, 58:*275–740.

Johnson, R. (1979). *Juvenile Delinquency and its Origins.* Cambridge: Cambridge University Press.

Johnson, R. (1986). "Family structure and delinquency: general patterns and gender differences." *Criminology, 24:*65–83.

Joseph, R. (1982). "The Neuropsychology of development: hemispheric laterality, limbic language, and the origin of thought." *Journal of Clinical Psychology, 38:*4–33.

Kagan, J., Reznick, S., and Snidman, N. (1987). "The physiology and psychology of behavioral inhibition in children." *Child Development, 58:*1459–1473.

Kalil, R. (1989). "Synapse formation in the developing brain." *Scientific American,* December:76–85.

Kamin, L. (1974). *Science and the Politics of IQ.* New York: Wiley.

Kammeyer, K. (1969). "Birth order as a research variable." In Borgata, E. (ed.), *Social Psychology: Readings and Perspectives.* Chicago: Rand McNally.

Kandel, E. (1983). "From metapsychology to molecular biology: Explorations into the nature of anxiety." *American Journal of Psychiatry, 140:*1277–1293.

Kandel, E., Mednick, S., Kirkegaard-Sorensen, L., Hutchings, B., Knop, J., Rosenberg, R., and Schulsinger, F. (1988). "IQ as a protective factor for subjects at high risk for anti-social behavior." *Journal of Consulting and Clinical Psychology, 55:*224–226.

Kaplan, R. (1985). "The controversy related to the use of psychological tests." In Wolman, B. (ed.), *Handbook of Intelligence: Theories, Measurements, and Applications.* New York: John Wiley.

Kaufman, A. (1976). "Verbal-performance discrepancies on the WISC–R." *Journal of Consulting and Clinical Psychology, 5:*739–744.

Keiser, T. (1976). "Schizotype and the Wechsler digit-span test." *Journal of Clinical Psychology, 31:*303–306.

Kernberg, O. (1974). "Barriers to falling and remaining in love." *Journal of the American Psychoanalytic Association, 22:*486–511.

Khan, A. and Cataio, A. (1984). *Men and Women in Biological Perspective: A Review of the Literature.* New York: Praeger.

Klaus, M. and Kennell, J. (1982). "Labor, birth, and bonding." In *Parent-Infant Bonding.* St. Louis, C. V. Mosby.

Klopfer, P. (1971). "Mother love: What turns it on?" *American Scientist, 59:*404–407.

Konner, M. (1982). *The Tangled Wing: Biological Constraints on the Human Spirit.* New York: Holt, Rinehart and Winston.

Kraemer, G., Ebert, M., Lake, C., and McKinney, W. (1983). "Amphetamine challenge: Effects on previously isolated rhesus monkeys and implications for animal models of schizophrenia." *Progress in Clinical Biology Research, 131:*199–218.

Kreppner, K. (1988). "Changes in relationships with the birth of the second child." *Marriage and Family Review, 12:*157–181.

Lamb, M. and Hwang, C. (1982). "Maternal attachments and mother-neonate bonding:

A critical review." In Lamb, M. and Brown, A. (eds.), *Advances in Developmental Psychology,* Vol. 2. Hillsdale, NJ: Erlbaum.

Lancaster, J., Altman, J., Rossi, A., and Sherrod, L. (1987) "The Biosocial Perspective." In Lancaster, J. et al. (eds.), *Parenting Across the Life Span: Biosocial Perspectives.* New York: Aldine De Gruyer.

Lazar, L. and Darlington, R. (1982). "Lasting effects of early education: A report from the Consortium for Longitudinal Studies." *Monographs of the Society for Research in Child Development, 47* (2–3, serial No. 195).

LeFrancois, G. (1990). *The Lifespan.* Belmont, CA: Wadsworth.

Levine, S., Halmeyer, G., Karas, G., and Denenberg, V. (1967). "Physiological and behavioral effects of infant stimulation." *Physiology and Behavior, 2:* 55–59.

Lewis, D., Shanok, S., and Balla, D. (1979a). "Parental criminality and medical histories of delinquent children." *American Journal of Psychiatry, 136:* 288–292.

Lewis, D., Shanok, S., and Balla, D. (1979b). "Perinatal difficulties, head and face trauma, and child abuse in medical histories of seriously delinquent children." *American Journal of Psychiatry, 136:* 419–423.

Lewin, M. (1980). "Science with taboos: An inherent contradiction." In Sagarin, E. (ed.), *Taboos in Criminology.* Beverly Hills, CA: Sage.

Lewin, R. (1975). "Starved brains." *Psychology Today, 9:* 29–33.

Leyton, E. (1984). *Hunting Humans: Inside the Minds of Mass Murderers.* New York: Pocket Books.

Lidberg, L., Modin, I., Oreland, L., Tuck, R., and Gillner, A. (1985). "Platelet monoamine oxydase activity and psychopathy." *Psychiatry Research, 16:* 339–343.

Liebowitz, M. (1983). *The Chemistry of Love.* New York: Berkley.

Linn, M. and Petersen, A. (1986). "A meta-analysis of gender differences in spatial ability: Implications for mathematics and science achievements." In Hyde, J. and Linn, M. (eds.), *The Psychology of Gender: Advances Through Meta-Analysis.* Baltimore: Johns Hopkins University Press.

Linn, R. (1982). "Individual differences, prediction and differential prediction." In Wigdor, A. and Garner, W. (eds.), *Ability Testing: Uses, Consequences, and Controversies.* Washington, DC: National Academy Press.

Lipsitt, S. (1979). "Critical conditions in infancy: A psychological perspective." *American Psychologist, 34:* 973–980.

Loro, B. and Woodward, J. (1976). "Verbal and performance IQ for discrimination among psychiatric diagnostic groups." *Journal of Clinical Psychology, 32:* 106–114.

Loury, G. (1987). "The better path to black progress: Beyond civil rights." In Barnes, L. (ed.), *Social Problems.* Guilford, CT: Dushkin.

Lyons-Ruth, K., Connel, D., and Grunebaum, H. (1990). "Infants at social risk: Maternal depression and family support services as mediators of infant development and security of attachment." *Child Development, 61:* 85–98.

MacIver, R. (1960). "Juvenile delinquency." In Ginsberg, E. (ed.), *The Nation's Children.* New York: Columbia University Press.

Marlatt, G., Baer, J., Donovan, D., and Kivlanhan, D. (1988). "Addictive behaviors: Etiology and treatment." *Annual Review of Psychology, 39:* 223–252.

Marx, K., and Engels, F. (1956). *The Holy Family, or Critique of Critical Critique.* London: Foreign Language Publishing House.

Maslow, A. (1954). *Motivation and Personality.* New York: Harper & Row.

Matarazzo, J. (1976). *Wechsler's Measurement and Appraisal of Adult Intelligence.* Baltimore: Williams and Wilkins.

Matarazzo, J. and Herman, D. (1985). "Clinical uses of the WAIS–R: Base rates of differences between VIQ and PIQ in the WAIS–R standardized sample." In Wolman, B. (ed.), *Handbook of Intelligence: Theories, Measurements, and Applications.* New York: John Wiley.

Matas, L., Arendt, R., and Stroufe, L. (1978). "Continuity of adaptation in the second year: The relationship between the quality of attachment and later competence." *Child Development, 49:*547–556.

Mawson, A. and Mawson, C. (1977). Psychopathy and arousal: A new interpretation of the psychophysiological literature." *Biological Psychiatry, 12:*49–73.

May, R. (1980). *Sex and Fantasy: Patterns of Male and Female Sexual Development.* New York: Norton.

Maccoby, E. (1988). "Gender as a social category." *Developmental Psychology, 24:*755–765.

Maccoby, E. and Jacklin, C. (1974). *The Psychology of Sex Differences.* Stanford: University of Stanford Press.

Macionis, J. (1989). *Sociology.* Englewood Cliffs, NJ: Prentice-Hall.

Masters, R. and Robertson, C. (1990). *Inside Criminology.* Englewood Cliffs, NJ: Prentice-Hall.

McClearn, G. and Defries, J. (1973). *Introduction to Behavioral Genetics.* San Francisco: W. H. Freeman.

McCord, J. (1983). "The psychopath and moral development." In Laufer, W. and Day, J. (eds.), *Personality Theory, Moral Development, and Criminal Behavior.* Lexington, MA: D. C. Heath.

McCord, W. and McCord, J. (1959). *Origins of Crime.* Montclair, NJ: Patterson Smith.

McEwen, B. (1981). "Neural gonadal steroid actions." *Science, 211:*1303–1311.

McFie, J. (1973). "Intellectual imbalance: A perceptual hypothesis." *British Journal of Social and Clinical Psychology, 12:*433–434.

Mednick, S. (1979). "Biosocial factors and primary prevention of antisocial behavior." In Mednick, S. and Shoham, S. (eds.), *New Paths in Criminology.* Lexington, MA: Lexington Books.

Mednick, S. et al. (1982). "Biology and crime." In M. Wolfgang and N. Weiner (eds.), *Criminal Violence.* Beverly Hills, Sage.

Mednick, S. and Finello, K. (1983). "Biological factors and crime: Implications for forensic psychiatry." *International Journal of Law and Psychiatry, 6:*1–15.

Mednick, S., Gabrielli, W., and Hutchings, B. (1984). "Genetic influences in criminal convictions: Evidence from an adoption cohort." *Science, 224:*891–894.

Mednick, S., Higgins, J., and Kirschenbaum, J. (1975). *Psychology: Explorations in Behavior and Experience.* New York: John Wiley.

Mellen, S. (1981). *The Evolution of Love.* San Francisco, W. H. Freeman.

Menard, S. and Morse, B. (1984). "A structural critique of the IQ-delinquency hypothesis: Theory and evidence." *American Journal of Sociology, 89:*1347–1378.

Merton, R. (1938). "Social structure and anomie." *American Sociological Review,* 3:672–672.

Miller, J. (1984). "The development of woman's sense of self." Working paper, Stone Center for Developmental Services and Studies, Wellesley College, Wellesley, MA.

Miller, L. (1987). "Neuropsychology of the aggressive psychopath: An integrative review." *Aggressive Behavior, 13:*119–140.

Moffitt, T., Gabrielli, W., Mednick, S., and Schulsinger, F. (1981). "Socioeconomic status, IQ, and delinquency." *Journal of Abnormal Psychology, 90:*152–156.

Moffitt, T. and Silva, P. (1988). "IQ and delinquency: A test of the differential detection hypothesis." *Journal of Abnormal Psychology, 97:*330–333.

Montagu, A. (1970). "A scientist looks at love." *Phi Delta Kappan, 51:*463–467.

Montagu, A., (1981). *Growing Young.* New York: McGraw-Hill.

Montagu, A. (1974). *The Natural Superiority of Women.* New York: Collier.

Montagu, A. (1978). *Touching: The Human Significance of the Skin.* New York: Harper & Row.

Murchison, C. (1926). *Criminal Intelligence.* Worcester, MA: Clark University Press.

Murrell, S. (1974). "Relationship of ordinal position and family size to psychosocial measures of delinquents." *Journal of Abnormal Child Psychology, 2:*39–46.

Nachshon, I. and Denno, D. (1987). "Violent behavior and cerebral hemisphere function." In Mednick, S., Moffitt, T., and Stack, S. (eds.), *The Causes of Crime: New Biological Approaches.* Cambridge: University of Cambridge Press.

Naftolin, F. (1981). "Understanding the bases of sex differences." *Science, 211:*1263–1264.

National Institute of Justice. (1987). "Sourcebook of criminal statistics." Washington, DC: U.S. Government Printing Office.

Nelson, N. (1971). "Trebly sensuous woman." *Psychology Today, July:*48–52.

Nettler, G. (1978). *Explaining Crime.* New York: McGraw-Hill.

Netler, G. (1982). *Explaining Criminals.* Cincinnati: Anderson.

Newman, G. (1979). *Understanding Violence.* New York: Harper & Row.

Norton, E. (1987). "Restoring the traditional black family." In Barnes, L. (ed.), *Social Problems.* Guilford, CT: Dushkin.

O'Conner, S., Vietze, P., Sherrod, K., Sandler, H., and Altmeier, W. (1980). "Reduced incidence of parenting inadequacy following rooming-in." *Pediatrics, 66:*176–182.

Offer, D. (1975). *From Teenager to Young Manhood: A Psychological Study.* New York: Basic Books.

Olds, D. (1984). Final report: Prenatal/early infancy project. Washington, DC: National Institute of Health.

Olweus, D., Mattsson, A., Schalling, D., and Low, H. (1988). "Circulating testosterone levels and aggression in adolescent males: A causal analysis." *Psychosomatic Medicine, 50:*261–272.

Omenn, G. and Motulsky, A. (1972). "Biochemical genetics and the evolution of human behavior." In L. Erhman, S. Omenn, and E. Caspari (eds.), *Genetics, Environment, and Behavior.* New York: Academic Press.

Oreland, L. (1983). "Why do alcoholics have low platelet monoamine oxidas activity?" In Hesselbrook, V., Shaskan, E., and Meyer, R. (eds.), *Biological/Genetic Factors in Alcoholism.* Washington, DC: U.S. Department of Health and Human Services.

Pardes, H. (1986). "Neuroscience and Psychiatry: Marriage or coexistence?" *American Journal of Psychiatry, 143:* 1205–1212.

Pearsall, P. (1987). *Superimmunity.* New York: Fawcet.

Peele, S. (1990). "Second thoughts about a gene for alcoholism." *Atlantic, 266:* 52–58.

Platt, T. and Takagi, P. (1985). "Biosocial criminology: A critique." In Marsh, F. and Katz, J. (eds.), *Biology, Crime, and Ethics.* Cincinnati, OH: Anderson.

Plomin, R., DeFries, J., and Loehlin, J. (1977). "Genotype-environment interaction and correlation in the analysis of human behavior." *Psychological Bulletin, 84:* 309–322.

Plomin, R. and DeFries, J. (1980). "Genetics and intelligence: Recent data." *Intelligence, 4:* 15–24.

Plomin, R. and Daniels, D. (1987). "Why are children in the same family so different from one another?" *Behavioral and Brain Sciences, 10:* 1–60.

Prescott, J. (1975). "Body pleasure and the origins of pleasure." *Bulletin of the Atomic Scientist, 31:* 10–20.

Purves, D. and Lichtman, J. (1980). "Elimination of synapses in the developing nervous system." *Science, 210:* 153–157.

Radzinowicz, L. and King, J. (1977). *The Growth of Crime: The International Experience.* London: Penguin.

Rahav, G. (1980). "Birth order and delinquency." *British Journal of Criminology, 20:* 385–395.

Rankin, J. (1983). "The family context of delinquency." *Social Problems, 30:* 466–479.

Rapaport, D., Gill, M., and Schaefer, R. (1968). *Diagnostic Psychological Testing.* New York: International Universities Press.

Reid, S. (1990). *Criminal Justice.* New York: MacMillan.

Reige, M. (1972). Parental affection and juvenile delinquency in girls." *British Journal of Criminology, 12:* 55–73.

Reite, M. (1987). "Some additional influences shaping the development of behavior." *Child Development, 58:* 596–600.

Restak, R. (1979). *The Brain: The Last Frontier.* NY: Warner.

Restak, R. (1986). *The Infant Mind.* Garden City, NY: Doubleday.

Rice, R. (1977). "Neurophysiological development in premature infants following stimulation." *Developmental Psychology, 13:* 69–76.

Roberts, D. and Bachen, C. (1981). "Mass communication effects." In Rosenzweig, M. and Porter, L. (eds.), *Annual Review of Psychology,* Vol. 21. Palo Alto, CA: Annual Reviews.

Robinson, J. and Shaver, P. (1973). *Measures of Social Psychological Attitudes.* Ann Arbor, MI: University of Michigan Survey Research Center.

Rohner, R. (1975). *They Love Me, They Love Me Not: A Worldwide Study of the Effects of Parental Acceptance and Rejection.* New York: Hraf.

Romig, D., Cleland, C. and Romig, L. (1989). *Juvenile Delinquency: Visionary Approaches.* Columbus, OH: Merrill.

Rose, R. (1978). "Neuroendocrine correlates of sexual and aggressive behavior in humans." In Lipton, M., Di Mascio, A., and Killam, K. (eds.), *Psychopharmacology: A Generation of Progress.* New York: Raven.

Rose, R., Holaday, J. and Bernstein, R. (1971). "Plasma testosterone, dominance rank and aggressive behavior in male rhesus monkeys." *Nature, 231:*366–368.

Rose, S. (1976). *The Conscious Brain.* New York: Vintage.

Rosen, L. (1985). "Family and delinquency: Structure or Function?" *Criminology, 23:*553–573.

Rosen, L. and Neilson, K. (1982). "Broken homes". In Savitz, L. and Johnson, N. (eds.), *Contemporary Criminology.* New York: Wiley.

Rosenbaum, J. (1989). "Family disfunction and female delinquency." *Crime and Delinquency, 35:*31–41.

Rosenfeld, A. (1981). "Tippling enzymes." *Science, 81*(2):24–25.

Rosenzweig, M., Bennett, E., and Diamond, M. (1973). "Brain changes in response to experience." In Greenough, W. (ed.), *The Nature and Nurture of Behavior: Developmental Psychobiology.* San Francisco: W. H. Freeman.

Rossi, A. (1977). "A biosocial perspective on parenting." *Daedalus, 106:*1–31.

Rossi, A. (1984). "Gender and parenthood: American Sociological Association, 1983 presidential address." *American Sociological Review, 49:*1–19.

Rossi, A. (1987). "Parenthood in transition: From lineage to child self-orientation." In Lancaster, J. et al. (eds.), *Parenting Across the Life Span: Biosocial Perspectives.* New York: Aldine De Gruyter.

Rothbart, M. (1971). "Birth order and mother-child interactions in an achievement situation." *Journal of Personality and Social Psychology, 17:*113–120.

Rowe, D. and Osgood, D. (1984). "Heredity and sociological theories of delinquency: A reconsideration." *American Sociological Review, 49:*526–540.

Rubin, R., Reinisch, J. and Haskett, R. (1981). "Postnatal gonadal steroid effects on human behavior." *Science, 211:*1318–1324.

Rushton, J., Fulker, D., Neale, M., Nias, D., and Eysenck, H. (1986). Altruism and aggression: The heritability of individual differences." *Journal of Personality and Social Psychology, 50:*1192–1198.

Rutter, M. and Madge, N. (1976). *Cycles of Disadvantage.* London: Heinemann Educational Books.

Rutter, M. (1972). *Maternal Deprivation Reassessed.* Hammondsworth, England: Penguin.

Rutter, M. (1979). "Maternal deprivation, 1972–1978: New findings, new concepts, new approaches." *Child Development, 50:*283–305.

Saccuzzo, D. and Lewandowski, D. (1976). "The WISC as a diagnostic tool." *Journal of Clinical Psychology, 32:*115–124.

Sack, W., Mason, R., & Higgins, J. (1985). "The single-parent family and abusive child punishment." *American Journal of Orthopsychiatry, 55,* 252–259.

Sagarin, E. (1980). "Taboo subjects and taboo viewpoints in criminology." In E. Sagarin (ed.), *Taboos in Criminology.* Beverly Hills, CA: Sage.

Salzinger, S., Kaplan, S., Pelcovitz, D., Samit, C., and Kreiger, R. (1984). "Parent and teacher assessment of children's behavior in maltreating families." *Journal of the American Academy of Child Psychiatry, 23:*458–464.

Sampson, R. and Laub, J. (1990). "Crime and deviance over the life course: The salience of adult social bonds." *American Sociological Review, 55:*609–627.

Scar, S. (1980). *Race, Social Class, and Individual Differences in IQ.* Hillsdale, NJ: Lawrence Erlbaum Associates.

Scarr, S., Pakstis, A., Katz, S., and Barker, W. (1977). "The absence of a relationship between degree of white ancestry and intellectual skills within a black population." *Human Genetics, 39:* 69–86.

Scarr, S. and Weinberg, R. (1976). "IQ test performance of black children adopted by white families." *American Psychologist, 31:* 726–739.

Scarr, S. and Weinberg, R. (1978). "The influence of 'family background' on intellectual attainment." *American Sociological Review,* 674–692.

Scar-Salaptek, S. (1971). "Race, social class, and IQ." *Science, 174:* 1285–1295.

Scar-Salaptek, S. and Williams, M. (1973). "The effects of early stimulation on low-birth-weight infants." *Child Development, 44:* 94–101.

Selye, H. (1956). *The Stress of Life.* New York: McGraw-Hill.

Selye, H. (1970). "The evolution of the stress concept." *American Journal of Cardiology, 26:* 289–299.

Schalling, D. (1978). "Psychopathy-related personality variables and the psychophysiology of socialization." In Hare, R. and Schalling, D. (eds.), *Psychopathic Behavior.* New York: Wiley.

Schalling, D., Edman, G., and Asberg, M. (1983). "Impulsive cognitive style and inability to tolerate boredom: Psychobiological studies of temperamental vulnerability." In M. Zuckerman (ed.), *Biological Bases of Sensation, Impulsivity and Anxiety.* Hillsdale, NJ: Erlbaum.

Schalling, D. (1987). "Personality correlates of plasma testosterone levels in young delinquents: An example of person-situated interaction?" In Mednick, S., Moffitt, T., and Stack, S. (eds.), *The Causes of Crime: New Biological Approaches.* Cambridge, Cambridge University Press.

Schuckit, M. and Rayses, V. (1979). "Ethanol ingestion: Differences in blood acetaldehyde concentrations in relatives of alcoholics and controls." *Science, 203:* 54–55.

Scott, J. (1958). *Aggression.* Chicago: University of Chicago Press.

Sherman, J. (1978). *Sex-Related Cognitive Differences: An Essay on Theory and Evidence.* Springfield, IL: Charles C Thomas.

Shinn, M. (1978). "Father absence and children's cognitive development." *Psychological Bulletin, 55:* 295–324.

Simons, R. (1978). "The meaning of the IQ-delinquency relationship." *American Sociological Review, 43:* 268–270.

Skeels, H. (1966). Adult Status of Children with Contrasting Early Life Experiences. Monographs of the Society for Research in Child Development.

Skinner, B. (1966). "The phylogeny and ontogeny of behavior." *Science, 157:* 1205–1213.

Skinner, P. and Shelton, R. (1985). *Speech, Language, and Hearing: Normal Processes and Disorders.* New York: Wiley.

Snyderman, M. and Rothman, S. (1988). *The IQ Controversy, the Media and Public Policy.* New Brunswick: Transaction Books.

Solomon, R. (1980). "The opponent-process theory of acquired motivation." *American Psychologist, 35:* 691–712.

Sorokin, P. (1954). *The Ways and Power of Love.* Boston: Beacon Press.

Spitz, R. (1945). "Hospitalism." In *The Psychoanalytic Study of the Child.* New York: International Universities Press.

Sroufe, A. (1979). "The coherence of individual development: Early care, attachment, and subsequent developmental issues." *American Psychologist, 34,* 835–841.

Steelman, L. and Doby, J. (1983). "Family size and birth order as factors on the IQ performance of black and white children." *Sociology of Education, 56:* 101–109.

Strickland, S. (1971). "Can slum children learn?" *American Education, 7:* 3–7.

Sutaria, S. (1985). *Specific Learning Disabilities: Nature and Needs.* Springfield, IL: Charles C Thomas.

Sutherland, E. and Cressey, D. (1970). *Criminology* (8th Ed.) Philadelphia, Lippincott.

Sutton-Smith, B. and Rosenberg, B. (1970). *The Sibling.* New York: Holt, Rinehart & Winston.

Tarter, R., Hegedus, A., Winsten, N., and Alterman, A. (1985). Intellectual profiles and violent behavior in juvenile delinquents." *Journal of Psychology, 119:* 125–128.

Taylor, G. (1979). *The Natural History of the Mind.* New York: E. P. Dutton.

Taylor, I., Walton, P., and Young, J. (1973). *The New Criminology.* New York: Harper & Row.

Taylor, L. (1984). *Born to Crime.* Westport, CT: Greenwood.

Terkel, J. and Rosenblatt, J. (1972). "Hormonal factors underlying maternal behavior at parturition: Cross transfusion between freely moving rats." *Journal of Comparative and Physiological Psychology, 80:* 365–371.

Thiessen, D. (1976). *The Evolution and Chemistry of Aggression.* Springfield, IL: Charles C Thomas.

Thoman, E., Barnett, C., and Liederman, P. (1971). "Feeding behaviors of newborn infants as a function of parity of the mother." *Child Development, 42:* 1471–1483.

Thornburg, H. (1971). *Contemporary Adolescence.* Belmont, CA: Wadsworth.

Thornhill, R. and Thornhill, N. (1987). "Human rape: The strengths of the evolutionary perspective." In C. Crawford, M. Smith, and D. Krebs (eds.), *Sociobiology and Psychology.* Hillsdale, NJ: Lawrence Erlbaum.

Townson, M. (1984). "Paid parental leave." Paper presented at the Colloquium on the Economic Status of Women in the Labor Market, Montreal, Quebec.

Tracy, P., Wolfgang, M. and Figlio, R. (1985). *Delinquency in Two Birth Cohorts.* Chicago: University of Chicago Press.

Trasler, G. (1978). "Relations between psychopathy and persistent criminality." In Hare, R. and Schalling, D. (eds.), *Psychopathic Behavior.* New York: Wiley.

Trojanowicz, R. and Morash, M. (1983). *Juvenile Delinquency: Concepts and Control.* Englewood Cliffs, NJ: Prentice-Hall.

Trunnell, E., Turner, C., and Keye, W. (1988). "A comparison of the psychological and hormonal factors in women with and without premenstrual syndrome." *Journal of Abnormal Psychology, 97:* 429–436.

Udry, J. (1988). "Biological predispositions and social control in adolescent sexual behavior." *American Sociological Review, 53:* 709–722.

Udry, J. R. (1990). "Biosocial models of adolescent problem behaviors." *Social Biology, 37:* 1–10.

United States Department of Justice. (1988). *Report to the Nation on Crime and Justice.* Washington, D.C.: Bureau of Justice Statistics.

Utain, W. (1980). *Menopause in Modern Perspectives.* New York: Appleton-Century-Crofts.

Valliant, P., Asu, M., Cooper, D. and Mammola, D. (1984). "Profile of dangerous and nondangerous offenders referred for pre-trial assessment." *Psychological Reports, 54:*411–418.

Vandenberg, S. and Volger, G. (1985). "Genetic determinants of intelligence." In Wolman, B. (ed.), *Handbook of Intelligence: Theories, Measurements, and Applications.* New York: John Wiley.

Van Dussen, R. and Zill, N. (1976). *Basic Background Items for U.S. Household Surveys.* Washington, DC: Social Science Research Council.

van Praag, H., Kahn, R., Asnis, G., Wetzler, S., Brown, S., Bleich, A., and Korn, M. (1987). "Denosologination of biological psychiatry or the specificity of 5-HT disturbances in psychiatric disorders." *Journal of Affective Disorders, 13:*1–8.

Van Voorhis, P., Cullen, F., Mather, R., and Chenoweth Garner, C. (1988). "The impact of family structure and quality on delinquency: A comparative assessment of structural and functional factors." *Criminology, 26:*235–261.

Venables, P. (1987). "Autonomic nervous system factors in criminal behavior." In Mednick, S., Moffitt, T., and Stack, S. (eds.), *The Causes of Crime: New Biological Approaches.* Cambridge: University of Cambridge Press.

Virkkunnen, M., DeJong, J., Barkto, J., Goodwin, F., and Linnoila, M. (1989). "Relationship of psychobiological variables to recidivism of violent offenders and impulsive fire setters." *Archives of General Psychiatry, 46:*600–603.

Vold, G. and Bernard, T. (1986). *Theoretical Criminology.* New York: Oxford University Press.

Waber, D. (1977). "Sex differences in mental abilities, hemispheric lateralization and rate of physical growth at adolescence." *Developmental Psychology, 13:*29–38.

Wadsworth, M. (1976). "Delinquency, pulse rates, and early emotional deprivation." *British Journal of Criminology, 16:*245–256.

Wallis, C. (1987). "Children having children." In L. Barnes (Ed.), *Social Problems* (pp. 10–16). Guilford, CT: Dushkin.

Walsh, A. (1981). *Human Nature and Love: Biological, Intrapsychic and Social-Behavioral Perspectives.* Lanham, MD: University Press of America.

Walsh, A. (1983). "Neurophysiology, motherhood, and the growth of love." *Human Mosaic, 17:*51–62.

Walsh, A. (1986). "Love and human authenticity in the works of Freud, Marx, and Maslow." *Free Inquiry in Creative Sociology, 14:*21–26.

Walsh, A. (1987). "Cognitive functioning and delinquency: Property versus violent offenses." *International Journal of Offender Therapy and Comparative Criminology, 31:*285–289.

Walsh, A. (1988a). *Understanding, Assessing, and Counseling the Criminal Justice Client.* Pacific Grove, CA: Brooks/Cole.

Walsh, A. (1988b). "'The people who own the country ought to govern it:' The Supreme Court, hegemony, and its consequences." *Law and Inequality: A Journal of Theory and Practice, 5:*431–451.

Walsh, A. (1990). *Statistics for the Social Sciences with Computer Applications.* New York: Harper & Row.

Walsh, A. (1990). "Illegitimacy, child abuse and neglect, and cognitive development." *Journal of Genetic Psychology, 151:*279–285.

Walsh, A. (1991). *The Science of Love: Understanding Love and its Effects on Mind and Body.* Buffalo, NY: Prometheus.

Walsh, A. and Balazs, G. (1990). "Love, sex, and self-esteem." *Free Inquiry in Creative Sociology, 18:*37–41.

Walsh, A. and Petee, T. (1987). "Love deprivation and violent juvenile delinquency." *Journal of Crime and Justice, 10:*45–60.

Walters, G. and White, T. (1989). "Heredity and Crime: Bad genes or bad research?" *Criminology, 27:*455–485.

Warren, J. (1969). "Birth order and Social Behavior." In Borgata, E. (ed.), *Social Psychology: Readings and Perspectives.* Chicago: Rand McNally.

Watters, J. and Stinnett, N. (1971). "Parent child relationships: A decade review of research." *Journal of Marriage and the Family, 33:*70–103.

Wechsler, D. (1958). *The Measurement and Appraisal of Adult Intelligence.* Baltimore: Williams and Wilkins.

Weis, J. (1982). "The invention of the new female criminal." In Savitz, L. and Johnson, N. *Contemporary Criminology.* New York: John Wiley.

Weisenfeld, A., Malatesta, C., Whitman, P., Granrose, C., and Uili, R. (1985). "Psychophysiological response to breast- and bottle-feeding to their infant's signals." *Psychophysiology, 22:*79–86.

Wells, B. (1980). *Personality and Heredity.* London: Longman.

Wells, E. and Rankin, J. (1986). "The broken homes model of delinquency: Analytic issues." *Journal of Research in Crime and Delinquency, 23:*68–93.

Werner, E. and Smith, R. (1982). *Vulnerable but Invincible: A Study of Resilient Children.* New York: McGraw-Hill.

West, D. (1982). *Delinquency: Its Roots, Careers and Prospects.* Cambridge, MA: Harvard University Press.

West, D. and Farrington, D. (1977). *The Delinquent Way of Life.* New York: Crane Russak.

Wexler, H. et al. (1988). "A criminal justice strategy for treating cocaine-heroin abusing offenders in custody." National Institute of Justice. Washington, DC: U.S. Department of Justice.

Whitman, D. and Thornton, J. (1987). "A nation apart." In Barnes, L. (ed.), *Social Problems.* Guilford, CT: Dushkin.

Widom, C. (1989). "Child abuse, neglect, and violent criminal behavior." *Criminology, 27:*251–271.

Wiesel, T. (1982). "Postnatal development of the visual cortex and the influence of the environment." *Nature, 299:*592.

Wilkin, H., Mednick, S., Schulsinger, F., Bakkestrom, E., Christiansen, K.,

Goodenough, D., Hirshhorn, K., Lundsteen, C., Owen, D., Philip, J., Rubin, D., and Stocking, M. (1977). "Criminality, aggression, and intelligence among XYY and XXY men." In Mednick, S. and Christiansen, K. (eds.), *Biosocial Bases of Criminal Behavior.* New York: Gardner Press.

Wilkinson, K., Stitt, G. and Erickson, M. (1982). "Siblings and delinquent behavior: An exploratory study of a neglected variable." *Criminology, 20:*223–239.

Wilson, C. (1984). *A Criminal History of Mankind.* London: Panther.

Wilson, E. (1978). Foreword. In Caplan, A. (ed.), *The Sociobiology Debate.* New York: Harper & Row.

Wilson, E. (1978). "Academic vigilantism and the political significance of sociobiology." In Caplan, A. (ed.), *The Sociobiology Debate.* New York: Harper & Row.

Wilson, G. (1981). *Love and Instinct.* New York: Quill.

Wilson, W. (1987). *The Truly Disadvantaged.* Chicago: University of Chicago Press.

Wilson, J. and Herrnstein, R. (1985). *Crime and Human Nature.* New York: Simon and Schuster.

Winikoff, B. and Laukaran, V. (1989). "Breast feeding and bottle feeding controversies in the developing world: Evidence from a study in four countries." *Social Science and Medicine, 29:*859–868.

Wish, E. and O'Neil, J. (1989). "Drug use forecasting." National Institute of Justice. Washington, DC: U.S. Department of Justice.

Witelson, S. (1976). "Sex and the single hemisphere: Specialization of the right hemisphere for spatial processing." *Science, 193:*425–426.

Witelson, S. (1987). "Neurobiological aspects of language in children." *Child Development, 58:*653–688.

Wolfe, D. (1987). *Child Abuse: Implications for Child Development and Psychopathology.* Beverly Hills, CA: Sage.

Wolfgang, M. (1958). *Patterns in Criminal Homicide.* Philadelphia: University of Pennsylvania Press.

Wolfgang, M., Figlio, R. and Sellin, T. (1972). *Delinquency in a Birth Cohort.* Chicago: University of Chicago Press.

Wolkind, S. and Rutter, M. (1973). "Children who have been 'in care'—an epidemiological study." *Journal of Child Psychology and Psychiatry, 14:*97–105.

Wolman, B. (1985). "Intelligence and mental health." In Wolman, B. (ed.), *Handbook of Intelligence: Theories, Measurement, and Applications.* New York: Wiley.

Woodger, J. (1948). *Biological Principles.* London.

Woolverton, W. and Kleven, M. (1988). "Multiple dopamine receptors and the behavioral effects of cocaine." In Clouet, D., Khursheed, A., and Brown, R. (eds.), *Mechanisms of Cocaine Abuse and Toxicity.* Washington, DC: U.S. Department of Health and Human Services.

Wrong, D. (1968). "The oversocialized conception of man in modern sociology." In S. McNall (ed.), *The Sociological Perspective.* Boston: Little, Brown.

Yablonsky, L. (1990). *Criminology: Crime and Criminality.* New York: Harper & Row.

Yablonsky, L. and Haskell, M. (1988). *Juvenile Delinquency.* New York: Harper & Row.

Yochelson, S. and Samenow, S. (1976). *The Criminal Personality*. New York: Jason Aronson.

Young, M. (1975). *The Rise of the Meritocracy*. Harmondsworth, England: Penguin.

Zarrow, M., Denenberg, V., and Sachs, B. (1972). "Hormones and maternal behavior in mammals." In S. Levine (ed.), *Hormones and Behavior*. New York: Academic Press.

Zuckerman, M., Buchsbaum, M., and Murphy, D. (1980). "Sensation seeking and its biological correlates." *Psychological Bulletin, 88:* 187–214.

# NAME INDEX

## A

Ader, R. 135
Adler, F. 130
Allen, S. 77
Alterman, A. 71
Anastasi, A. 26, 65, 72
Andersen, M. 128, 133
Andrew, J. 68, 71, 72, 73, 111, 189
Applewhite, P. 15, 21, 161, 164
Arendt, R. 109
Arrehenius, S. 12
Asberg, M. 141
Asso, D. 135, 136, 141
Austin, P. 135
Austin, R. 68, 69

## B

Bachen, C. 170
Balazs, G. 112
Balla, D. 114
Baltes, P. 108
Banton, M. 41, 42, 100
Baratz, J. 59
Baratz, S. 59
Barfield, A. 136
Barrash, D. 3
Bennett, E. 55
Barnett, R. 73
Bensch, M. 72
Bernard, T. 103, 108, 121
Berndt, T. 91, 92
Berne, E. 116
Bernstein, R. 137
Black, J. 179
Blau, A. 108
Bliss, E. 137
Block, N. 30

Bogdanovich, P. 165
Borduin, C. 143
Bouchard, T. 34, 35, 38, 57, 90, 95
Boucher, C. 167
Braginski, D. 26
Braginski, M. 26
Bridgeman, P. 9, 10, 100
Brody, N. 31, 47
Brodie, B. 12
Brown, D. 131
Brown, S. 177
Brunner, J. 50
Buchsbaum, M. 140, 163
Buikhuisen, W. xi, 77, 80, 109, 112, 119, 126
Buri, J. 112
Burt, C. 33

## C

Cadoret, R. 144
Camp, B. 67, 94
Casler, L. 58
Cataio, A. 129, 134, 135, 147, 148, 168
Cernkovitch, S. 155
Chaprin, I. 64
Chase, T. 64
Chein, I. 161
Clelland, C. 7
Cloninger, C. 144, 172
Cloward, R. 96, 97
Cohen, A. 95, 96, 97
Cohn, A. 177
Coleman, J. 185
Collins, 162
Comte, A. 12, 107
Connel, D. 182
Cooke, W. 135
Cornell, C. 185, 187
Corning, W. 64

# SUBJECT INDEX